ART OF THE WORLD

EUROPEAN CULTURES

THE HISTORICAL, SOCIOLOGICAL

AND RELIGIOUS BACKGROUNDS

THE ART OF
THE MODERN AGE

by

H. G. EVERS

translated by J. R. FOSTER

CROWN PUBLISHERS, INC., NEW YORK

Title-page:

PLATE 1 – Hans von Makart. Sketch in oils for the huge painting *Entry of Charles V into* Antwerp, 1878. Oil on canvas. *Height $26^3/_{10}$ in., length $42^1/_{10}$ in., Kunsthalle, Hamburg. (The finished picture is also in the Kunsthalle, Hamburg.)*

FIRST PUBLISHED IN GREAT BRITAIN BY METHUEN & CO. LTD.

LIBRARY OF CONGRESS CATALOG CARD NUMBER: 72–125038

PRINTED IN HOLLAND

CONTENTS

LIST OF COLOUR PLATES

The photographs were kindly put at our disposal by: Aerofilms Ltd., London, p. 46; Klaus G. Beyer, Weimar, p. 96; J. Blauel, Munich, pp. 173, 209; M. Chuzeville, Vanves, p. 133; H. Engelskirchen, Krefeld, p. 77; Photo Giraudon, Paris, p. 134; Foto Hinz, Basle, pp. 113, 135, 174, 208, 210, 230; J. F. Kersting, London, 66; R. Kleinhempel, Hamburg, 3; Foto Kühle, Hagen, 48; J. A. Lavaud, Paris, 47, 65, 116, 163, 175, 185, 186, 195, 196, 197, 198, 207, 219; Publications Filmées d'Art et d'Histoire, Paris, 23, 146, 164; Schweizerischer Verkehrsverein, Zurich, 33; Max Seidel, Mittenwald, 12, 13, 14, 34, 45, 75, 76, 77, 95, 115; Dr. J. Steiner (Schnell & Steiner, Munich), 78; O. Vaering, Oslo, 176; Zentrale Farbbildagentur, Düsseldorf, 24; Züricher Kunstgesellschaft, Zurich, 220.

SOURCES OF THE PLATES

LIST OF FIGURES

PREFACE

This book is the twenty-first volume in the (Western) series 'ART OF THE WORLD'. It will be followed by three further volumes on the architecture, sculpture and painting of the twentieth century, and twenty-three volumes on non-European art have already appeared or are planned. It is we Westerners who have explored this 'art of the world'; it is on our knowledge that the whole undertaking is based. However, I do not draw the conclusion that the spirit of civilization has finally descended on us and that we form a sort of culmination to all that has gone before. Nor do I draw the conclusion that this 'imaginary museum' of twenty-four volumes stands at our disposal to do as we like with, as if it were established that we were not only the living generation, but also the only one entitled to hold any views. On the contrary, I feel as if I were being watched by twenty-four other not basically unfriendly yet reserved centuries; I feel as if I were being watched by Cheops and Sesostris and wonder if I could make my views comprehensible to them. Every utterance that I venture is checked, so to speak, from the distance of the Pyramids.

Anyone who has stood on the mound covering the buried remains of an ancient city like Babylon or Troy knows how difficult it is to separate the strata of the various millennia once everything has fallen into ruins. We have learnt from the last war that our cities too can fall into ruins like these. This time the cracks were quickly closed (except for divided Berlin), because the same states, the same families, companies and industries that produced the architecture of the nineteenth century also continue to create the architecture of the twentieth century. All the terms and concepts of sculpture and painting have remained the same: art, art societies, art exhibitions, art journals, art criticism, the market value of works of art, the individuality of the artists – all these things link the nineteenth century to the present, but none of them existed in the time of the men who built the Pyramids. What would Cheops think of them?

I. ARCHITECTURE

THE BIG OPERA-HOUSE

On 21 June 1868 Richard Wagner received the applause of the opera-going public of Munich for his *Mastersingers;* on 23 September 1964 Marc Chagall received similar applause from a similar public for his ceiling in the Paris Opéra.

The two tributes, which were separated by a hundred years, resembled each so closely that it might have been the same period – except that on one occasion it was a king who introduced the artist and on the other a minister, and that on the first occasion the newspapers depicted the event in a woodcut and on the second in a photogravure illustration. And it is indeed the same period: that is the assumption on which this book, *The Modern Age*, is based.

APPX. PL. 1
APPX. PL. 2

It could be argued that the nineteenth century (if we were willing to equate it with historicism) is over, and that the twentieth century (which would then have to correspond to functionalism) is a totally different period; but in that case the tribute paid to Chagall under the dome of the Opéra would be incomprehensible, for the painting of domes is after all not one of the favourite practices of functionalism. Could it be that the twentieth century regards itself as so autocratic that the change of ceiling makes it permissible gradually to replace the whole opera-house? But no, not even the most perfervid admirer of contemporary art would provoke any applause if he suggested touching a building that is one of the wonders of Paris and the masterpiece of academicism. On the contrary, it was precisely in this great Opéra that Chagall wished to be honoured; he did not want to tear it down but to be admitted to its precincts. On the whole, the painter's contribution to the theatre tends to be concentrated on scenery and settings; many painters have worked in this field, for after all the theatre is contemporary and creative. Perhaps it was not a very sound idea to put Chagall's setting on the dome instead of on the stage, where it really belonged; on the ceiling it disturbs a whole which has been wonderfully well preserved. There can be no doubt that Chagall is a far greater painter than Lenepveu, even if Chagall's ceiling is only an enlargement of themes, forms and colours developed in easel pictures; but there can be no doubt either that Lenepveu's painted ceilings are much better than contemporary taste will allow, that they enshrine genuine inspiration and a genuine tradition, and that, in a context which is still intact, they are superior to any painting that could be substituted for them today.

APPX. PL. 42
APPX. PL. 4b

The Opéra is rhetorical, balletic, musical; it is hospitable and adaptable, and has room for many, even for Chagall. It has the continual capacity for change of the genuine work of art. In every generation quite different, unexpected, sparkling facets appear.

Of the two concepts 'historicism' and 'functionalism', historicism is by far the richer and more comprehensive. 'One can imagine', says the composer Hans Werner Henze, 'a short harmonic and rhythmic progression which at no point contains any reference at all to the past. And within thirty seconds, I should say, it becomes so deadly boring and you feel such a longing for the past that – if the piece does not stop then – you either fall asleep or go away, or else simply say to yourself "Now I should like a bit of past." For I think that every person, even the youngest and most progressive, has something to do with the past.'

We know that new art only arises and develops out of earlier art. It contains an element of historicism just as a plant has roots. On the other hand, the naming of an artistic period after functionalism is a transitory phenomenon and one that will probably not recur. It is quite obvious that people could not for long be so occupied with *function* that they would want to see their own period named after it.

The illusion that anyone who is a pretty good painter can therefore also decorate opera-houses is as old as the Paris Opéra itself, and Chagall's attempt is, so to speak, a late execution of the wishes of the Impressionists. 'They ought to have let Degas decorate the Opéra,' said Manet. The longing for the operatic, the theatrical, overcame even the Impressionists. However, we shall see in a moment how curiously the Opéra and Impressionism hung together, how they both belonged simultaneously to the Parisian bourgeoisie. In nineteenth-century opera, with the music of Mozart and Beethoven, Auber and Rossini, Meyerbeer and Halévy, Verdi and Wagner, this rhetorical, Terpsichorean, religious element had its great moment, one perfectly comparable with the days of Greek tragedy and the choral songs performed at holy places. The big opera-houses were built at the same time; there are many of them, in every big city from Moscow to Rio de Janeiro, from Cairo to Chicago, yet they are also few enough in number for everyone of them to be important; and so from a living cult arose a living architecture. The Paris Opéra is by far the most dazzling achievement of them all, and it is wonderful, not only for Paris but also for the culture of the whole world, that this great opera-house is still preserved intact down to the smallest detail. What was exceptional about the architect, Charles Garnier, was precisely that he was able to exploit traditional ideas in such a masterly way. The history of theatre construction in Europe was a story of continuous advance. Foyers and staircases had been developed in the old Comédie Française. Architectural theorists such as Jacques-André Roubo *fils*, court carpenter, had aided the plans with their folios of drawings. Between 1772 and 1780 Victor Louis had built the Bordeaux theatre, which is also still standing today, though the interior has been somewhat altered. From 1764 to 1770 Pierre-Louis Moreau had put up the opera-house in the Palais Royal. This theatre was burned down thirteen years later. These were the first two such projects on which really big sums of money were spent: 2,381,553 *livres* in Paris, 2,436,523 in Bordeaux.

FIG. 1

The basic ideas of these big buildings – staircases, division of the foyers, the circular dome over the *salle* (auditorium), the resting of the shell on pairs of coupled columns in the four diagonals – were also retained in the two provisional buildings erected after the destruction by fire of Moreau's opera-house (1781) and the assassination of the Duc de Berry (1820): first in the Salle Richelieu, built by Victor Louis for a business woman, confiscated from her

Edgar Degas, *Foyer de Danse (Ballet School). C.* 1879/1880. Oil on canvas. *Height 17 in., width 19½ in. In the W.A. Clark Collection, Corcoran Gallery of Art, Washington.*

Schloss Herrenchiemsee, unfinished north staircase. Built according to the plans of Georg Dollmann in 1878/9. The foundation stone was laid on 28 May 1878. *Cf. p. 20.*

Schloss Herrenchiemsee, south staircase, decorated in 1886. Designs for the sculptural decoration by Franz Widmann, carried out by Philipp Perron.
Cf. p. 20.

Federal Polytechnic at Zurich, original front. Built by Gottfried Semper. 1859–1865. *Cf. pp. 22, 26.*

by the Directory during the Revolution, given to the nation, and demolished after the murder of the Duc de Berry in 1820; and then in the opera-house in the Rue Lepelletier subsequently improvised by Debret within a year in the mansion and garden of the Duc de Choiseul. The amount of intellectual activity that the bourgeoisie put into this centre of Parisian life can be seen from Balzac's novels; one could almost say that his whole *Comédie humaine* takes place in the boxes of the opera and that it was only for the sake of completeness that the destinies of the boxes' occupants were followed to other scenes as well.

On 13 March 1861 Richard Wagner experienced his great *Tannhäuser* scandal, in which he really won a great victory ('Oh, if only Heaven would grant me one flop like yours,' said Gounod to him enviously). Wagner, who could not see the real background to the affair, thought that the *jeunesse dorée* had only fought for the insertion of the ballet in the first or second act. In reality they were fighting for their own rights in the theatre. They knew that the new building plans were already drawn up and that the imperial decree authorizing them had been signed since 29 September 1860. They were used to treating the erstwhile dancing arena as the festive hall of the old palace, as a place in which they felt themselves at home – dukes, ministers, diplomats, journalists, as Charles Garnier himself recounted; he might have added painters like Edgar Degas. The young aristocrats did not want to be forced out of this salon, and this is just what Wagner did want, like all reform movements since the days of Lessing, Schinkel and Semper. They wanted to separate the theatre from the noble's palace, to curtail the sovereignty of aristocratic society and to put in its place an absolute art which could only be enjoyed from reserved seats. The audience was to sit in the dark, silent and motionless.

The enumeration of traditions, of contents, of splendour would be unimportant if Charles Garnier had not united and heightened all these things in his building, so that he must be regarded as the most inspired interpreter of tradition who has ever lived; this one building alone makes him immortal. It would be impossible to describe all the factors that contribute to produce the total effect. The exterior setting begins in the planning of the city, far outside the Opéra itself: in the Avenue de l'Opéra, which was pushed through from the Louvre, in the hexagon of boulevards round the building, in the façade with its famous *Dance* group by Carpeaux. In contrast to the design of the Bordeaux theatre the ballroom is omitted and replaced by the much more effective grand foyer. On the other hand the administrative building for the Opéra was added, the seven-storey mansion round the Cour d'Honneur at the back: this goes back to the earlier Hôtel Choiseul. That the building was carried out in various styles and in various materials, that the main foyer is baroque in style while the ante-room displays the mosaics of imperial Byzantium, is all part of the hospitality of opera; theatrical, in fact. But the same hospitality is extended to functional engineering, of which the Opéra is also one of the high-water marks. Where does iron construction speak out more clearly than in the three tiers of seats, one above the other, which are welcomed right in the middle of the public rooms? These tiers are not disguised in any way; they are just like the cabin decks in an ocean liner.

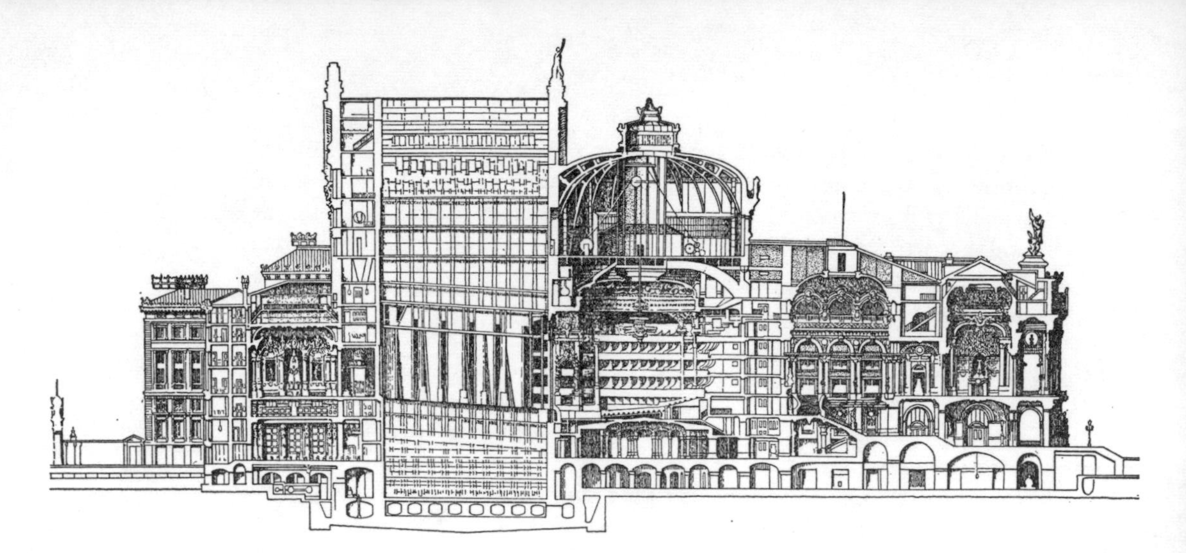

FIG. 1 – *Cross-section of the Opéra, Paris. Cf. p. 10.*

FIG. 2 We have therefore put a cross-section of the Opéra alongside that of an ocean liner, so as to make it clear that the various functions of a great building like this are arranged and co-ordinated in just the same spirit and with the same mastery, and to show how homogeneous nineteenth-century architecture is, how the erection of opera-houses and the construction of ships – historicism and functionalism – hang together.

DEGAS 'They ought to have let Degas decorate the Opéra'; so there was one painter to whom the Impressionists would have entrusted this task. Thus for us his life is a good example of the destiny, in the earnest nineteenth century, of a painter who had a genuine link with opera.

For Edgar de Gas came from the aristocracy. He had the entrée to the dancers' practice rooms and could have booed Wagner with the *jeunesse dorée.* His relatives in Italy belonged to the aristocracy of intellect and birth and his relatives in New Orleans to the capitalist society of the stock exchange. He was really supposed to become a banker and lawyer and it was some time before he gave up writing his name in the aristocratic fashion.

He began with grand portraits, pictures so precise in their drawing and discreet colouring, of such psychological penetration, that they are like jewels. Then (and this is the intermediate period when the question of decorating the Opéra would have arisen) he turned his attention to historical subjects, scenes from opera and ballet – Semiramis, Alexander. These pictures remained only sketches, and when one tries to visualize them in conjunction with architecture one realizes why they had to be abandoned. Not because they were historical, but because they showed no architectural feeling. In the imaginative world of Impressionism there was no connection with architecture, whether it be nineteenth-century architecture or that of today; unless one regards the emptiness of a running-track or a sports field (in *Young Spartans Exercising,* for example) as the point of departure of

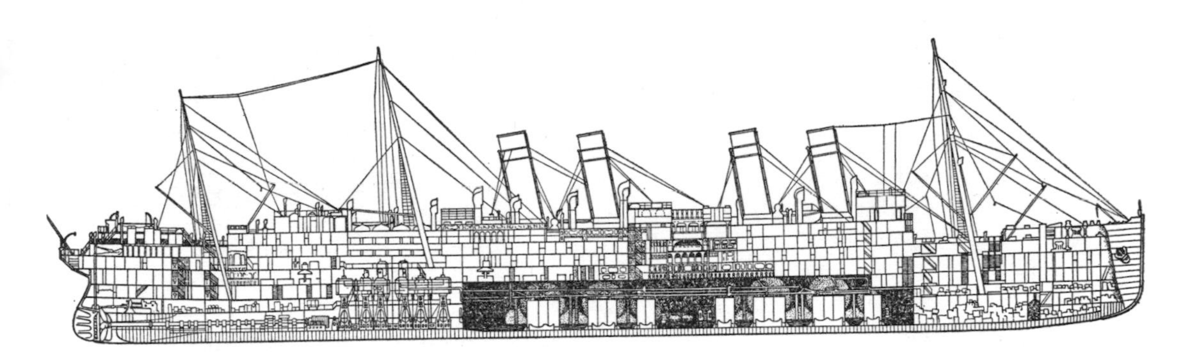

FIG. 2 – *Cross-section of an ocean liner. Cf. p. 16.*

contemporary architecture. In Impressionism there could be no room for a three-dimensional world – by which, of course, I mean one constructed out of building materials, something not to be confused with the construction of colours and lines on the given surface of the picture.

Yet the same Degas had close ties with the Opéra. First of all with the music of the orchestra. His intimate friendship with M. Dihaut, a bassoon-player, gave rise to a portrait. The picture shows the player's head, his instrument, and round him his colleagues, the performance, the whole orchestra; no longer, however, from the point of view of the aristocrat in the dress circle, who has the whole performance in front of him as if it were his own property, but from the point of view of the participant, below the footlights – the artist is incorporated in the rank and file.

It is the same with the dancers. Degas, with his talent for portrait-painting, could surely well have interested himself in one particular artiste, championed one single singer, as Toulouse-Lautrec did, for example, in the case of Mlle Guilbert, Mlle Lander or Mlle Avril. Degas had the entrée to the practice room, but where his equals dallied with the girls he discovered the world of hard work, of strict training by the dancing-master, of supervision by mothers drawing lines in the dust with their umbrellas from boredom, of shivering round the iron stove, of painful leg-joints and stiff backs. He studied the exercises in deportment, could demonstrate every dance-step with precision, talk expertly on the subject – and in doing this he was complying with the demands – just as severe – of his own art, painting. He was not the customer, but the artist.

A necessary, unavoidable path led him to his place in the Opéra, a path that led away from the aristocratic salon to the artists' canteen, away from the grandiose but superficial world of the audience to the ever greater concentration and intimacy of shared experience. There had of course been whole-page lithographs of festival performances, of the *La Muette de Portici (Masaniello)*, of the *Jewess of Toledo* or whatever the opera might be called, and of the big ballets, with the scene on the stage seen as a whole. There had been pictures of Fanny Elssler, of Taglioni, of the classical ballet, which was always related to a central axis to which all the choreography and every movement, however wide-ranging, had to return. Wide-ranging, eccentric movement was only possible if the counter-force was still at work in it, so that the gyrating top could stand up straight on its end again, so that leaning over did not end in a fall.

It was precisely this totality, this centralized survey that the history of painting was moving away from further and further, and necessarily so. More and more it was putting the special, characteristic detail in the place of the 'main action'. Degas, with his burning interest in ballet, was no longer in a position to paint the performance as a whole; instead he painted the oblique view from a box, the detail, and finally the individual limbs cut off by the edge of the picture. He no longer painted the dancers' intoxicating appearance on the stage but the hard training behind the scenes. Or if he did paint a scene on this side of the curtain, then it was the applause, the dancer curtseying between the footlights and the descending curtain, bouquet in hand, bending on tiptoe (it is worth noting that the young Degas' first big aristocratic portrait, the Bellelli family, is composed round a little baroness who has pulled one foot so far back under her seat that it looks as if she has only one leg).

The dancers' lives are followed to their homes, to the tub in which they prepare themselves or wash themselves off afterwards, to the simple dress which they put on. The first collage in the history of art is the little frilly dress on the *Fourteen-Year-Old Dancer*, the wax statue of 1884 – what an affront to the classical theory of art, which maintained that nothing 'real' could be taken over unchanged into the world of art. Moreover, the frilly dresses have to be ironed and pleated; so next it is no longer the dancers who are the subject but the laundresses, and in the end not even the laundresses' ironing, but their yawning. It will be noted what a curious springboard effect dominates this artistic world of Degas. What eccentricity; and it is always fatefully irreversible – from the splendour of a night at the opera, indeed from the whole presence of imperial Paris, to the yawning of the laundresses.

Could this eccentric artistic attitude finally remain related to a centre, could the pendulum swing back past the central point and the leaning dancer straighten up again? Not in the life and art of Degas, but certainly with the logic of art history, in the figurines of dancers by Oskar Schlemmer; at a price, however: they have become spinning tops, marionettes; they are no longer the 'ballet rats' of the Paris Opéra.

The problem of the 'whole' was given a remarkably different slant. If before it had been the 'whole' theatre, not just the scenery and performance but at the same time the 'whole' audience, every row of it, that together made the opera, now the new 'whole' consisted of a talented artist's whole work, in which the individual picture was only a recurring, disciplined unit, like the dancer's individual step, which only made up the dance in conjunction with many others. The great opera scenes of Delacroix, such as *The Death of Sardanapalus* and *The Entry of the Crusaders into Constantinople*, could be painted only once, and only the Louvre could have the picture. Degas' dancers on the other hand exist in more than one form and it is only in the whole work of Degas that one finds a unity again.

HISTORICISM

While people admit that in the case of grand opera, even when based on a historical libretto, the contemporary nature of the music holds the whole theatrical event together, the architecture of the same period is under strong suspicion of being what is called 'historicism'. It is difficult to see in it any contemporary element corresponding to the music in opera. Historicism produced these suspicions itself right from the start; even in the nineteenth century it provoked the expression of every kind of ridicule and contempt. If the 'angry young men' of 1910 had known how historical their criticisms of historicism were they would have been ashamed to be so unoriginal.
It is not my intention to seek a final definition of historicism that would fit all the uses of the term. I regard such a project as difficult because I am convinced that we are living in the middle of historicism and that the view that it was overcome and passed away with the nineteenth century is an error, indeed a nonsensical idea. The rebellion of Westerners against historicism was directed only against their own, western historicism, against the styles of the West. The very same artists who shouted down historicism found Negro art fascinating and learned from Japanese art. Is Japanese art not historical then? It is much older than European art; it is rooted in the prehistoric period and continually renews itself in the same recurring type. Courbet, who painted *The Wave*, like Hokusai, and Frank Lloyd Wright, who took the Japanese bungalow to Chicago, are not thought of as historicists, but why not? It is true that we do not call it historicism any more; we speak of 'the art of the primitives', of 'early man and late culture', but all these expressions are illusory; we do not know how far early man was primitive or to what extent we are a late culture.
Every event in history can be evaluated positively or negatively. I regard it as a fact that during the nineteenth century the civilization of Europe exerted its influence over the whole surface of the globe, that everywhere European clothing was worn and a European language used to make oneself understood, that to all intents and purposes no part of the material well-being and the industrial capacity which every country would today like to make its own is a product of Arab, Indian or Far Eastern civilization. I make the assumption that nineteenth-century Europe was overwhelmingly strong. I am continually amazed to find it described as weak; but I also see that it is characteristic of European man to have a split mind. I called opera 'hospitable', and I regard hospitality, when it is tinged with curiosity, interest and readiness to learn, as a pleasant quality; other scholars despise the same attitude as imitation, weakness, venality. I called opera a living cult; but Richard Wagner, when he was himself writing inaugural pieces on historical themes for the theatre at Bayreuth, called that part of the business which he could not control himself 'the dirt of the theatre, which I heartily detest, and of its repulsive routine' (to King Ludwig II, 1.3.1871).
I regard history as an ever necessary source; I do not believe that art arises out

of itself and it is therefore difficult for me to support the view that the art of the twentieth century is new and spontaneous while that of the nineteenth century was imitative.

Perhaps it is easiest if one first tries to consider the architecture of historicism as it is generally evaluated, i.e. as derivative and mere copying. Thus when in the nineteenth century a king (were there kings then? And are there kings even today? Are they all imitation kings?), when Ludwig II of Bavaria built Schloss Herrenchiemsee and in it created the purest architectural copy there was (but how do you make an architectural copy? It must have been a terribly complicated business, just as expensive and time-consuming as building the so-called original. If earlier periods had produced no architectural copies, surely the method, the artistic means, of producing a copy had to be invented?), quite apart from the 'style' of this castle (and in this book as a whole I shall only employ the concept 'style' when other scholars compel me to do so by speaking of *Jugendstil* or 'International Style', thus keeping alive the notion that art must be expressed in styles), it can be shown by simply comparing the two staircases of Herrenchiemsee, the ornate one and the one that has stood unfinished for a hundred years, that at any rate the assertion that the architecture of historicism is technically poor is just not true. When good patrons and good architects shared the responsibility this architecture was quite outstanding in quality. We have already said as much of the architectural quality of the Paris Opéra, which dates from the same period.

PLATES PP. 12, 13

The castle of Herrenchiemsee is a 'dream work'. We know that Ludwig II never actually slept in the state bedroom, any more than Philip Johnson will ever live in his glass house in Cambridge, Massachusetts, or a Japanese walk in the petrified stream of his garden. These are dream works of art, in the sense that Schopenhauer described the world as a dream, Wagner explained his whole work as the fruit of a dream and Nietzsche attributed the birth of tragedy to the Apollonian dream.

I have selected the staircase at Herrenchiemsee because it can be illustrated alongside the unfinished one; otherwise the Mirror Gallery or the 'Chambre de parade' would have been a better example. The Mirror Gallery, because it was to have been as close a copy as possible of the prototype at Versailles and yet could not be, because the materials were not the same (stucco instead of painting) and because the furnishings corresponded not to the present but to the short period of glory under Louis XIV. The bedroom, because it was a quite independent creation, newly thought out by architects, contractors and craftsmen, much bigger and more splendid than the corresponding room at Versailles. The staircase was a third variety of interior at Herrenchiemsee. It went back, it is true, to a staircase originally present at Versailles and designed by the same Lebrun who had designed the interior of the Mirror Gallery. But this staircase had been demolished in the eighteenth century and was only preserved in an engraving. Here the nineteenth-century execution did not attain at any point the seventeenth century's wealth of decoration; it was simpler and more friendly. Warlike and gradiose themes were excluded. Only the four quarters of the world were depicted on the walls and ceiling. A pleasant group of statuary showing Diana with two

nymphs was put in the place of the mighty bust of the king, which was there to represent him only when the king's actual throne did not stand on the central landing. For of course these staircases were not built for hurrying up and down, but as the scenes of important state events. The steps were occupied by stationary not moving people. Under Ludwig II the people were replaced by a profusion of flowers and plants. At Versailles there was no corresponding staircase in the other wing; thus no sharply-defined model filled the Bavarian king's dream and his architects could satisfy the nineteenth century's urge for symmetry – but for the same reason this second staircase was also only built, never decorated.
When the king was toppled from his throne, when the bourgeoisie grew agitated at the debt of twenty millions (fourteen years earlier Baron Haussmann had left the city of Paris debts amounting to seven hundred millions), when his buildings were adduced as evidence of his mental sickness, people did not know how many such castles had been built or extended in every country in western Europe, all in the same manner, but not all of them by persons in the same position as the king to continue a long enterprise. Herrenchiemsee was the most grandiose example of such a castle because its builder knew most precisely what he wanted, collaborated in the work most closely and watched over its quality piece by piece. In the meantime one after another of these castles has been brought to light – Pierrefonds, Liechtenstein, Hohenzollern, Anif, Hluboka, Medano al Lambro, Bergamo, Waddesdon Manor, Desio, Beylerbey, the Palais Talleyrand at Paris, Schwerin, Wartburg, Chillon, Torino, Barcelona; they appear in *avant-garde* periodicals such as *L'Oeil*. The most amazing piece of information to come to light in the last few years was the news that Sir Joseph Paxton, celebrated today as a 'pioneer of modern design' because he was the builder of the Crystal Palace, was by no means simply a herald of twentieth-century forms but also a traditional architect; in the very same year, 1851, he designed and built one of his historical castles, Mentmore Castle, for Baron Nathan Mayer Rothschild, in the purest English Renaissance style, with interiors in the styles of François I, Louis XIV, Louis XV and Louis XVI; in other words, the middle of the nineteenth century was broad enough to nourish both the engineer's approach and historicism in the same man's heart and at the same time. It would in fact be interesting to see in what sort of houses the accepted engineering geniuses, the great bridge-builders of the nineteenth century, themselves lived: hardly in architecture that we should describe today as modern. And *vice versa:* how furious William Morris would be if he thought that we classified him today as a forerunner of the industrial methods of production against which he fought so hard.
Of course, castles are exceptional, romantic cases; they are not historicism as a whole. We can leave out of account nineteenth-century patrons, but not the architects. Viollet-le-Duc and his contemporaries in France; Gilbert Scott, Butterfield, Street and Bodley in England; Camillo Boito and Luca Beltrami in Italy; Gottfried Semper, Friedrich Adler, Karl Schäfer in Germany – they are all exceptional men, equally important as writers and as architects.
Considerations of space allow us to look at only one of them more closely, by way of example. But first a remark is needed on the part that education can play

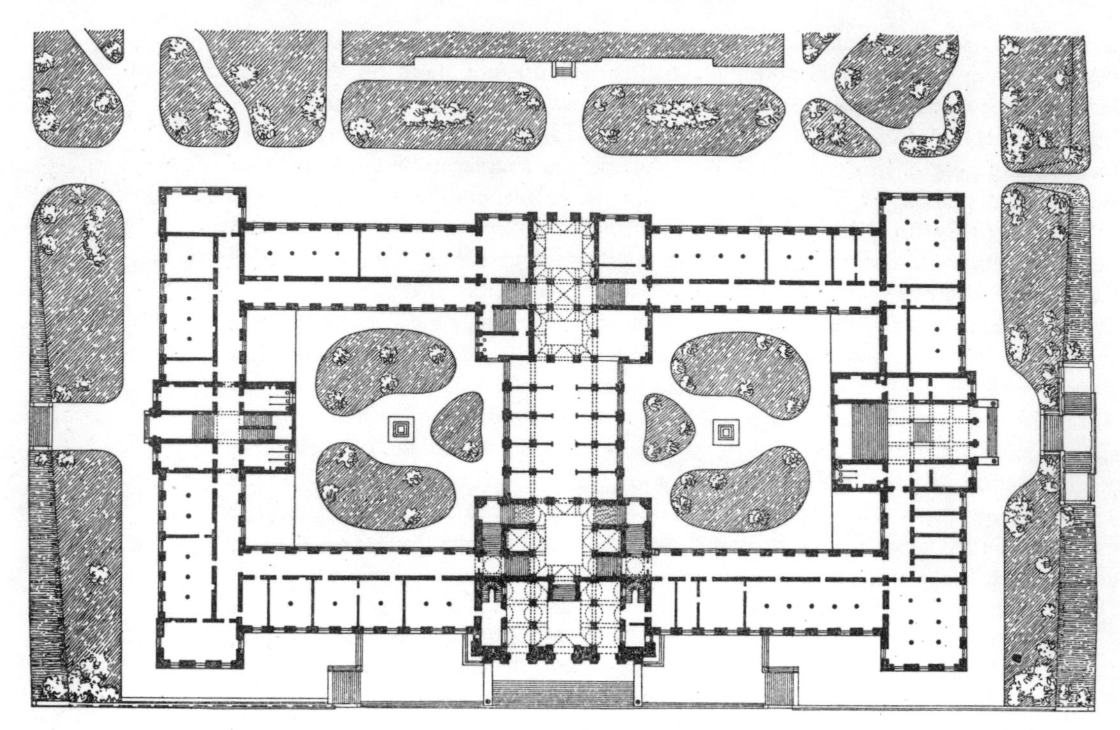

FIG. 3 – *Ground-plan of the Polytechnic, Zurich. Cf. below.*

in an artist's life. In the nineteenth century it was regarded as creditable to be educated, to have a wide enough view to be able to see one's work in the context of the culture of earlier times and other nations. People remembered Leon Battista Alberti, Raphael, Rubens, Fischer von Erlach. At the beginning of this century an antithesis was set up between 'historically educated' and 'creative' as if one excluded the other. I do not know to what extent it is still regarded as desirable to seem uneducated, but the architects of the nineteenth century were certainly not uneducated. A great many of them were educated, but otherwise only average architects. In the twentieth century a great many want to appear uneducated, but that does not make them good architects.

However, many men in both the nineteenth and twentieth centuries were not only highly educated but also exceptional architects. In the middle of the nineteenth century technical high schools were differentiated from other institutes of high education. The plan on which they were built could still be summed up quite briefly: staircase, hall, institutes, lecture-rooms, basements for machines, all connected by corridors and arranged round two interior courtyards. The Federal Polytechnic for Zurich (1859–1863) was very generously equipped by the city and the federal government; it cost 1.8 million to build. Above all, a splendid site was provided, close to the old city, on the edge of the Limmat valley, in front of still virgin rising ground, so that even today, when the peripheral site has

FIG. 3

PLATE P. 14

Claude Monet, *The Gare Saint Lazare in Paris*. 1877. Oil on canvas. *Height 2 ft. 6 in., width 3 ft. 4 in. Louvre, Jeu de Paume Gallery, Paris. Cf. pp. 27, 28, 141.*

become a central one, the façade still looks out unchanged and imperturbable into the distance. The citizens of Zurich realized that technology had become a central feature of life, and of art too.
Semper built a front that was still a real façade. I was brought up on the principle that a good façade must give some indication of what the interior architecture is like; then I found the façade being despised as unnecessary, indeed inartistic; after that people took the view that the interior and exterior could most easily be equated by replacing the outer skin with an open wall of glass; and finally biology (in the person of Adolf Portmann) informed architects (at the 1963 congress) that in nature the façade, the outer form, is independent of the inner organism; it does not obey functional laws but formal ones, which in the realm of human consciousness must be described as art, beauty. Thus after a hundred years the façade has been rehabilitated.
Semper himself complained that the best stone, the sort which he had recommended, was not used. Thus he was familiar with the quality of the material. He had not visualized his façade as so bald, but articulated and adorned with a *sgrafitto* painting. On the north side of the building it is preserved or restored. The wall would have become a fabric on its own account; it would have had a content, not just proportions. It would have acquired a rise and fall, a tinge of something more substantial; Switzerland preserved the memory, which had never quite disappeared, of the time of the great façade paintings of Hans Holbein and Tobias Stimmer. As we have said, Semper had had this sort of richness in mind. What now remains possesses calm, clear proportions, and concentration on the central projecting section; there lie the steps, and behind the columns on the top storey lies the hall, so that unity of exterior and interior in the nineteenth-century sense is achieved.
The Polytechnic was carefully extended from 1884 onwards, and the main building from 1915; naturally the present federal Technical High School cannot be accommodated on this site. This has often happened with nineteenth-century building plans; demands have changed and broadened to such an extent that the old, originally appropriate building is no longer suitable.
Gottfried Semper, born in Hamburg in 1803, had become famous through the Dresden Opera-House (1838–1841). In the competition for the restoration of the church of St. Nicholas after the dreadful fire at Hamburg in 1842 he had been dramatically defeated by the design of an Englishman, Gilbert Scott; this was the moment when Germans had to realize that the Gothic style had not arisen in Germany but in France, and neo-Gothic in England. Semper had begun to build the Gallery at Dresden – and with it decided how the Zwinger was to be incorporated in the town-plan – when with Richard Wagner he had to flee from the barricades of 1848, pursued throughout German territory by warrants for his arrest. In England he was concerned, as Prince Albert's adviser, in the Great

Track at Bradford Station.

Exhibition of 1851; at the same time, as author of a multi-volume work on 'Style', he became a central figure in nineteenth-century artistic theory: 'Art knows only one mistress: necessity.' Appointed professor at the Zurich Polytechnic, he put up the Polytechnic building from 1859 to 1865; simultaneously he built the very clever town hall at Winterthur, which is really a great hanging hall surrounded by offices and reached by solemn stairs; a link in the chain of festival buildings which stretches from Elias Holl's town hall at Augsburg in the seventeenth century to the Festival Hall in London, built by Robert H. Matthew and colleagues in 1951.

PLATE P. 14
FIG. 3

In 1871 Semper was summoned to Vienna and designed the new wing of the Hofburg, the Burgtheater and the two huge museums opposite the Hofburg. The Wagner festival theatre that he had designed for Munich was put up in Bayreuth, barrack-fashion, without his co-operation. Semper's buildings form an architectural *œuvre* that is always close to tradition and to subsequent developments; it is synonymous with the best that was built in the middle of the nineteenth century. He was an exceptional man; if we no longer recognize this, then we have lost sight of all sensible criteria.

ARCHITECTURE OF TRANSPORT

Nicholas Pevsner has suggested calling the nineteenth century not 'the Victorian Age', which means nothing outside England, but 'the Railway Age', a description which would be comprehensible anywhere in the world. It does indeed aptly describe a century in which the railway came into being, was developed to its fullest extent and in the end was succeeded by the car and the aeroplane. It is true that in the twentieth century railways are being improved and rationalized; but only a few miles are being added to the existing network and other stretches have been put out of commission.

With railways, too, we can introduce the concept of 'limited infinity' for the nineteenth century: 'infinite', because theoretically the network of lines and of world transport extends round the whole earth and returns upon itself; but 'limited', because the human imagination is still confined to the surface of the earth and does not go off at right angles into the depths of the earth or the spaces of the universe. In addition, the railway, with its permanent way, is still physically visible; it has not yet become invisible – trackless air, wave or beam.

The railway is the greatest constructional achievement of the nineteenth century. It possesses its own formative power; it alters the surface of the inhabited earth, alters man's feeling for his world, extends his vision, his speed of movement. It needs bridges, tunnels, stations, rolling stock, but this is all held together by what is expressed in the name, the railway, the network of lines. Of the twenty milliards spent on railways up to 1857, by far the largest part went on the track, which must therefore be regarded as building work, even if the other individual buildings were more spectacular and more easily related to previous architectural forms.

In the nineteenth century, thinking about art and works of art was firmly tied to quite definite objects and there was an insuperable barrier against anything that did not fit into these categories; against anything that was not a pure easel picture, pure sculpture or pure architecture. We, however, must find new methods in order to be able to think about art at all. In dealing with architecture the history of art can no longer restrict itself to glancing at picturesque corners in castle courtyards. Architecture has many layers, even where one single building is concerned. It was two thousand years before the curves in the stylobate of a Greek temple were seen, and they were only 'seen' after they were known and had been calculated; yet no one can doubt that the curvature is part of the artistic form of the temple. In the same way the line of the railway track, which is hardly visible above the surface of the ground, is part of the railway's appearance; it even contains artistic elements. They can be seen from an aeroplane: the relation between curve and speed, between embankment and cutting. It is true that railways are not really there to be seen, but they exert a powerful influence over our lives; they determine distance and proximity, public finance, holidays. Indeed, since we travel on them from childhood onwards their influence on us is more decisive than the compressed influence of a single visit to a museum.

Jean Renoir, in his book on his father, Auguste Renoir, tells this story: 'One fine morning Monet woke Renoir with a shout of triumph: "I've got it – the Gare Saint Lazare! When the locomotives start off, the clouds of smoke are so thick that one can scarcely make out anything. It's magical, an absolute fairy-tale atmosphere." He did not want to paint the Gare Saint Lazare from memory but to catch the play of the sunlight on the clouds of steam. "The train to Rouen must be held back. The light is better half an hour after it is due to leave according to the time-table!" He put on his best clothes, straightened his shirt cuffs, and, carelessly swinging his stick with the gold knob, proffered his card at the office of the manager of the Chemin de Fer de l'Ouest at the Gare Saint Lazare. The doorkeeper stiffened and took him straight in. The high-ranking official begged his visitor to take a seat. The latter introduced himself quite simply with the words, "I am the painter Claude Monet." The manager knew nothing about painting but did not dare to admit this. Monet left him in suspense for a moment before condescending to impart the great news to him. "I have decided to paint your station. I hesitated for a long time between the North station and yours, but I think now that yours has more character." Monet achieved all he desired. Trains were held up, platforms were closed and the locomotives were stuffed full of coal so that they emitted as much steam as Monet wanted. He behaved like a tyrant in the station, painted all day long amid universal respect and finally went off with a good half-dozen pictures. The whole staff, headed by the manager, bowed low as he departed. Paul Durand-Ruel bought the canvases of the Gare Saint Lazare and arranged things so that he could pay his protégés something on account.'

PLATE P. 23

Even if we do not accept old Jean Renoir's charming account as authentic in every detail, the whole episode illustrates clearly the difference between the nineteenth and twentieth centuries' conceptions of what art is. If Monet's attitude – that only painting could make something artistic out of the station – were valid universally, not just for him, then the railway would have only one side worth looking at, or rather it would have no artistic side of its own at all; it would

FIG. 4 – *Euston Station, London. Portico by Philip Hardwick, 1835–9. Demolished in 1963. Cf. below.*

simply be that the painter created something artistic by means of the locomotive smoke. But the railway carries us away; it influences and alters our lives, Monet's included. Every great artist has entertained the wish that his work could be powerful enough to alter men's lives – not just their aesthetic attitudes. Monet's picture is compressed art. A yard of railway line is almost nothing – a bit of ennobled raw material, a bit of technical form; it has no perceptible art about it, unless a contemporary sculptor is going to 'discover' the permanent way. But the Gare Saint Lazare as a whole, with its compression, scope, energies, spaces, times, is much more influential, and contains much more art, than Monet's picture. It is another kind of art, different from mimesis, recapture of the subject in a painted picture.

A railway station is not just a shelter from the rain, a place where tickets can be bought, and passengers, luggage and freight dealt with; it is the entrance and exit portal to a city. In using the word 'portal' we are naming the same architectural function as that fulfilled in religion and in political and art history by the bastion, pylon, propylaea, main gate, city gate. A station which was designed as a pure ancient gateway was Euston, long respectfully preserved, and demolished only with reluctance and sorrow when a change became necessary in 1963. King's Cross in London and the Gare du Nord in Paris were built as halls, huge ones even by present-day standards, the latter by Jakob Ignaz Hittorff, the most important architect to design a station in the nineteenth century. St. Pancras in London was built as a hotel, by Gilbert Scott. The concourses of stations in many cities, especially in North America, are monumental. The corresponding buildings today, when railway stations are tending to become smaller, are the great airports, such as those designed by Eero Saarinen for New York and Washington. Here we have a perfect example of the way in which the two halves, 'historicism' and

FIG. 4

'functionalism', hang together, the same yet ineradicably different – buildings erected before and after the turn of the century, or world transport by railway and world transport by aeroplane; but in both cases material for the history of art. It was for railway stations that the hall-like buildings of the nineteenth century were devised and developed. The great international exhibition halls usually mentioned as examples would have been impossible (apart from the Crystal Palace of 1851) but for the innumerable smaller station halls built before them. The three-section arch which appeared in Paris in 1889 had been developed in station halls since 1875. In general we must always remember that the whole problem of creating new traffic arteries had cropped up all at once in the decades before and after 1800; railways, canals and main roads, which we regard as quite different things, were all simply different solutions to the same urgent problem, that of transport or traffic.

What is transport? How is it connected with art?

In 1954 Ortega y Gasset wrote a prologue for a transport exhibition, in which he said: 'In fact, from wherever I happen to be at any given moment all the other places in the world coalesce in a living emotionally dynamic perspective, dynamic in its emotional tensions, the perspective "near-far".'

With all due respect for the great man, we must be allowed to contradict him: that is just what traffic is not. It is not a perspective, and it certainly does not consist in an 'I' that finds itself at the beginning of all philosophy, with all the rest organized as something far off; that is much rather the basic principle of the romantic imagination, which stands dreaming out into the distance.

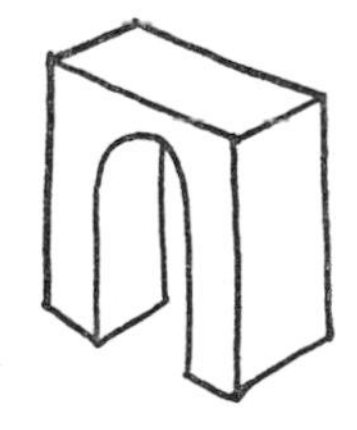

PORTAL BRIDGE-HEAD STATION	PEDESTRIAN HORSE COACH LOCOMOTIVE CAR	**LAND**	ROAD BRIDGE TUNNEL RAILWAY MOTORWAY	PORTAL BRIDGE-HEAD STATION
HARBOUR	SHIP	**WATER**	CHANNEL	HARBOUR
AIRPORT TRANSMITTER RADAR	AIRCRAFT CALL TELEGRAM IMPULSE	**AIR**	AIR CABLE VIBRATION WAVE	AIRPORT TRANSMITTER RADAR

No, fundamentally traffic knows no arrangement in which one pole is so dominant that it is 'the near' and all the rest is as vague and undefined as 'the far'. On the contrary, traffic starts at the same time from the same distances and the same bridge-heads, meets, passes and returns to the points of departure. There are two sides balancing the traffic with theoretically equal forces, masses, values and weights. And between the points of departure we find the real bearers of the traffic – the primitive elements of earth, water and air; we might add fire, in the shape of electricity, telegraphy, telephony etc.

Diagram of transport

At every spot inside the comprehensive diagram by which traffic could be represented architectural tasks occur. Demands and achievements grow greater every year. And what is the meaning, the human value of traffic? Surely not use and necessity, but order and communication, two highly intellectual concepts which are among the highest values accessible to man, values on which democracy is based.

Bridges have always been recognized as great architectural achievements; they are famous; works of literature have been devoted to them (Theodor Fontane, Thornton Wilder). How could there be anything more human, more friendly, more imaginative than a bridge? From the rainbow to the title of the Pontifex Maximus, bridges are linked with religious ideas.

If only one building from the last hundred years could be illustrated it would have to be a bridge. It would be wrong to attribute the great developments in bridge-building in the nineteenth century to the materials, as if cast iron and steel had produced the structures. The ideas which preceded the reality lay back in the eighteenth century. In the park at Wörlitz playful experiments were made with every type of bridge employed by the engineers of the following century – the Cyclopean bridge, the suspension bridge, the arched bridge, the girder bridge. The great wooden bridges of the Grubenmann brothers were the first to span more than a hundred yards, while those of Carl Friedrich Wiebeking rivalled the best of Maillart's in elegance. It is impossible here to give an accurate history of bridge-building; in any case this was done in outline by Mehrtens fifty years ago. The really big bridges, the decisive structures, are few in number; the innumerable others were all dependent on these. Yet even the smaller bridges, the unknown ones, possess an unexpected charm. People are always amazed when I show them a picture of Vilshofen bridge, built by the Augsburg-Nuremberg Engine Works in 1872 and photographed sixty years later in its original condition (it was subsequently destroyed during the war and has been rebuilt in a stronger but less beautiful form). They always find it difficult to believe the date, peer into the simple yet clearly differentiated strut-work, on whose lines the changing shadows rest; they are always struck by the magic way in which the girders coalesce and vanish, at the visual charm of the structure.

APPX. PL. 5

The pioneer age of bridge-building, the real break-through to new forms, to adventurous achievements, to the fulfilment of the dreams already current in the eighteenth century, was the nineteenth century. Around 1820 the first big suspension bridges were built, with chains at first and later cables (Telford's bridge across the Menai Strait). Around 1850 the solid piers of Stephenson's

'Britannia Bridge' across the same strait were erected, this time for the railway (and since then, for more than a hundred years, trains have been running daily between England and Holyhead between these girders – they have never had to be strengthened or altered). Around 1866 Gerber's first cantilever bridges were built; the greatest example of these was to be John Fowler's Forth Bridge (1882–9), but there have been many variations on the theme since then. Around 1867 John Röbling's great suspension bridges in Cincinnati and New York were finished or nearing completion. The nineteenth century also tried many other forms – crescent-shaped and lenticular piers, for example. The twentieth century has seen the appearance of bridges with unequal spans. The nineteenth century would never have built these; not because it would have been incapable of doing so but because they would not have fitted in with the basic artistic principle of symmetry. The asymmetrical bridge has only become a possibility since people have no longer regarded even the biggest bridge as a building in its own right but have seen it in the context of the landscape, the urban scene, transport as a whole.

A bridge can be one of two things.

It can be a building on the middle of which people abide and live. Then squares are laid out and *liwans* (arched halls) erected for the view, as on the Pol-i-Kadju in Isfahan; markets are set up, as on the Cornmarket bridge in Leyden; or workshops and houses built for goldsmiths, as in Venice, Florence, Paris or London. Often the approach roads on each side are quite steep. Or else a bridge can be so much a part of a long road that the traveller in his train or car does not notice that the valley has suddenly sunk away beneath him. Such is the case with the Europa Bridge near Innsbruck, which carries the autobahn across a deep Alpine valley. The pre-stressed concrete of which it is built is the material of the twentieth century. It is used in conjunction with steel, which was all the nineteenth century had at its disposal.

PLATE P. 34

Some of the big bridges lie far out in the countryside. A good example is Eiffel's viaduct at Garabit in Auvergne: it forms an integral part of the railway line, so much so that anyone sitting in the train simply does not see it. Other bridges, on the other hand, belong to the townscape; there are cities which are held together, given life only by their bridges. Fribourg in Switzerland was like a small medieval citadel until its whole character was altered by the suspension bridge. A city situated on a similar ridge, but one so much bigger – fifteen miles long and two and a half wide – that it can only be seen as a whole from an aeroplane is Manhattan, within New York. It was only through the bridges that Manhattan coalesced with the suburbs into a unified city. Other examples of the same sort of thing are the cities on both banks of a river – Rome, London, Paris, Cologne – where in the course of time the bridges have come to be lined up one after another like a row of bracelets. The river must be big enough to provide orientation, to give the city a centre. Just as the building of cathedrals held religions together, so the construction of roads, the development of transport, holds states together. A history of art that bases art on communications rather than on sensitivity must allow fundamental importance to the development of means of transport.

In prehistoric times there was the trackway, and even today there is the runway, wherever the wilderness is firm enough to support one. Gradually roads are built and strengthened. The Romans had a world-wide network of them and the only ancient map of the Roman Empire, the *Tabula Peutingeriana*, is a map of roads, not one of geographical features. The Rue des Pierres, which dates from the Middle Ages, is the most important street in Brussels. The strengthening of roads culminates in the iron track of the nineteenth century, which concentrates the heaviest loads on the smallest imaginable area of frictional contact. This is followed again in the twentieth century by the flattening and widening of the carriageway into a rolled surface with many tracks. The connected train is also broken down into a number of individual automobiles. The nineteenth century's solution was a very clever one: the assembly of many wagons into one single train. The fact that the twentieth century has departed from this optimum solution and surrendered to the caprice of the individual vehicle is probably due to deeper causes than purely technical or economic ones. We shall certainly have to think how to break this tyranny again, how to replace it with something equal to the railway in simplicity, even if it is no longer the railway itself.
Something that was laid on the surface of the earth in the nineteenth century in the shape of railway track, something that only almost imperceptibly, almost reluctantly contains an artistic element – an artistic element that is something communal, that does not arise out of the sensitivity of the individual and at the most can be appreciated by the individual only in his capacity as a representative of the community – this something is described by the individual in the twentieth century as a subjective experience, proclaimed to be obviously symbolic, a work of art. Moreover, this thing no longer lies on the surface of the earth, but follows (this is one of the motivations of the artist and the art historian) the trail made by the aeroplane through the air; it is like the cloud of condensation solidified in steel, as in the case of Norbert Kricke. The attempt to eternalize movement as such in a work also explains the constructions of Pevsner and Gabo, Calder's mobiles, the wire cages and curves of movement. The motif is legitimate, inevitable, it is the idiom of our time. How far posterity will recognize it, whether it will reveal completely new facets of which we as yet know nothing, remains to be seen. Only when it possesses this capacity for change, rather like the 'calving' of an iceberg, does a work remain a work of art. What pure technology is accomplishing is so exceptional in its formative power that art may have to give up the attempt to catch up or recognize technology – or the technological age – by technical means.

SHIP-BUILDING

The greatest marine painter was bound to be an Englishman: William Turner. He was more than just a marine painter; he was also a landscape painter and indeed, quite simply, a painter. But the fact that he included the whole business of the sea – its atmosphere, its history, its technology – in his picture of the world is nevertheless English in a narrower sense; it was part of the magnificent 'dilettantism', the intense and fruitful attention, with which the English aristocracy equipped itself to rule the world. The sea was calm, the sun was setting, its rays

The Alpine road over the St. Gotthard Pass. The hairpin bends have been built up since 1924.

The Europa Bridge near Innsbruck, begun in 1959 and completed in 1964. *Total length 880 yards, width 24 yards; height above the bottom of the valley 515 feet. Cf. p. 31.*

J. M. W. Turner, *The Fighting Téméraire*. 1839. Oil on canvas. *Height 36 in., width 48 in. National Gallery, London. Cf. pp. 37, 40, 127.*

The passenger liner *Rotterdam*, built in 1962. *Length 740 feet; beam 92 feet; height to sun-deck 100 feet; capacity about 1370 passengers.* *Cf. p. 39.*

reflected in a mirror image: the Dutchmen of the seventeenth century had already grasped the artistic problem implicit in the fact that a landscape picture always threatened to fall apart into a dark lower half and a bright sky above, which it was difficult to fill with a content equal in weight to the earth below. Yet Turner's solution was a new one: not simply a matter of the observing eye, but a matter of the explosions, the bursts of solar energy, the power of light, in place of impressionistic appearances. The Dutch painters had recognized the art of shipbuilding and concerned themselves with hull and sails, with shipyard and carpenter. What they had not been able to do in their own seventeenth century was to give recognition to the history of shipbuilding and to depict, by one magnificent example, how at this moment, when the *Téméraire* was towed off, a thousand years of shipbuilding were coming to an end.

The *Téméraire* had originally been built in a French yard at Brest. The British had captured the ship in the battle of the Nile (Abukir, 1801) and incorporated her into their own fleet. Chivalrously they allowed the previously hostile ship to retain her name. She had subsequently fought under Nelson, as second flagship, in the battle of Trafalgar on 21 October 1805. She continued in service after that, first as a ship of the line and later as a training ship for cadets. Finally she succumbed to the fate of all ships. The materials of which she was built were still so valuable that she was broken up. (That is why there is almost no memorial to the great ages of shipbuilding; that is why it was so splendid that the *Gustavus Vasa* could be raised, and so praiseworthy that ten years ago the American Navy did not allow the battleship *Repulse* to be broken up, but decided to preserve it as a memorial for posterity).

A smoky tug towed the *Téméraire* away; it was a legendary moment, comparable with the Doge's voyage, the annual marriage of Venice to the sea. Much greater than the reminder of the fight between French and British was the reminder of the transition from sailing ship to steamship. The seafaring of five thousand years, during which the elements had been conquered by the sail, was replaced by modern machines built of iron. The new victory was still achieved with a visible effort, by means of the paddles which pushed the tug forward; the day was still to come of underwater propulsion – screw or jet – invisible and impossible to represent optically. The new age drew its power from the same heat that made the sun blaze. In Turner's picture, where the sails still hang the colours are blue, white, yellow. Where heat and the steam power derived from it hold sway, red lies like molten iron over the water. The ships which the tug and her tow passed, all the way from Portsmouth to Gravesend, broke out in the dull, wailing whistle that had only become possible with steam power.

PLATE P. 35

How should a structure express that it is swift and powerful? Should it look like a sailing-ship whose expanses of canvas are blown along by the wind? Or like a castle or a hotel? Should the windows of the cabins be round like bull's-eyes – the best shape to keep out heavy seas – or big and square, with panes of ordinary glass, so that from inside you do not notice that you are on a ship? Should the masts be retained when the rigging has become superfluous? Should the funnels be raked, as if drawn back by the forward movement, although the rake is quite unnecessary against the wind, which in any case blows from various directions? Or should they stand straight up like the towers of a medieval castle? Should the stem be straight, or bend forward at the top, or jut out at the bottom like a ram? How should the upperworks be shaped? For in a short time ships were to be bigger and stand higher out of the water than a town hall or a church; they would not fit into any of the squares of London, Paris, Rome or Vienna, for old cities do not possess squares three hundred yards long. These are some of the questions which were to occupy the naval architects of the next few decades, apart from the alterations forced on designers by changes in seafaring technique.

In Turner there is still the poetry of the sea, a poetry that has now become melancholy; there is no resistance to the new age, but insight and admission that the new is the more powerful. In the original painting one can even make out the men on the tug, the engineers – they can no longer be called sailors – standing about on deck.

That was in 1837. In 1852 the keel of the *Great Eastern* was laid down: 27,000 tons, 11,000 horsepower, 680 feet long. At the end of five years the ship could not be launched in the usual fashion; it had to be pushed into the water by hydraulic rams, a task which took months. Seven years' work and £ 732,000 had been expended on the ship. It was the decisive step into the gigantic: in the domain of architecture real size also has real significance, real consequences and real value, even for the history of art. For the first time a double bottom and watertight bulkheads were incorporated. The builders, Isambard Kingdom Brunel and John Scott Russell, were among the engineers who made the history of transport in the first half of the nineteenth century.

The career of this giant steamer was somewhat chequered. Technically the ship was a success; its trials could be shortened and the crossing to New York was accomplished punctually. But the shipping company's calculations turned out to be unsound; it was found impossible to book for every voyage the 800 first-class, 2,000 second-class and 1,200 third-class passengers needed to make the ship a profitable concern. It had to be hired out on charter for individual voyages. It was just going to be broken up when a fresh, apparently quite different job turned up: the ship was big enough to hold the first submarine cable to be laid between Europe and America, with its 2,500 miles of plaited wire, which had to be sunk on the bed of the Atlantic. What a decline, one might say if one were thinking in classical terms: instead of men, the lords of creation, the proud ship now had to embark and reel out oily coils of wire. But the person who sees the task and history of world communications as a unity would answer, no: the exchange of news was just as much a part of communications as the exchange of travellers or goods. The cable served communications as much as the ship did. The steamer's function changed, but it was still a piece of architecture, part of the whole group of buildings and structures connected with traffic and transport. The *Great Eastern* was finally broken up in 1889; the scrap realized £ 16,000, one-sixtieth of what it had cost to build her.

The *Great Eastern* was not equalled or surpassed in size until forty years later, around the turn of the century. At the moment (1966) the record stands at 205,000 tons and a length of 1,100 feet. People are now talking of 300,000 tons, no longer for a passenger liner or even an aircraft-carrier, which for some time was the biggest kind of ship, but for a tanker – so quite clearly for world communications again.

Do we realize all the famous buildings that could be accommodated in a hull of this size? Four Parthenons would fit in lengthways. The question is not an idle one. A hall in Stephenson's Hotel in Chicago was bought by the management from the wreckage of the *Normandie* and transferred to the hotel. The cinema incorporated in the *Rotterdam* has 456 seats; it has its own place in the story of architecture. If the interior of the cinema belongs to architecture, surely the exterior must, too? Or are we dealing in the twentieth century with an architecture which must be asked whether it is interior or exterior before it can be included in the history of art?

Obviously we cannot enumerate all the ships built in the last hundred years or name all the types of ship in existence, for we should have to include big and little warships as well, with all their variations in size, armour, speed and shape above and below the waterline. Take the *Rotterdam:* built in 1962, 38,645 gross registered tons, length 740 feet, beam 92 feet, height to the sun-deck 100 feet, passenger-carrying capacity 580 first class, 789 tourist class. She is a good example of the hotel building, the 'bachelor flat', the *unité d'habitation:* superimposed storeys, single rooms arranged for transitory occupation, streets of shops, public rooms, cinema, baths and sun-lounges, all accommodated in the same building. Large floor-spaces can be arranged in 'decks' in the same way and furnished with hundreds of desks and typewriters; then you have the tower office-block. Or as sick rooms; then the operating theatres would have to be enlarged. These are obviously not lacking in a ship, but they have to be kept within modest proportions. The whole area could also be made into cargo space, perhaps for complete trains. All these possibilities belong to the field of interior architecture, a special department of contemporary architectural training. It goes without saying that today everything is air-conditioned. There are old sailors who would rather do their North Cape cruise in the oldest possible ship than in a modern one because they hope that on the old ship they will still breathe the sea air directly. The more modern the ship the more probable it is that one will only see the sea and fjords from behind panes of glass. On the other hand it is also more likely that the trip will adhere to its timetable!

PLATE P. 36

What still gives ships such magic is the necessity for them to be self-sufficient units. However vast a ship may be, once it has cast off and is floating on the ocean it must still assert itself, it must be an individual, it must have a stout exterior, a clearly defined shape and a very complicated interior. If one wished to compare it to an animal, the comparison should be with a turtle rather than with a fish; in the same way an aeroplane would have to be compared with an insect rather than with a bird. A ship does not need a spine but a stout exterior shell which supports itself and makes life within possible. It has more cells than most of the buildings which go to make up present-day architecture. The outside must be strong enough to stand up to all kinds of buffeting. What enormous, changing

tensions arise when a ship's hull is lifted from one wave to the next, when it has to withstand the thousands of tons of water that a breaker can hurl against it. Aeroplanes have to stand up in the same way to the pressure of the winds and the resistance of the air. Only satellites are subject to different laws.
Naturally the propulsion machinery and the crew's quarters have always to be fitted in somewhere, but the greater the tonnage the smaller the proportion of it needed for propulsion. The cargo capacity, quite small in a rowing boat or a Viking ship, was a good deal greater in the big-bellied ships of Greece and Rome now being raised from the bed of the Mediterranean and in the high-pooped ships of the Hanseatic League. Today the use of high-performance metals permits cargo space that seems almost limitless. It really makes very little difference to the shipbuilder whether the empty space is filled with oil tanks or a fish factory, as is the case with a whaling ship.
The difference between modern shipbuilding and the *Great Eastern* of a century ago is considerable. But the idea, the prophetic spirit already existed in those days. What has followed in between springs from the technical expertise which naval architects have acquired from the building materials and the specialized tasks which have arisen. But the dividing line between the five-thousand-year-old sailing ship and the machine-driven vehicle, between the *Téméraire* and the paddle steamer, can be drawn round about 1830. That was when the great revolution in shipbuilding occurred, not at the turn of the nineteenth and twentieth centuries. Any attempt to exclude the art of shipbuilding from a survey of architecture would be quite useless. The history of art has always had to take into account this brilliant chapter in the story of man's building activities, and today it would be quite impossible to ignore it. The different branches of the construction industry are too closely connected with each other, and young architects obviously see too many pictures of ships. They influence our sense of form. Seeing that modern architecture has been described at times as 'streamlined', it would be illogical to exclude from the history of art those very forms which must on all accounts be shaped in accordance with the streams of water and air.

WORLD EXHIBITIONS

'There is art in everything': this was the principle – though it was never formulated in so many words in those days – followed by the organizers of the Great Exhibition of 1851. It was industry's optimistic principle throughout the century. After the sharp counter-attack at the beginning of this century, when people wanted to separate art completely from technology, nature and any kind of imitation, we are returning to the earlier principle, if with much more reflection and greater caution. There is art in everything; otherwise world art could not be compiled in the way it is, with examples from pottery, religious ritual, portraiture and aqueducts. We know that in every age theologians have resisted the idea of allowing their church to be regarded as a work of art, or predominantly as a work of art, on the ground that it is much more a building in the service of God: art is subordinate to religion. Our principle, 'There is art in everything', does not subordinate anything but simply asserts that in all man's products his sense of art plays some part. They all contain, however small the admixture, an artistic element.

A certain amount of composition is involved in this book, but neither the author nor his publishers would claim to have produced a work of art. Let the expenditure be a little greater and the publisher is soon competing to have his book mentioned among 'the most beautiful books of the year'. Just a little more care still and book illustrations become predominantly works of art; they are only secondarily books of hours and objects of religious use, and that is true from the moment of their creation. Theologians would not succeed if they tried to claim them back for the service of God. The precious golden manuscripts of the Middle Ages were always intended for preservation, not use; otherwise they would not have been kept in such mint condition.

There is art in everything, even in world exhibitions. It is well known that the glass palace of 1851 was the first nineteenth-century building to re-appear over the horizon of aesthetic consciousness. When did this happen? Was it the art historians – Giedion, Pevsner, Zevi – who first raised it again into the ranks of works of art? Or was it inquisitive architects looking for ancestors? In any case, it is no longer possible to write a history of nineteenth-century art without giving the place of honour in it to the Crystal Palace.

And rightly so, for there are moments of genius in the history of art when ideas that have long been in the air can at last be fulfilled. The fairs of the Middle Ages, the national exhibitions of the industrial age were bound eventually to produce the idea of a world exhibition for, as Prince Albert, the Prince Consort, said in his inaugural speech, 'We live in a wonderful age of transition, which is hastening towards the attainment of the great goal of all world history, the demonstration of the unity of mankind.' A building had to be devised which would house ten thousand exhibitors (in the end there were seventeen thousand) and provide room for a million visitors (in the event six million came). An international invitation to architects brought in 240 designs; but none that could have been turned into reality; and the design which the Commission eventually patched together out of them could not have been built in the time available. It would not even have been possible to bake quickly enough the seventeen million bricks needed for the walls. We may hazard the guess that the history of architecture was bound to reach an end like this. It had begun with the mighty mountain – the pyramid and the stepped temple or ziggurat – which scarcely contained any room at all, and was thus bound to end in a building which was all space and transparent envelope and needed hardly any mass to stiffen the envelope. One day, perhaps, frozen air or a dome of light that is not just the reflection of a search-light may push the boundary of architecture yet further out, but in principle it was reached in 1851. There appeared on the scene, just at the right moment, the landscape gardener (and architect!) Joseph Paxton, who had experience with glass-houses, knew how to put them together out of prefabricated sections of cast iron and glass, possessed the energy to suggest and execute the shapes possible with these materials, the prudence to test the resistance of the individual sections (in such a human, beginner's way – he made a company of soldiers double across the trial pieces of his iron struts!), and the organizing ability to supervise the erection of a building over 600 yards long, 130 yards wide and 107 feet high.

(We have already mentioned above that at the same time Paxton was building the traditional castle of Mentmore.)
The history of world exhibitions, which is well enough known in outline but still remains to be studied and told in detail, brings two further basic ideas to the big buildings of the technological age.
One of them is French: the connection with town planning. With each of their international exhibitions the French took a decisive step forward in the perfecting of their city of Paris. In 1855 they created the general purpose hall, the permanent building. Even though Napoleon III had made it a condition that it must be capable of holding 18,000 troops and 6,000 horses – he had in mind the control of the city if street fighting with barricades were to break out – the Palace of Industry was never used by the military, but it was employed every year for events of all kinds. (In 1900 it was replaced by the present Grand Palais and Petit Palais.) In 1876 the Trocadero was built on the heights of Passy (to be reconstructed in 1937 as the present museum buildings). 1889 saw the addition of the Eiffel Tower and the Machinery Hall, which – alas! – fell a victim twenty years later to the zeal of the aesthetes, torn down in cold blood through the temporary predominance of people who were not yet capable of fitting nineteenth-century architecture into their picture of the world, and were convinced that Paris would be improved by the removal of this hall.
The other idea was an Anglo-Saxon one: that it was not possible to depict the unity of the world in one single building, whose symbolic form would have to be, in accordance with a two-thousand-year tradition, a dome. It was thought on the contrary that the way to govern was to leave carefully what had grown up independently where it was. In short, that not the dome, not the individual building, but the garden was the humane symbol of the world, and that consequently a world exhibition must be set in a park. Here the British and the Americans were certainly at one with the oldest tradition; but it was not a western tradition. The most beautiful parks in the world were those of imperial China, perishing at that same moment – the middle of the nineteenth century – amid the chaos of war.
In eighteenth- and nineteenth-century Europe far more parks were laid out than is commonly realized – by the Prince of Dessau at Wörlitz, by Prince Pückler in Muskau (Silesia), Pegli near Genoa, the Bois de Boulogne in Paris, Linderhof in Upper Bavaria and many others. The first world fair was staged in Hyde Park, on condition that the trees were spared, and the Philadelphia Exhibition of 1876 and the Chicago Exhibition of 1893 were both made the occasion for laying out magnificent parks; subsequently this Anglo-Saxon concept has become the traditional one for the setting of international fairs.
Another regular feature of every big exhibition, at any rate since 1878, is the historical village, in which the pleasure buildings are concentrated. In 1878 there was a reconstruction of medieval Paris.
The *borgo medioevale* put up at Turin in 1882 is still standing today; so is Barcelona's *pueblo español* of 1929. At Paris in 1900 a 'Swiss town' was opened, at Brussels in 1958 a *cité joyeuse*, and at Los Angeles in 1955 'Disneyland'. In other words,

international exhibitions mirror our picture of the world, our self-consciousness, in a gay and reflective manner. From them we can learn, not very methodically perhaps, but hence all the more naturally, what art means for mankind.
From this series of international exhibitions one could illustrate at least the history of 'industrial design' and indeed the whole history of architectural technology: for example, in 1878 it was possible for the first time to keep an exhibition open after dark – in 1851 the Crystal Palace had had to be closed at nightfall – and the main hall of 1878 marked the beginning of Art Nouveau (a subject which has not yet been studied in detail). However, here we shall deal only with the Paris Exhibition of 1889 and we shall concentrate on the Eiffel Tower and the Machinery Hall.
Why did the Parisians build the tower? 'The Eiffel Tower, which not even business-like America wanted to have, is a disgrace to Paris,' declared many artists in a communal protest. They comforted themselves with this thought: 'If our warning is not heard, if our reasons are not understood, if Paris obstinately persists in disgracing itself, at any rate you and we will have done what we could. It is a protest that does us honour.' Why then did the Parisians build it? The answer is that it is the purest tower ever erected by mankind. But the question why men build towers at all cannot be answered in a single sentence. It is certain that there is some connection with the fact that man stands upright, but this is obvious. For five thousand years the tallest building in the world was the Pyramid of Cheops, which was primarily a tomb. The Pharos of Alexandria was one of the wonders of the world, but it was primarily a lighthouse. The towers of fortresses were tall, but they were intended for defence. So were the family towers of Bologna and San Gimignano. And what about the pagodas of China, the towers of cathedrals? What arguments would their medieval builders have used to defend the latter? Would they have just said that the bells had to be hung somewhere high? The longing for towers is very hard to analyse. The skyscrapers of America are certainly also towers and expressions of national pride, but essentially they are living spaces piled on top of each other on a cramped site. And television towers: do they have to be high in order to transmit their signals?

PLATE P. 45

The Eiffel Tower is the most 'tower-like' of all these buildings. It is nothing but a tower and therein lies its appeal to the imagination. It is built, of course, in a material that is firmer and tougher than any stone, but, more than that, it is built to a design that makes it the very symbol of upward striving. It was probably clear to Gustave Eiffel himself that from a technical point of view the tower could have been built quite differently, as a perpendicular lattice girder without any arches or curvature. But what his imagination suggested to him was this particular tower, which has an almost mythical quality. Before the Eiffel Tower was built, if you had asked any Parisian which building best typified his city he would have replied 'the Cathedral of Notre Dame'. Ever since, he has said – you can confidently bet on it – 'the Eiffel Tower'. What other building has impressed itself so immediately (and so rightly) on the national consciousness? It has been copied innumerable times; in tiny toys, in liqueur bottles (which are to be found in the drawing-offices of the cleverest, most modern architects), in the wishful dreams of ambitious Englishmen (cf. the competition in the very same year of 1889), and full-size in Japan; there is never any doubt that the Eiffel Tower is the prototype.

The situation was not the same as in Paxton's case. Even without the tower Gustave Eiffel would be an important engineer – a bridge-builder like Telford, Stephenson, Röbling or Gerber. He had built the Garabit viaduct, the bridge over the Garonne downstream from Bordeaux, and other bridges in Portugal, India and Hungary. He also built the iron framework of the Statue of Liberty at the entrance to New York harbour. The trust placed in him when he suggested building something twice as high as anything yet in existence was already established; it did not have to be won.

The construction is absolutely typical of Eiffel's time. The material is iron in the form of mild steel; long past the stage of cast iron, but not yet endowed with the degree of hardness attained by modern alloys. It is the angle iron that gives the additional stability, and every four such angle girders are joined together by oblique struts to form a box beam. The joining was still done with hammered rivets, not by welding the edges as it is nowadays. Today box sections would be used rather than braced girders and of course the whole four-legged structure, with its ground-plan of a square with sides of 135 yards, would be dispensed with. However, this would also mean dispensing with the visual impression which is – and was from the start – based on artistic, not constructional principles.

The large number of these girders makes the construction of the Eiffel Tower clear and comprehensible, yet at the same time confused and eye-defeating, according to the angle from which one looks at it or photographs it.

Precisely the same assemblage of steel girders was the basis of the mode of construction employed by Dutert and Contamin for the Machinery Hall. At the first international exhibitions the machines were shown working and were demonstrated and sold on the spot (in this respect the exhibition of 1889 was the last real fair; the exhibitions of today are only sample demonstrations of industries, not vending-places for manufacturing firms, which otherwise, extending over the whole range of the modern industrial world, would overstep the bounds of any possible site), but since 1855 the halls containing them have been separated from the main building. The size and noise of the machines had become too great.

Indeed, 1867 was the last occasion on which any attempt was made to represent the world by means of a building. An oval was chosen and concentric rings apportioned to the individual branches of industry, while the various nations were given sectors of the oval. A fine patriarchal idea – if only the distribution of industry had been the same in each country. But, apart from that, the idea could only be realized as a ground-plan. There was no longer any actual building; the centre was an open garden with fountains.

Between 1867 and 1889 the so-called triple-jointed arch was developed. The great expansion and contraction of iron in changing daily temperatures had to be considered. Rigid joints were replaced by three roller bearings, in which the girders stretching between could move. The triple-jointed arch with roller bearings inserted in it had been invented and first employed by C. Knoll in 1875.

The Eiffel Tower in Paris. Erected between 1885 and 1889 by Gustave Eiffel for the Paris Exhibition of 1889. *Height 975 feet. Cf. pp. 43, 44.*

Aerial photograph of the industrial town of Saltaire in England. Built from 1853 onwards by Sir William Fairbairn, who was commissioned by Henry Salt. *Cf. p. 52.*

Eugène Vallin, Dining room for M. Masson in Nancy. 1903–5. Leather wall-covering, ceiling and carvings on the fireplace and sideboard by Victor Prouvé. Design for the copper light fittings by Vallin, glass by the Brothers Daum from Nancy. *Musée de l'École de Nancy.*

Henry van de Velde, Four-piece silver tea service with boxwood handles. 1905/6. Made by the court jeweller Theodor Müller, Weimar. *Karl-Ernst-Osthaus-Museum, Hagen i.W.* *Cf. p. 55.*

Now, in the Machinery Hall of 1889, the dimensions became vast: 460 yards by 125 by 35. These have only been exceeded once since then, at the Chicago Exhibition of 1893, and then only slightly. This 'clear space', too, verges on the fantastic; it may be that, just as the Eiffel Tower has remained the purest tower, so the Machinery Hall would have remained the purest 'clear space', if it had been left standing.

The impression created by this hall must have been tremendous. There is a famous photograph of it, reproduced again and again since 1925 (Siegfried Giedion, *Bauen in Eisen*), but it is the only usable shot of it so far discovered. In other words, the hall was demolished before photographers had seen what an artistic task lay before them here – that of providing a proper record of the building.

Today many halls are built for the most varied purposes. The first large-scale hall in the new material, reinforced concrete, was the Jahrhunderthalle in Breslau, designed by Max Berg in 1913. Since the arrival of pre-stressed concrete as well, halls which must provide a large open space are erected in this material, though it is already being replaced by an artificial material (chemically produced polyester), which can be inflated. The business of erecting halls belongs to the age when it was still important to have built the 'biggest' hall. This ambition has passed away.

As everyone knows that enlarging or reducing the dimensions is only a matter of arithmetic, every task, every production, every exhibition is broken up into a number of small halls. 'Small' means up to the size of a football field.

Advances are continually being made: the astonishing hanging ceiling of the Raleigh hall, by Nowicki; the magical stresses of Pier-Luigi Nervi, made of prefabricated sections – the first public hall in this style was the one at Turin (somewhat spoilt, alas, by an unfortunate exterior), but it had been preceded by aircraft hangars. Then there are the sports halls with a single instead of a double arch, for example, the 1965 one in Tokyo, by Kenzo Tange. On the whole, the fantastic halls of today are built more often for sport than for exhibitions.

The creations of Konrad Wachsmann and R. Buckminster Fuller defy classification. Wachsmann is known for his studies of joints. How many halls have been built according to his patents, and how big they are, is simply not known, since they are used for military purposes. The same is true of Buckminster Fuller's geodetic domes. There are said to be two thousand of them, the biggest 33 yards in diameter. They certainly hold all kinds of possibilities. It lies in the nature of these recurring structures that they leave the world of size behind; they reach out into an infinity that returns upon itself.

In 1966 the assembly shed at the John F. Kennedy Space Center was described as the biggest complex of buildings in existence at the time, but it is not an open hall and the roofed space is far smaller than in the Machinery Hall of 1889. On the other hand, the height has been increased to 390 feet so that, according to the newspapers, thunderstorm equipment has become necessary on the inside. The framework consists rather of hardened honeycombs than of an outer skin.

Meanwhile the business of arranging exhibitions – deciding what will be shown and how it will be shown – has become an art in itself; it cannot be included in

FIG. 5 – *The layout of the Ringstrasse in Vienna. Cf. below.*

architecture or sculpture or painting. And it certainly could not be found in a system of aesthetics such as Hegel's or Schelling's.

TOWN-PLANNING

FIG. 5

A word more about Semper: his buildings in Vienna belonged to the context of the Ringstrasse. A big nineteenth-century city gave itself a new look. Vienna, which had twice acted as a bastion for the whole of Europe and twice held back the Turks, knew the importance of fortifications. For this reason it had kept its ring of forts and the glacis in front of them longer than other cities; or at any rate other cities like Bordeaux, Paris and Antwerp did not use the exceptional opportunity provided by the dismantling of their fortifications in the same way as Vienna. The suburbs had had to stay some distance outside the city; the land in between belonged to the state. It was a chance that could occur only once in the city's two-thousand-year history – the chance to create a new environment in a belt 650 yards wide right round the centre of the city. The sale of land provided the means to erect on this ring road all the big buildings needed by a national state in the nineteenth century: city church, university, city hall, ministry of justice, theatre, imperial palace, opera-house, big museums, academy, parliament, barracks, many parks, library, record office and markets, all connected by a splendid thoroughfare. It was in 1857 that the emperor announced his intention of having the fortifications razed and laid down the general lines on which building was to take place. The competition was won by C. F. L. Förster in 1858, and the distribution of the sites was finally decided in 1872. There have been examples in these

days of the foundation of new capitals – Canberra, Brasilia, Chandigarh – but Vienna was a better proposition since it did not have to be started from scratch but could be filled out at the most favourable point. Moreover, the population was there already, and there was no doubt whether the old and new cities would coalesce. Slowly, remarkably slowly, the Ringstrasse is rising in the estimation of art historians. The tasks of a capital city have remained approximately the same; and this confirms yet again our view that historicism and functionalism belong together, that they both form part of a unified century. The solutions adopted to solve the problems raised by capitals are various. The work of the Viennese architects (several were involved) hung together well; the stylistic unity of historicism was greater than the stylistic unity of the twentieth century was to be. At any rate Chandigarh was entrusted to one single architect, probably because otherwise unity would not have been achieved. (An example of the contrary in the twentieth century is the Hansa district in Berlin, put up in 1957 on the basis of a building exhibition.)
Other assumptions underlay the transformation of Paris carried out by the Emperor Napoleon III and Baron Haussmann, prefect of the Seine. It may be that the basic ideas came from Napoleon III himself; along with Ludwig I of Bavaria he was one of the very few really fertile patrons of the middle of the century. But he could not have realized his plans but for Haussmann, the energetic, unscrupulous local politician who guided the credit facilities of a period of continual expansion, the building industry of a whole epoch, in the direction of town-planning. The Paris which they created is the Paris we see today; by far the biggest part of the city centre proper dates from the nineteenth century. This capacity to go on building without a halt by continually raising new loans can be compared only with the financial policy of the popes in the Baroque age. The clearance of the boulevards, the bulwarks, the walls of earlier fortifications, to make way for wide straight streets had already begun in previous centuries. The Rue de Rivoli dated from the time of Napoleon I, but as yet it did not connect with the Rue St. Antoine; it still stopped at the Louvre. The Rue Turbigo and the railways with their stations dated from the reign of Louis-Philippe.
In Paris circumstances were different from those in Vienna. It was not a question of finally building on open land that already belonged to the state; a thickly populated district had to be bought up, demolished and re-developed. The emperor may have been concerned to open up the twisting streets of the old city, where he wished to prevent further fighting at the barricades, but the prefect was similarly interested in the traffic problems which, with remarkable vision, he foresaw. Jakob Ignaz Hittorff, who had remodelled the Place de la Concorde, the Champs-Élysées and the Place de l'Étoile, thought he was doing something quite exceptional when he suggested a width of fifty-two yards for the Avenue Bois de Boulogne. Baron Haussmann pushed the esteemed architect of the previous régime, and his plan, to one side and widened the avenue to 120 yards. A completely new north-south axis was created, in the shape of the Boulevard Sébastopol and the Boulevard St. Michel. As for the Opéra and its surroundings, the Avenue de l'Opéra was driven through from the Louvre. The whole middle of the Île de

Paris, the oldest part of the city, was rebuilt; only right at the west end, round the Place Dauphine, and right at the east, to the north of Notre Dame, were Baroque sections left standing.

The façades framing the new streets were not really 'historicist' but rather academic or classicist. The French Academy should not be under-valued, nor should the quality of the training which it gave its pupils and the quality of the attainments which it demanded of them. French classicism, developed by France in place of Italo-Habsburg Baroque, was far more suitable for adaptation to contemporary forms. The versions employed for these façades were skilful, self-evident and reserved; they resulted in completely homogeneous streets, which were later painted on numerous occasions by the Impressionists. The uniformity of Parisian building during the nineteenth century was so great that one must hesitate to call it 'historicist'. At any rate, buildings which were 'historicist' in the strict sense of the term, such as the church of St. Clotilde, make a far stronger impression in Paris than the corresponding Votivkirche does in Vienna.

The uncontrolled growth of the English industrial towns, the sticking together of similar units, the refusal to provide a water supply, drains, made-up streets, illumination or hygiene of any kind was, even in the nineteenth century, not only the subject of novels preaching social reform (Charles Dickens) but also a source of worry to town councils. And as the councils were composed in those days almost exclusively of middle-class people it was the business man with patriarchal feelings who took the real step forward into the future by founding the first factory with a housing estate belonging to it and planned at the same time, the first self-sufficient industrial town. The first and most important building was the factory itself. The name Saltaire was made up from the name of the River Aire and the name of the employer, Henry Salt.

PLATE P. 46

The next achievement which I want to mention, the industrial town of Tony Garnier, certainly plays a part from the beginning in the history of art, that is, in man's consciousness of art, but – almost in instructive contrast to the town of Saltaire, which no one knows because it is only an existing reality – it is a town that only exists in literature, in the public mind. Here we have an excellent example of the extraordinary power of literary expression in the nineteenth and twentieth centuries – something to which one can never give too much thought. Tony Garnier conjures up, in pure theory, in a frenzied Utopia, before his own eyes and those of others, the picture of a possible, a future town, just like a film, a 'Metropolis', with all its feasibilities, with a maze of industry, confusing, but no longer negative as in the descriptions of English industrial towns, with the evocative power of the factory city as opposed to the imposing look of the imperial, the bourgeois city. Movement and energy in the place of power and property. In imperial Paris the street had still been an open space, a place for the enjoyment of life, now it is becoming a traffic artery, a channel from which the city draws life, but through which it also bleeds away.

ART NOUVEAU

Within the nineteenth century – of whose density, compactness, power of expansion we no longer possess an adequate conception – within a restless activity

which on the one hand was historicism but on the other – quite apart from stylistic categories – building frenzy, enterprise, speculation, industrialization (all of which is not directly connected with the history of art but must be understood in all its abundance and inevitability, lest one should think that artists hankered for *l'art pour l'art* on an island of their own, in a vacuum), within this mass society opposition arose at either end of the social hierarchy. At one end there was the opposition of the oppressed, the proletarians, the organized unions; at the other, the opposition of the completely esoteric, the determinedly isolated, the individuals. Among them (important names could obviously be mentioned in every country) William Morris in England glowed with a special intensity. His aims, when given in his own words, can be seen to be contradictory; they were really unattainable from the outset. He asserted that industrialization could be opposed by re-introducing handicrafts (this was after Karl Marx's volumes on capitalism and the proletariat had appeared in this very England); that one must live from handicrafts (he could not even do this himself; Morris's so-called handicrafts could only exist by courtesy of rich men who earned their money in industry); that the old materials could be used (aniline dyes had already been introduced and year by year chemistry was transforming the science of materials with revolutionary analyses and syntheses); and finally that in the late Middle Ages artists had been uneducated but happy craftsmen, and that works of art had simply been passed from hand to hand, more or less by barter (which, in view of the Burgundian court and such aristocratic personages as the chamberlain Jan van Eyck, was bound to make any historian shake his head). It was not what Morris said that was fascinating, but the way in which he said it, the way in which he acted, namely as a quite individual maker of highly cultivated articles which could not themselves become mass-produced goods but were suited to become models for industrial design.
Morris for his part chose the same sort of models as the Pre-Raphaelites: slender but lascivious girls; strapping, ascetic heroes enclosed in shining armour. If the theory that historicism is weakness were at all tenable, then Morris would have to be charged with this weakness, for he did not strive to reshape the content of his work but, beginning with the texts which he set up on his presses, drew everything from the Middle Ages. Thus everything he made would be, in terms of *Weltanschauung*, second-hand – if this whole line of argument were not in fact false, for it was not a question of first- or second-hand but of the intensity with which life was lived. The canvassing for his ideas and products was intensive, too, and so was the consciousness of a prophetic role (it was in imitation of this that French painters later called themselves Nabis, prophets). Intensity and versatility: these were characteristics of English dilettantism in its most fruitful form. Such multiplex activity was only possible because the multiplicity lay not in the end product, the final specialization, but in a communal beginning which Morris conceived and propagated personally, as if this were the hand that held everything together. His was certainly the mind, if not the hand as well, that applied itself to everything: house-building, interior decoration, weaving, book production, glass-painting – much too much to make a profession that others

could have taken over; yet all rooted in an autophagous dilettantism which by its very intensity fertilized and stimulated other steadier and more conventional talents.

Museums for art and industry were founded in every country, in London, Vienna, Paris, Berlin, Nuremberg. They were all meant to provide models for handicrafts, but they soon changed into showcases of historicism and finally into special kinds of art galleries.

The 'Red House', built for Morris by Philip Webb, should not be compared with town houses; it is one of the country houses, the cottages, which always existed, even in the middle of the nineteenth century, from which American country houses in the 'shingle style' were also developed. It looks surprising today simply because the other houses amid which it stood are no longer to be seen.

The word 'handicraft' which Morris used must be interpreted quite differently. It should be set alongside his assertion that art is joy in life, that indeed work is joy in life; alongside Richard Riemerschmid's statement, 'We are simply making a start.' One should see the cupboard which Gauguin made for his family in 1881 and which is still preserved by his family. It is not the carving on the cupboard door that is important; this is a ludicrous imitation of the iron-work on medieval wooden chests, shallowly incised in the living wood, with a mixture of plant forms, and thus hideous to any purist with a knowledge of materials. What is important is that the enthusiastic dilettante Paul Gauguin hankered after this personal activity, that he made the cupboard himself – and at the same time made pottery himself; all this was really one of the first manifestations of Art Nouveau. He was a dilettante in the noble sense that he longed to do everything himself. So, that he himself might be active, he reconstructed everything, last but not least his own life.

Thus we can define Art Nouveau *(Jugendstil)* as a movement similar to the 'do-it-yourself movement' of the twentieth century, filled with the same reforming zeal, the certainty that there is something moral, healing, reforming in this activity. Hence the connection with the social programme, with the feeling that doing things yourself was the gateway to a primitive paradise. Hence the impulse to keep going back to the beginning – in Gauguin the impulse to move out of Europe into a pre-European, extra-European environment.

If we discuss Henry van de Velde more fully than others, that is because he and his activities are particularly good examples, because he remained a 'do-it-yourself' man far longer and much more consistently. For this reason he was very influential, while the Art Nouveau activity of other artists was limited to a relatively short period, which was succeeded by other periods of activity as pure architects or painters or sculptors.

The connection with painting is often interpreted as if Art Nouveau was mainly an affair of painting, indeed almost only graphic art, and as if this is proved by the fact that van de Velde (and other men of the same stamp) were first painters. But what was the situation for an enquiring mind between 1880 and 1890? There was as yet no *numerus clausus* for professional training. Whoever felt the urge towards artistic activity turned first to the field where it was easiest. This was painting, which demanded least in the way of handicraft and left most room for theory, for studio discussions. If van de Velde turned away from painting before he had really achieved any eminence in it, that was because he was more interested in the things themselves than in painting them, because reality, the hardness of the material, three-dimensionality fascinated him.

PLATE P. 48

What is Art Nouveau? German art history is full of works by scholars who have considered the problem on the basis of printed graphic art and paintings and have found in these aspects of it formal elements that can be precisely defined. Hence their conclusion, that Art Nouveau is a two-dimensional style, and their continuing refusal, even today, to allow the definition Art Nouveau (in German, *Jugendstil*) to be applied to anything that is not two-dimensional.

Henry van de Velde certainly did not move over to architecture in order to make it two-dimensional, but in order to live, and to surround his own life, and that of his young wife, with objects and a house appropriate to them; and to accustom others to live amid these simple but powerful forms. The lines which he drew were not like those made by a rake on a flat surface; they were links, outlines, often intertwined, which arose in his imagination as three-dimensional as the movement of cigarette smoke in the air. They were streams of energy, not mere pleats or folds.

On the one hand it is moving to hear that the simplicity of his house at Uccle was so striking that the sombre mood of mourners (there was a cemetery nearby) always changed to excited pointing and disapproval. On the other, it is a fact that his furniture, both before and after the turn of the century, was welcomed by aristocrats (Count Kessler), by industrialists (Karl Ernst Osthaus) and by elegant shopkeepers (the Haby hairdressing salon in Berlin), not just by art historians (Meier-Graefe) – who in any case were not traditionalists either, but progressive spirits. In Weimar, whither van de Velde was summoned by Count Kessler, he found a closely-knit, open-minded circle, with the Nietzsche Archiv and the art school, where in the middle of the nineteenth century the young Böcklin, the young Preller and the young Reinhold Begas had been active. On the other hand, he also had the misfortune to be dependent on an unpleasant prince who sought to extend the behaviour of the Emperor Wilhelm II to the city of Goethe; who allowed his artist to be insulted and even added a few insults of his own into the bargain. Thus van de Velde fell between two stools in the matter of countries: Germany could have become his adopted home, but in 1914 he lost his job because he was a foreigner and in 1917 he was deported; while from 1939 to 1945 Belgium reproached him with being a friend of the Germans. Such was the career of an artist sadly wronged by politics.

In Darmstadt it was the other way about. Two temperaments worked alongside each other, at first quite independently, almost unaware of each other, and later jointly. The commoner was Alexander Koch, a publisher who followed the new movement in art attentively and furthered it with publications. He founded the periodical *Deutsche Kunst und Dekoration*, which tells us much about Art Nouveau from 1900 onwards. The prince was Grand Duke Ernst Ludwig, who, as a grandson of Queen Victoria, had had close ties with England since his childhood

FIG. 6 – *Peter Behrens, Dedicatory page from his book 'Feste des Lebens und der Kunst', 1900.*

and was also related by marriage to the Tsar of Russia. Young and high-spirited, he was interested in living with artists and really keen to be able to help the young idea in art. While later societies of artists were only formed when the members were fairly old and had proved themselves, the oldest of the seven artists whom he collected in an 'artists' colony' in 1899 was thirty-two and the youngest twenty; and two of them, Olbrich and Behrens, turned out to be exceptional men. 'And I was in the midst of them – for that my position was useful, since I could help the artists where they could not have made their mark alone.'

Olbrich, who died in 1908 at the early age of forty-one, was the only academically trained architect among the seven artists. He never renounced ornament – he handled it with a lightness of touch that was reminiscent of Mozart – and why should he renounce it? As the arguments adduced by the Viennese Adolf Loos in his book *Ornament und Verbrechen* ('Ornament and Crime') were far too much tinged with rigid self-condemnation, and as Loos introduced window-boxes full of flowers in place of ornament, one could call him, of one wished to be spiteful, the inventor of 'planting out'. At the same time Olbrich was a decided innovator. He was given the task of making an entrance to the exhibition on the Mathildenhöhe in 1901. On each side, opposite each other, he placed the ticket offices, like the wings of a Punch-and-Judy show; the visitors on paying to go in walked between them. A very clear piece of thinking, once one decided to regard architecture as a loosely arranged happening, not as a house with exterior walls. In between – an unparalleled piece of boldness for that time – he stretched a tapestry as a dipping roof. On the other hand, he arranged the flat planks, nailed together over a transitory exhibition space, in layers one above the other and prolonged their supports upward with coats of arms, like the pinnacles in Gothic architecture. At that time it was done playfully; all kinds of ideas can be tried out playfully in exhibition architecture. But when, sixty years later, both concepts, the hanging roof and the rows of supports, were employed and now turned into something *aere perennius* by Eero Saarinen in the great reception hall of the John Foster Dulles airport in Washington, the brilliance of the ideas thrown out by Olbrich became apparent. His own house was just as playfully daring: apparently a quite conventional shape within four walls, in reality it was a sophisticated hanging design, with a sloping roof on the mountain side and a free-hanging loggia on the valley side. Even more functional was the studio building further up the slope for all seven artists (the Ernst Ludwig House, the only building restored today more or less in its original form, at any rate outwardly), really consisting of one single huge slab of wall with a slanting glass roof leaning against it on the sloping (north) side and a connecting passage – with a view – on the valley side. Again, where else at that time could one have found such nonchalant and decided asymmetry posing as official architecture?

APPX. PL. 9

The Darmstadt artists had made a catalogue for every house, since the houses themselves and all their furnishings, from the door-mat to the cutlery, were the subject of the exhibition. They had combined the individual catalogues in a general catalogue. Suddenly a 'super-general' catalogue appeared with caricatures guying precisely those points where Olbrich's architecture passed into the extraordinary. The House of the Flat Arts appeared as the House of Flatness, with upstanding choppers instead of coats of arms; the tapestry was hung out like a carpet waiting to be beaten; and the hanging loggia was made to look like a row of biscuits. Subsequently people were so unfamiliar with this period that for half a century it was no longer known for certain who the authors of this witty and biting piece of criticism really were: Munich cabaret artists, perhaps? But no, it was the Darmstadt artists themselves indulging in an orgy of parody. They themselves argued more keenly than anyone whether they had chosen a breakneck or a promising path.

APPX. PL. 10

APPX. PL. 11, 12, 13

They themselves also criticized Behrens's house; the brick pilasters, they said, which emphasize its character on the outside, were quite superfluous; if one wanted to employ supports in architecture they should be clearly visible. Behrens

– previously a painter, a graphic artist; his *Kiss* forms an indispensable link in the transition from Rodin to Brancusi – had built a 'cube', that is, in the literal sense of the word a stereometric shape. This calls for a word about the difficulty of employing the term 'cube', a description which the association of the term 'cubism' with painting has rendered unusable in other contexts. Behrens's house is not cubist, but cubic, stereometric. That the corners are picked out in colour like pilasters and therefore look like the shafts in Gothic architecture is a mode of expression; it has nothing to do with functional architecture.

The stereometric style has close affinities with the classicist style; in the work of Ledoux and his contemporaries one merges into the other. Thus Behrens is one of the main representatives of that branch of Art Nouveau which, all over the world, round about 1908, turned back towards classicism. It made no difference whether the architects and interior decorators concerned had previously been practitioners of Art Nouveau, historicists or constructors in concrete, whether they were called Adolf Loos, Auguste Perret or Frank Lloyd Wright: around 1908 they were all employing flat ceilings with coffers and circular pillars without entasis; and if they were building roofs, these all had a slope of 45 degrees. This style was particularly well suited, and still is, to the expression of political power. Between 1911 and 1914 Peter Behrens built the Imperial German Embassy in St. Petersburg; it was burned down by the Russians at the beginning of the war. They need not have bothered to do this, for in 1937 they erected a building in very much the same style, as a Palace of Soviets.

This contribution alone would not have made Peter Behrens significant, but he is in fact important because he became the first 'industrial designer'. In 1906 he was invited by Emil Rathenau, the president of the Berlin General Electric Company (AEG), to become the designer of the firm's whole equipment, from writing-paper to turbine house, from lamp fitting to instrumental panel. Such extensive influence on such a big firm has seldom since been wielded by one designer. And Behrens was broad-minded; he trained younger men and gave them their head. Around 1910 Walter Gropius, Le Corbusier and Mies van der Rohe were all working in his office.

SKYSCRAPERS

The Americans have by now done all the work that can be done on the history of skyscrapers. As often with important events, everything in this field happened so naturally that historians find it difficult afterwards to come to any firm conclusions. Attempts have been made to establish from business documents when the first passenger lifts were put on the market – but where are they preserved? And again, how long has it been known that the lift was one of the preconditions for the creation of the skyscraper, such an important one that for a time it was uncertain whether the new type of building would be called an 'elevator building' or a skyscraper? The term 'elevator building' must have originated from the thought that the whole building hung together round a perpendicular shaft; the expression would have been no more obscure than the expression 'corridor train', still used to describe a whole train with a horizontal passage running right through it. A lift to carry passengers had been constructed in England in 1854; naturally

FIG. 7 – *Louis Sullivan, architectural ornament.*

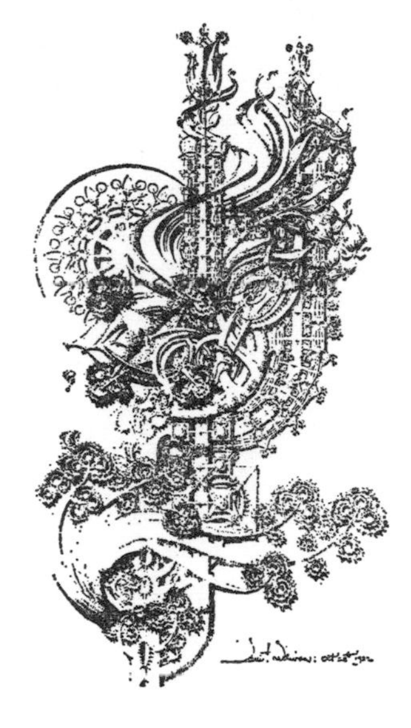

it was still driven in those days by steam. It was introduced into America in the very next year and developed further. But for the possibility of making the many storeys easily accessible the skyscraper could not have been developed; from the same principle followed the need to keep the storeys equidistant.
How many storeys must there be before you can speak of a skyscraper? Who used the name for the first time? These are questions to which only approximate answers can be given. The Montauk building in Chicago (1882), by Burnham and Root, was ten storeys high; the Monadnock building (1889–1891), by the same architects, had sixteen storeys and these certainly possessed the necessary height. But both these buildings still had massive brick walls, which had to be made so thick in the lower storeys that the rooms inside were reduced in area. The sky-scraper proper did not appear upon the scene until the moment when a steel skeleton carried the weight, made uniform storeys possible and speeded up the process of erection. The first real skyscraper was the Home Insurance Building in Chicago; built between 1883 and 1885 by William Le Baron Jenney, it had twelve storeys. Steel skeleton? One has only to go and look in streets that are still standing for iron pillars and iron frames supporting upper storeys – in the out-side walls, that is, for on the inside of buildings floors had been supported by cast-iron posts since the eighteenth century; in English cotton-spinning mills, for example. Iron frames were still made of cast iron, for it had only been possible to produce mild steel in large quantities since 1856.
The origin of the skyscraper is linked with the history of the United States of America, and with the fact that during the nineteenth century the settlement of the country westward to the Pacific was pushed on further and further, for the population increased faster than that of European countries. Towns had to be founded swiftly and were consequently very similar to each other all over the continent, spreading out from the typical 'Main Street'. There were few towns

built around a natural nucleus or so closely linked to a geographical site that their individual layout was dictated by it.
Skyscrapers would not have been possible if the anonymous mass society had not created all the preconditions. The problem of the growing population, the modern money and credit economy, the labour market with its unemployed, its labourers and skilled workers, steel, building machinery – all these things go to make the building industry, which is at the architect's disposal. But for this context he would not be able to build. It would be ridiculous to try to write a history of modern architecture which mentioned only architects and not the building industry.
As to the origin of skyscrapers, the old answer that tall buildings were simply a result of the high cost of land is no longer sufficient. An aerial photograph of New York shows that the skyscrapers are not distributed over the whole built-up area at all; they were concentrated at first on the tip of Manhattan. It was only later that a new collection of tall buildings grew up in the centre of the city. The argument that the number of people was great and the ground dear is certainly sound, but there was also another factor involved. American sociologists call it the 'market'. They say that it was not that many people wanted to live in one spot, but that they were looking for a place where they could be side by side in a sort of market, just as in antiquity and in the Middle Ages people met in the market-place, which was the real centre of urban life. Thus the tip of Manhattan was the place where the urban life, the marketing, the banking of the great city concentrated.
The best known partnership of architects in the 'Chicago School' was that of Dankmar Adler and Louis Sullivan, the former talented primarily as an entrepreneur, the latter as an artist. Their co-operation began in 1879 and ended in 1895. The Auditorium Building, erected between 1887 and 1889 at a cost of 3,145,291 dollars, ten storeys high and occupying a whole block, with a theatre seating 4,237, was the crowning achievement of their first manner of building; it still recalled the principles of the French École des Beaux-Arts and was still influenced by H. H. Richardson. The lower storeys were built of blocks of granite and there were huge Greek columns binding four storeys together, with the bases and attics of the order each spreading over three storeys; such was Sullivan's first response to the demands of a tall building. In the three main doors, the foyer jutting out over them and the interior decoration his own personal manner was already more clearly visible.
The buildings erected in the 'nineties by Sullivan in Chicago and Buffalo are in a style that is decidedly his own but just as decidedly not one that points forward to the twentieth century. On the contrary, each building is conceived as a unity that can be extended neither sideways nor upward. The storeys are not concealed or masked by colossal columns as they still had been in the Auditorium Building. But neither are they conceived as a grid which can be continued at pleasure. That is a concept quite alien to Sullivan. On the contrary, the main part of the building, comprising twelve or fourteen storeys, is precisely planned to be a certain height and width. Underneath is a broad base, two storeys high, and the building is topped by a vigorous attic storey with a massive cornice over a continuous row

of differently shaped attic windows. Above all, Sullivan's buildings possess ornament, an almost lush decoration, an intensive, wordless idiom of the beautiful. He developed tiling, the covering of the surface with glazed moulded tiles. He would not have agreed with Gottfried Semper that art proceeds from necessity; he was convinced that it needed superfluity. On the Transport Pavilion which he built for the Chicago Exhibition of 1893 he used fifty-one different ornaments, which could be stamped and repeated in moulded bricks. That could only be done by someone who felt the surface of the building as a special part of architecture in which the architect must show his mettle. This provides food for thought, for in 1908 the Viennese Adolf Loos wrote: 'Ornament is not only the product of criminals; it commits a crime itself in that it harms man in his health, in his national resources and therefore in his cultural development.' Obviously he said this because he did not think it possible to give ornamentation a special task of its own, to endow it with a separate language of its own owing nothing to historical idioms.

Sullivan on the other hand was able to do this; his later development is inconceivable except on this basis: a fundamentally architectonic form and – applied to the stereometric form, the cube – a floating ornamentation that is yet linked to the cube.

The wall of the Carson-Pirie-Scott store (1899, 1906) is made or composed of a tiled surface such as this: down below, on the pedestrian level, a lush maze of ornamentation; on the eleven storeys, broad areas of glass between strips of tiles, with a unifying band on top. The concluding storey originally planned was never built or was altered later; that is why it looks as if Sullivan erected a grid building. When architecture had gone over completely to the grid the building was praised as 'the first example'. But it was an error to adopt Sullivan as an ancestor.

A few more words about ornament. Adolf Loos said: 'Every age has its style; shall our age alone be denied a style? By style people meant ornament. Whereupon I said, "Weep not, it is precisely the greatness of our age that it is not in a position to produce a new kind of ornament. We have overcome ornament, we have broken through to the point of doing without ornament. Behold, the time is near, fulfilment awaits us. Soon the streets of cities will gleam like white walls. Like Zion, the holy city, the capital of Heaven. Then fulfilment will have come".' It is difficult to quote these words calmly, for it is a paradox that, to brand ornament as a crime, to renounce the historical style, anyone should employ the flowery rhetoric of a purely historical language. Loos has modelled his style on the Old Testament or Nietzsche's *Zarathustra* – second-hand historicism.

Sullivan's words were these: 'Think of the unity of your own thought. All social power, for good or evil, rests on the thought of the people. That is the only lesson in human history worth learning. And so, as soon as your basic thinking changes, a philosophy, a poetry, an art of expression become visible in all things. Then you will have learnt that a characteristic philosophy, poetry and art of expression are the vital elements for the healthy growth and development of a democratic people.'

These two statements of principle were written at approximately the same time.

Do they necessarily represent opposite extremes, so that one could say that mankind had to decide in favour of one or the other? Either to allow itself to be led by Sullivan along the path of ornament or, with Loos, to forswear all ornament? Can we not perceive behind both assertions – after an interval of sixty years – the same glowing, challenging, would-be prophetic sensitivity of the opening years of the twentieth century, differing only because men themselves differ? Both declarations speak a language that could be employed in this way only at the beginning of our century.
At the time (1908) when the Steiner House was being built in Vienna, the architect, Adolf Loos, was told by the police, as a result of protests by the occupants of neighbouring villas, that his building had to acquire ornamentation within a prescribed period. Well, the prescribed period was too short, but some twenty years were sufficient for the growth of ornamental flowers; he had planned window-boxes not only here but also for other buildings (such as the house in the Michaelerplatz, 1910). Now Loos's house does not look very different from a building by Sullivan. It is true that Loos would not have agreed; according to his definition, ornament was historicist and nothing else. Our definition of ornament runs like this: it is connected with festivals and the festive; it fits a building for the holding of a festival in it or in front of it. And it is our contention that the nineteenth century was just as capable as any other century of finding (not inventing, but just seeing arise) such festal decoration. Thus when Adolf Loos put window-boxes in front of his façades he was certainly relying, contrary to his own assertion, on ornamental factors.
To take one example: just as the Greeks created the acanthus leaf as a festal decoration, so the nineteenth century created the Christmas tree as a festal adornment.
In 1893 the Ninth or Tenth International Exhibition (according to whether or not you count the smaller exhibitions) was organized in Chicago; the whole broad strip of the city along the shore of Lake Michigan was remodelled for the occasion. Sullivan declared that this international exhibition had put back the development of architecture in America fifty years, because it brought with it an invasion of the Chicago School by the École de Paris, an influx of the playful, rich, hospitable architecture of Europe. But Sullivan did build the Transport Pavilion for this exhibition, profusely adorned with his own kind or ornamentation, which could be put together like strips of wallpaper and could be repeated. For Sullivan himself did not wish to build meanly, but richly, as long as it was with his own forms. However, the economic crisis which developed in the next few years – certainly not as a result of the exhibition, but just coincidentally – proved too much for the firm of Adler and Sullivan. Adler became the sales manager of a company that made lifts and Sullivan, left to himself, gained no more commissions that would have enabled him to develop further.
The following twenty years were not so empty or devoid of incident as present histories of the skyscraper would have us believe; these are all biased, not cool, objective studies. Extraordinary buildings were erected and in fact the history of the skyscraper developed quite evenly; this is indeed not so much a history of

architects as a history of the building industry and the volume of the buildings. It was the turn of the so-called classicists – Burnham and Root, for example. Today Root is regarded as an architect as talented as Sullivan. It is true that no texts of his like the *Kindergarten Chats* are extant; we shall find again and again how very much the view people take of our own century depends on the existence of texts and the use made of them. In 1900 Burnham and Root drew up a comprehensive building-plan for Chicago. This plan was intended to give the city, which had so far grown up without any artistic aim, a definite shape and breathing-space for its traffic. Burnham and Root saw in what was happening, in the essence of a city, something different from what the purists saw; they saw that their city had a number of quite different aspects, that it could not be built up and controlled from one single point of view. Things had not yet come to the point where air traffic re-united everything and cities were planned to provide the best aerial view. The people who inhabited cities were still on the ground. But they were either below in the street – in which case architectural forms had to be found which made the entrances of stores and banks attractive and comprehensible from street level – or else in the upper storeys, or rather on the roof – when they saw an urban landscape which could not be compared with anything which had previously existed in architecture: the tips of buildings, literally towering out of the fog, 'cloud-splitters' like Olympus in days gone by, with abysses in between where nothing could be seen. It was a question of rounding off these giant cliffs, of giving them a climax that was both uniform and individual. The great blocks were topped with structures in every conceivable vein: these were not just historicist in style, but anthropomorphic, theriomorphic and, increasingly, abstract in inspiration. There were globes of the world used for advertising purposes, glittering metal caps, gilded spires, illuminated signs that revolved or spelled out slogans – a half-unreal, surrealistic landscape. (The contemporary roofscapes of Gaudí and the present-day ones of Le Corbusier repeat this surrealism on a small scale, protected against neighbours.)
Between top and bottom, as the real core of the building, stood the ten, twenty or thirty storeys of offices or apartments. For these a clear ground-plan was developed, the large area with movable partitions – fully developed between 1900 and 1910, and what is more by the so-called classicists. Their task consisted of creating clear exterior walls with a practical, lasting facing. Architecture in the narrower sense was confined to the top and the bottom of the building. But this very division of the skyscraper into these three sections had been created by Sullivan; it was his own school that was continued and developed by his competitors.
The biggest compendium of the ideas about skyscrapers entertained by this period – the years between 1900 and 1920 – is to be found in the folio volume published by the *Chicago Tribune* as a report on their international competition with prizes of 100,000, 50,000 and 20,000 dollars. 275 architects from all over the world took part, the great majority of them naturally Americans; their ideas were almost exclusively variations on the model described above. The best of these American designs, by the firm of I. M. Howells and R. M. Hood, was only not awarded the first prize but was also built straightaway: the skyscraper proper,

in the middle, is supported on a base like a Loire château and is crowned – for the 'roofscape' – with a tower resembling the tower of the church of St. Germain l'Auxerrois in Paris, opposite the Louvre. As this tower was built in the middle of the nineteenth century, there was thus a period of seventy years between the first and second examples of this piece of historicism. The second prize was won by Eliel Saarinen from Finland. His entry had actually arrived too late, but in view of the great distance involved arrangements were nevertheless made for it to be considered and it was awarded a prize. It was on this occasion that Eliel Saarinen moved to America with his five-year-old son Eero.

In this competition the 'modern' designs – that is, the ones that gave the skyscraper neither a base nor a 'roofscape' but instead saw the interrelationship of the storeys themselves as the real problem and sought to attain a new form simply from the way in which they were piled up – came from Germany, from Gropius, Adolf Meyer, Bruno Taut and others. At that time they had no chance of success. The decision in favour of this conception of the skyscraper did not come until ten years later, with the arrival in America of a whole series of emigrants – Mies van der Rohe, Gropius, Mendelssohn, Hilberseimer, Neutra and others.

Simultaneously with the first Chicago School and quite separately from it (the patrons were not quite the same and most of the architects were different) there arose another group of buildings in America which were just as independent, and are just as famous today; these were likewise earlier than the corresponding buildings in Europe: country houses in the so-called 'shingle style', which was derived from the widespread custom of facing the walls of wooden houses with shingles.

An architect who made an important contribution to both kinds of building was Henry Hobson Richardson (1838–1886), one of the men who developed a feeling for the material. Apart from their urban office blocks the Americans built much more in wood than Europeans did. In Europe, building in wood has only lasted in real mountain districts, and even there only for farm houses. The Americans on the other hand stuck to wooden buildings; they were always looser in their style of living, used to greater expanses of meadow, garden and forest around them.

In addition to their liking for wood they have just as direct a feeling for stone, in the shape of boulder-flints, which are set in mortar and built up to form whole walls. These are used for the chimney-pieces and the main passages. The arrangement of the chimney determines the shape of the room and the grouping of the chimneys determines the layout of the whole storey; with shingle houses, every ground-plan, every elevation would have to be analysed individually.

In some examples the materials – planks, flint walls, shingles – are deliberately used alongside each other. In other words, we have here already the beginnings of something that goes beyond the rustic style, namely, joy in the primitive, the natural. It is the awakening of pleasure in the differing structures of materials, the start of amorphism, which plays such a big role in the art of the twentieth century.

Richardson is an intermediary between the French École des Beaux-Arts and this

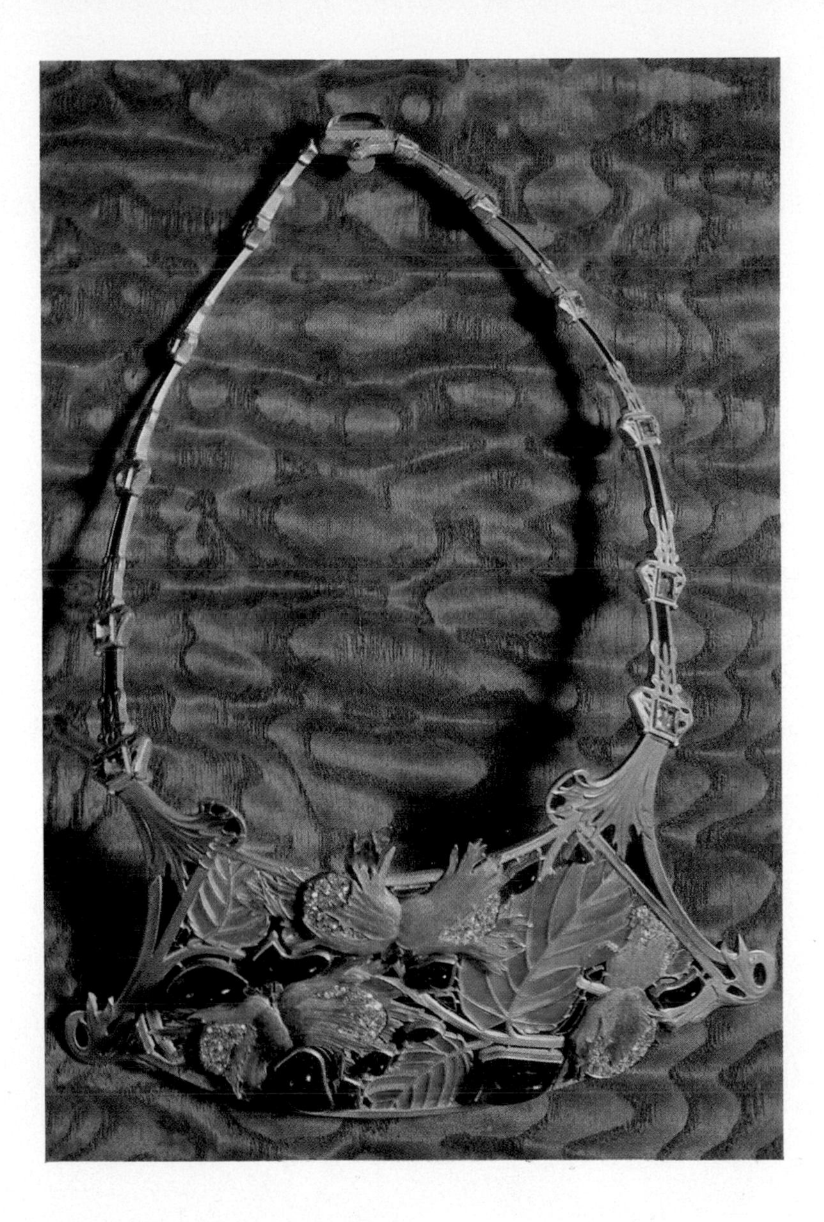

René Lalique, necklace consisting of a hoop divided into movable links and carrying a plaque shaped like the segment of a circle with an openwork relief of hazelnut blossoms and leaves. About 1900. Gold, enamel and diamonds. *Average diameter 5 in., height of plaque 2 in. Musée des Arts Décoratifs, Paris.*

Card Corner

newly developing feeling for material. He was influenced by Italian palaces of the so-called Florentine Early Renaissance. They were good examples of the use of different materials. The so-called 'High Renaissance' style, especially in its Venetian form, was particularly well suited to the superimposition of one storey upon another; Venetian tradespeople had already had to put several equally important floors one on top of another. By modelling his work on prototypes like these Richardson himself became a stern teacher, an impressive figure who laid people under an obligation to him.
The model for the shingle house lay neither in Italy nor in France; it was not a town house transferred to the country but a cottage-style house developed in England. The most important names in this school of architecture are Charles Follen McKim (1847–1909), Stanford White (1853–1906) and William Rutherford Mead; their firm was active from 1879 to 1915. One of their followers was Frank Lloyd Wright (1869–1959).

GAUDÍ

Pevsner calls Gaudí 'the only genius of Art Nouveau'. He was certainly a genius, but whether he can be assigned to the Art Nouveau movement is disputable. He was an architectural genius, with his roots in historicism and presentiments of the forms to come in the twentieth century, a pious Christian, and ceaselessly active, like Viollet-le-Duc perhaps before him and Le Corbusier perhaps after him. But he differs from these two in that he wrote nothing, so that we lack this key to his buildings – buildings to be found almost solely in one single city, Barcelona. He was not the sort of artist who must be regarded as essential to the development of a style, but the sort who exists in his own right. If Gaudí had never lived no one would have missed him, but since he did live and design buildings it is impossible to disregard his work.
A pious Christian: perhaps this phrase best sums up Gaudí's genuine roots in a genuine historicism. His thinking is not scientific; there is no evidence that he had absorbed the science of his time. He does not go in for technical experiments; he would never have consulted a material-testing laboratory in connection with any commission. His urgent, piercing architectural intelligence reaches as far as he can put something together himself by his own unaided ideas and efforts. Gaudí's thinking is not sociological; he did not go in for town-planning or satellite settlements. It is extremely individualistic and thus typically nineteenth-century. It is also typological, and, precisely for this reason, Christian. The world that Gaudí depicts is not the world of mass populations (hence he never devised or built unit forms, as everyone does who instinctively uses right angles – the basic form of any unit, any plan for multiplication – or as Konrad Wachsmann and Buckminster Fuller do); it is a world which proceeds from a central point and

Street scene in the City of London. View down Queen Victoria Street and Cannon Street. In the foreground, the Albert Building by F. J. Ward, 1871; behind it, the modern buildings Bucklersbury House and Temple House.

is organized round it – as Christianity is organized round Christ or a flower round the calyx. Gaudí's world is like both these arrangements.

Christ as the apex of a typological building, as the central tower five hundred feet high, with the towers of the four Evangelists ranged round it, then the four naves of the Christian church pointing to the four points of the compass, their façades heightened by three groups, each of four Apostle towers: such was Gaudí's design for the famous church of the Holy Family at Barcelona. In the west the façade of Grace, in the north that of the Passion, in the south that of the Glory, the Birth. Only this last façade is complete, with the southern group of four Apostle towers rising above it. The programme of the design as a whole is so comprehensive that a doctoral thesis has already been written on the iconology alone of this church. And although the three façades would have assumed quite individual forms they remain unquestionably historicist in spirit; they have no connection with anything that can be called a façade in the twentieth century. The vow to build this church was made in 1872 by a Catalan on his return from a pilgrimage to Rome. The foundation stone was laid in 1882, the architect at that time being one Francisco de Pilar de Villar. A year later the task was handed over to Gaudí, then thirty-one. In 1911, in a crisis brought on by illness and self-examination, Gaudí made up his mind to renounce all secular building and to devote himself to ecclesiastical architecture alone. In 1926, after forty-five years of work, he died. Even today the site remains more or less as he left it; the outer walls of the choir and the façade of the southern transept have been completed, but that is all. Gaudí reckoned confidently on the continuation of the work – had not all the medieval cathedrals been hundreds of years a-building and yet been completed? – but today there is considerable strife or bickering on the subject among his successors: should this pious work be continued, people ask, since the plans can at any rate be deciphered (though in 1936 both the site and Gaudí's papers were ravaged) and since the entrance fees paid by tourists reach a satisfactory level; or should this hybrid work be abandoned and the money used instead to build parish churches of average size and banality? The editors of the *Münster* write: 'The arguments advanced by both sides are worthy of consideration.'

PLATE P. 75
FIG. 8

Close attachment to Christian Gothic is not Gaudí's only historicist characteristic, and indeed this would be impossible, for historicism is always multiplex in style. The first building in Barcelona with which his name is associated, a dam with a waterfall in a public garden, would have to be called Baroque. The curious palace at Astorga is an English keep with towers at the corners; in the middle of it, over a central hall, are placed the cruciform gables of a kind of central tower. There is already present here a Moorish element which in other country houses is unmistakable. Gaudí has all the wealth of the man who inherits a varied past and, instead of rejecting it and casting it aside, adapts it to his own purposes.

And soon we are no longer dealing with the mastery of the ready-made Gothic style, but with the intensity of a constructor who regards his inner momentum as 'Gothic'. Gaudí becomes a thinker in lines of thrust; is this really historicism or is it already functionalism? At any rate there is no historical evidence that a

Gothic architect ever came upon the idea of experimenting with the thrust-lines of his arches in this way; that, instead of letting the force of gravity push upward, he turned the whole design upside down, that he anchored it to the surface of the ground so that the force of gravity pushes downward.
Now the wires and chains implicit in the later pillars and arches hang downwards, forming angles which guarantee stability. It is an idea as simple as Gutenberg's notion of printing a text in movable type – and one just as difficult in technical execution and scientific exploitation; an architect's whole life would not be sufficient to exhaust this idea completely. (It has subsequently been shown to be present in embryo in the Mannerist school.)
At any rate this procedure means the end of the temptation to see a wall as necessarily 'perpendicular'. Pillars and arches are no longer related to the perpendicular. On the other hand they are certainly related to the horizontal, the level on which man stands and which forms when a sheet of water is left undisturbed. In other words, Gaudí does not hesitate about recognizing gravity as the law governing life on earth. But he no longer agrees that, in building, this horizontal must be balanced by a perpendicular modelled on a plumb line or on the perpendicular fall of a weight. As for allusions to the apparently perpendicular growth of trees and plants, Gaudí would have rejected them, for he does in fact relate his artistic thinking to observation of the plant world, which is tumid, gristly, speedy, bulbous, but not rectangular. In other words, in this – central – part of his thinking Gaudí belongs beside Rodin, who likewise recognizes the force of gravity but does not conclude from this that man must always stand upright. Both artists, Rodin as well as Gaudí, teach us the lesson that the idea of perpendicularity (and with it the idea of the right angle) is not a natural assumption but rather an intellectual conception thought up by man.
The product of this attitude seems to many people to be simply a plastic fantasy, a Baroque lump of clay kneaded by the hand of a sculptor. This is not so; it is through and through the constructive fantasy of an architect, not a sculptor; the fantasy of a man who thinks in materials. The forms into which Gaudí has bent his wood, his iron-work, his stones, his furniture and his casts exceed in proved legitimacy, in possibilities, in curiosity the principles of the basic instruction given at the *Bauhaus*. Gaudí would have to occupy a place between Fröbel's kindergarten and Itten's basic courses.
The shafts of his pillars are blocks of basalt and they exploit the distortions of the quarry. Or else they are tilted drums of stone. What contemporary archaeology demonstrated in Greek temples, the inward inclination of the columns, was employed by Gaudí on a much more robust scale – because he wanted to counter quite different pressures, the real pressures of upper terracings, not just an aesthetic fading in the bright light of the sky. The curves of his arches are parabolas and seem to be made of concrete, but if one cuts into them one finds that they are built up of bricks. The ceilings of his spiral staircases seem to be as thin as metal foil, but they are actually made of quite flat tiles stuck together horizontally. Gaudí must have inspired with enthusiasm for himself a group of craftsmen of incredible reliability. He accomplished what Morris and other theorists de-

manded, the resurrection of the 'guild', the renovation of building through the medieval crafts. This achievement was probably only possible at that time in Spain, where such craftsmen, such industry and such devotion still existed, while the building industry on the other hand had not developed to the same extent. Everyone seeing the façade of Gaudí's Casa Milá for the first time takes it for concrete, so genuinely does it seem to be conceived in terms of concrete. In fact, it is built of the best hewn stone. What Adolf Loos's houses have gradually acquired – deliberately or shamefacedly – in the course of decades, namely, window-boxes, was built in from the start by Gaudí in stone and metal latticework.

As for the vegetable world, if Gaudí had been familiar with the following generation's mode of expression he could have said with justice: I do not create after Nature, I create parallel to her. Although he did not say so in print (for he scarcely made himself heard and was disproportionately reserved; at any rate, until now no essays or letters in which he speaks theoretically about his work have come to light), his attitude to architectural problems was quite independent and extremely creative. He remained childlike in the sense that he saw his goal clearly before his eyes, knew quite clearly what the final solution would be, but in order to reach the solution found unexpected, unorthodox ways – ways of childlike genius, in fact.

His most brilliant idea was probably that of buying up the débris from potteries, or rather having it transported to him, for the factories were glad enough to get rid of the rubbish, and of covering his shapes with these fragments. This is easily said, but Gaudí thereby found a solution for one of the great symbols of the whole century, for the rubbish dump, the heap of ruins, to which he gave a fresh meaning; he created restrained, controlled Dada long before the aggressive but baffled Dada of Zürich. If one pursued this idea into the abstract, one could quote the saying of the poet Stefan George:

> Bangt nicht vor Rissen, Brüchen, Wunden, Schrammen,
> Der Zauber, der zerstückt, stellt neu zusammen,
> Jed' Ding wie vordem heil und schön genest,
> Nur dass unmerkbar neuer Hauch drin west.*

One would then have, from the same period, a magic formula that points the way from a previous, disintegrating form to a newly developing wholeness.

When one sees the products oneself, one is overcome once again with amazement at the quality of the work: what fantastic colleagues Gaudí must have had! They knew how to handle the binding cement, and how to match the colours to every surface – in a mode of construction which, so far as our experience extends, leads in the vast majority of other cases to wretched, botched work.

These surfaces include the most abstract forms: spiral shapes on top of the Casa Milá, towers that end as bishops' crooks on the Holy Family, railings like snakes

* Shrink not from cracks, breaks, wounds, scratches.
The magic that breaks things up unites them anew.
Everything recovers, grows sound and fair again.
Except that imperceptibly a new spirit dwells in it.

FIG. 8 – *Antoni Gaudí, Church of the Holy Family, cross-section. Cf. p. 68.*

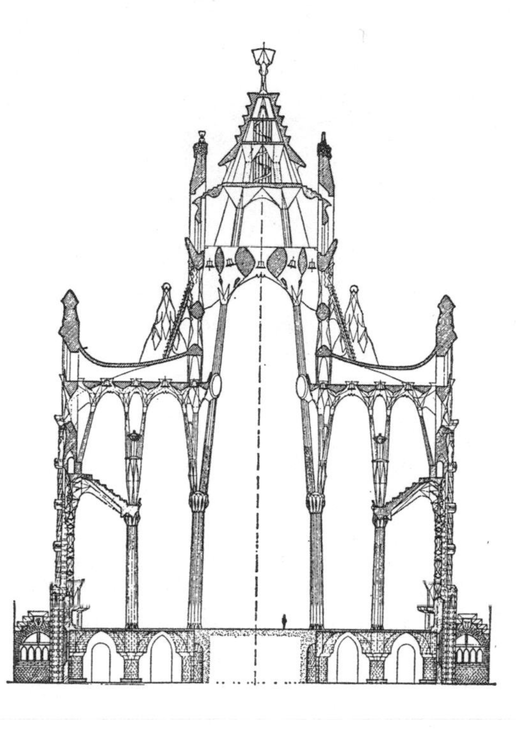

in the Güell Park, apparently without any regard to symmetry but in reality once again following precise rules.

PLATE P. 76

Count Eusebio Güell, a rich industrialist, put a park at the disposal of the city of Barcelona and thereby gave Gaudí as important an opportunity to show what he could do as at the church of the Holy Family. For the houses and villas which Gaudí had so far built were for rich people, like Frank Lloyd Wright's contemporary villas in America. These villas could only influence present building by the indirect route of publication. The creation of a park, on the other hand, was an immediate form of architecture – joining on again to the nineteenth century and leading on quite evenly to the present of the twentieth century. Güell Park was set in the hollow of a hill, leading down to a great central expanse which had to be built up on a substructure and was supported by columns which were playfully Doric in style, while other substructures were shaped vaguely like trees.

BAUHAUS

The Bauhaus style is as closely connected with the new ideas of the twentieth century as with the historicism of the nineteenth century. It is sufficient to see the design which Lyonel Feininger prepared for the first programme – a medieval Gothic cathedral, topped by three stars, between canyon-like streets formed by skyscrapers; it is sufficient to take the name Bauhaus itself, which succeeded the medieval word *Bauhütte* (guild). Or consider the text of Gropius's first proclamation: 'Architects, sculptors, painters, we must all get back to our crafts ... Let us will, conceive, create in common the new building of the future, which shall be everything in one, architecture and sculpture and painting, which shall one day rise up to heaven from millions of craftsmen's hands as the crystalline

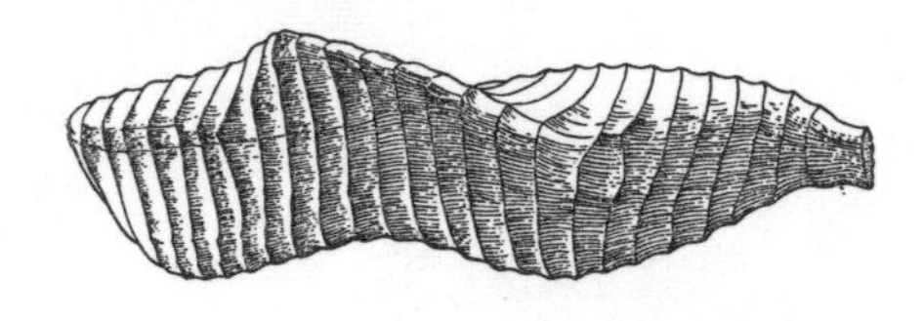

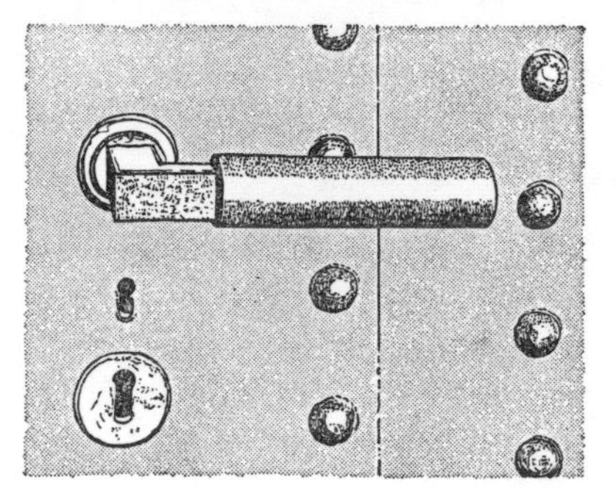

FIG. 9 – *Shoe-last (made at Alfeld before 1911; Carl Benscheidt); Door-handle (Alfeld factory, 1911; Walter Gropius). Cf. page 74.*

symbol of a new faith.' This enthusiastic formula was replaced four years later – a complete change – by the new motto: 'Art and technics, a new unity' – and even this formula was not new, but a continuation of the nineteenth century's efforts. At the same time the Bauhaus movement felt itself to be as new as Dada, Dada with the noisy, literary, merely aggressive element stripped off, transferred to the patient mode of thought and behaviour of architects, who do not isolate themselves but like to co-operate with others. However, it agreed with Dada that the past was to be rejected, that a new start was possible, that it was superfluous to examine the nineteenth century. To that extent what has been said here of the Bauhaus movement is true of many others. A Utopian mood prevailed after the First World War, which it was thought would be the only world war.

We must certainly not underestimate the extent of the changes that had in fact occurred, but since a balanced judgement can only be made after the opposing arguments have been heard, in this book emphasis will be laid on the things that had not changed. Political influence had shifted to other centres, for example from Europe to America and Russia, or from nationalistic hereditary enmities to ideological rivalries such as that between capitalism and communism or white and coloured. But things had not changed to the extent of making politics unnecessary. Industry's mode of operation and the appearance of its products had altered; but industry and mass production were still necessary. The form of works of art had altered; but they were still shown by art clubs in exhibitions, art magazines still reported on them and prices were still assigned to them.

What had changed was that people no longer talked, as they did in the nineteenth century, in periphrastic, indirect, anecdotal terms. On the contrary, it had become possible to speak about every aspect of life from God to genes with a directness and lack of concealment that were bound to shock the previous generation. We suggested the concept 'limited infinity' for the nineteenth century; the equivalent formula for the first half of the twentieth century would be 'isolating directness'. For this is the basis underlying many phenomena of human relationships and fine art. The possibility of isolating a procedure, of preparing one's attitude to a task, enabled people to see colour, light, line and three-dimensionality with a clarity resembling the cultivation of individual viruses in science. The social position of the artist, too, the components of a building, the building material, the individual problem in each architectural commission, the business of living in a house, the kinetic element in any activity, could all be perceived and discussed with a clarity which went beyond any previous formulation. Compared with the unsparing, blunt way in which the younger generation expressed itself, the important men of the nineteenth century all seemed to have lived amid plush and door-curtains. For example, it was possible to assert that it was the twentieth century that had first made the concept of 'art' comprehensible again; in the nineteenth century the place of art had been occupied by convention, imitation, emptiness. And to some extent this assertion was correct. The only thing was that the angry young men of 1920 were not capable of seeing that their own directness would very quickly become conventional; that convention too was a presupposition of art, was indeed even a part of art itself; that without convention there would never have been a sonata, a Dutch group portrait or a Gothic cathedral; and that indirect language, allusion to examples, was not merely to be interpreted as weakness but also contained age-old wisdom and even goodness.

The notion that it was enough to make a start oneself, completely abandoning the past, whereupon an 'international style' would come into being, indeed had already done so, was in fact Utopian – and really incomprehensible. Precisely because these young men were in reality highly educated, historically trained people – try to name an artist of that time who was uneducated; Brancusi, perhaps? – they must have known all the time that no one can step out of the past. To wish to alter the past is legitimate, but to wish to live without the past is an attitude half-way between folly and nihilism. How remarkable this attempt will seem in a hundred years' time, especially in the West, the continent pregnant with history.

The fitness of individual processes for isolation was the presupposition for the first decisive achievement of the Bauhaus movement, the design of the basic instruction. It was not as if there were no tradition of this education-through-work. From the time of Fröbel and his kindergarten (which was important in the development of Frank Lloyd Wright), and indeed, to go further back, from Pestalozzi onwards, the nineteenth century had been accustomed to a basic course in manual skills alongside vocational training. Van de Velde had incorporated one in his industrial art school at Weimar and Adolf Hölzel had developed it at Stuttgart. It reached the Bauhaus through Johannes Itten. Itten met Gropius through Alma Gropius, Alma Mahler, a woman with an exceptional instinct for the charisma of the creative men of her time. She had become acquainted with him in Vienna.

The insoluble contradiction inherent in a course of basic instruction can be seen more clearly in music, although it is talked of far less in that field. On the one hand there must be a sober preliminary test to find out how talented a young person is, for in instrumental music it is impossible to keep up the fiction that every person is musical. Finger exercises on an instrument have little to do with humanity – they are more like drill – yet they are indispensable and must start very early. On the other hand even the least personal artistic activity – dancing a folk dance or whistling through one's fingers – is a release of creative faculties, and really it is a question of a psychologically effective unblocking of the human element, leading not to artistic achievement but to a more rounded humanity. This can become an end in itself. Naturally this kind of education is itself not without its associations; however, they lead not to the medieval guild but to the Indian, Chinese and Japanese philosophies. In the early days of the Bauhaus not only was a costume designed by Itten worn, but the cooking was also done in the Itten style, that is, according to the teachings of the *Mazdaznan*. Tension was bound to arise between Gropius and Itten over the final direction of the school. The danger of sectarianism, of over-zealousness, was not far away. It was certainly only Gropius who could hold together this band of very different personalities; he alone could protect the young institute against political attacks. But it is just as certain that via the basic course, that is, via Itten (and after him Moholy-Nagy and Albers), the Bauhaus influenced the whole world.

The second decisive achievement of the Bauhaus is the architecture of Walter Gropius. It is clearly and soberly developed in the building at Dessau, but it can be more distinctly and more validly demonstrated in the earlier – more prophetic, one might say – Fagus works in Alfeld.

PLATE P. 77

In the shoe-last factory (the problems involved in which have for once been thoroughly investigated and made clear by Helmut Weber, as opposed to many other essays on the architecture of our century, which are just about as ill-founded and as much based on hearsay and memory as Vasari's essays in the sixteenth century on the art of the Renaissance), – in the shoe-last factory one can see in the simplest items, things for the foot and the hand, two quite separate possibilities of fashioning. On the one hand in the shoe-last itself we can see the form appropriate to 'natural' growth, the form resembling it (earlier one would have said 'imitated from it'). The mechanical engineer has shown amazing ingenuity in producing such variable, tense forms and of achieving them by the milling, scrubbing, rotation and guidance of the wood-turning machines. Forms like this shoe-last are the basis of that section of modern architecture which might be called 'streamlined'.

FIG. 9

FIG. 9

On the other hand we find in the door-handle the deliberate employment – forced through against any idea of 'naturalness' – of the right angle. If we add to this the right angles prevailing in the glass structure of the whole factory, we are led back to the origins of all human building. In the grey dawn of history it was the right angle that had made possible the invention of the squared stone and the brick. Now in the twentieth century it acquired once again a necessity, a fascination, a mythical significance which is nowhere near caught or summed up in the term 'functionalism'. Gropius himself admits that his use of the right angle, of glass, of the 'curtain-wall' was intuitive, not planned or functionally calculated.

Antoni Gaudí, Church of the Holy Family at Barcelona, in its present uncompleted state. Foundation stone laid in 1882. When the first architect, Villar, withdrew, the direction of the building was taken over by Gaudí in 1883; after his death in 1926 work was halted. *Cf. p. 68.*

Antoni Gaudí, Steps in the Güell Park at Barcelona. Commissioned by the industrialist Count Eusebio Güell for the people of Barcelona. Work begun in 1900, halted in 1914. *Cf. p. 71.*

Pag. 77 below. Walter Gropius and Adolf Meyer, factory for the Fagus Works in Alfeld, built between 1911 and 1914. *Cf. pp. 74, 79.*

Pag. 77 above. Mies van der Rohe, Dwelling house for Ulrich Lange at Krefeld. Built in 1935. *Cf. p. 85.*

FAGUS

Le Corbusier, Pilgrimage church of Notre-Dame-du-Haut at Ronchamp. Built 1950–1955. *Cf. p. 85.*

FIG. 10 – Walter Gropius, Isometry (design for furnishing) of the director's room in the Weimar Bauhaus, 1923. *Cf. p. 85.*

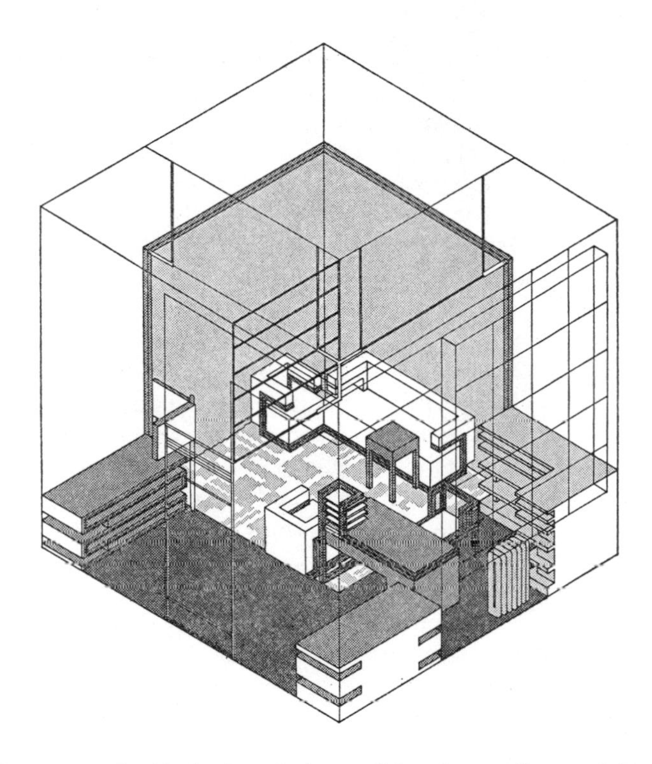

Architects have themselves created a kind of mythology of the glass wall, especially Frank Lloyd Wright, who said that the aim and result of transparency was freedom. There is no similar myth for the right angle. The mythical quality here lies in the possibility of adding on, of community, of co-operation. The right angle facilitates adding to a building at any time, even retrospectively; it opens the way to union by addition as opposed to chemical fusion or organic coalescence. It brings the possibility of teamwork – and that has remained one of the watchwords, one of the basic achievements of Gropius as an architect. One would be alienated, even repelled by the stiffness, the impatience with which the right angle was insisted on and applied, against all reasons, in the decade of the Bauhaus, of 'style' – there is nothing more irrational than the Rietveld chair tilted at right angles – if one did not realize what skill, what humanity, what flexibility, what democracy is made possible by the right angle.

PLATE P. 77

To return to the Fagus works: the process of manufacture was developed by the clear-thinking industrialist Carl Benscheidt, and the layout inside the new building was precisely planned by the local architect Eduard Werner, who was familiar with the manufacturing processes; the basement had already been excavated from the soil. The young Gropius – who had broken away from Peter Behrens without wishing to reject his teaching – had offered his services. It was part of the patron's genius that he looked upon the subsequent erection of the factory as a separate task, and that he chose the young architect for this task, let him go his own way and backed him up in his dealings with the building authorities and police regulations. Such co-operation between patron and architect, like that earlier between Emil Rathenau and Behrens, only occurs at happy moments in the history of architecture.

The careful way in which the glass façade is designed, down to the last centimetre, with tilts in it (which one only sees when one's attention is drawn to them, from the difference in the fall of the shadow between glass and pillars; it is uncertain whether the idea for these tilts came from the much more decided slant of the walls in the AEG turbine factory by Behrens or from the news about the slanting of Greek temple columns with which archaeologists surprised attentive artists at that time), the precision demanded of the craftsmen who made the window-frames, which really ought to be made by machine in order to attain the necessary regularity – these are the things that make this building exceptional. This factory can thus serve as an example for all the architecture subsequently developed by co-operation between architects and the building industry. The result of this co-operation is that today the advertisements and accompanying specifications in the building journals are just as important as the text itself and will form an equally important source for future historians of present-day architecture.

The third achievement of the Bauhaus movement was its planning for mass production (an aim that was only a secondary development) or, in the words of Gropius's second principle, 'Art and technics, a new unity'. This is an aspect that tends to be over-emphasized today, when publications on the Bauhaus are coming to resemble the catalogues of mail order firms, as if many decisive elements had been moulded in the Bauhaus. This achievement would make the Bauhaus only one of the many groups which have tried to further good taste and sales since the industrial art museums of the nineteenth century, indeed since the factories established in the days of enlightened absolutism, since Colbert in France.

On the contrary, it is the fourth achievement which really made the Bauhaus so influential all over the world, namely, the collaboration of so many exceptional men over so many years in such coherent activities. The 'idea' of the Bauhaus, summed up definitively by Mies van der Rohe, is that they lived this idea in daily intercourse, instruction and discussions – in two little towns which could offer them nothing that might help them in their task: Weimar only an old-fashioned atmosphere, and Dessau not even that. But stop: just as Carl Benscheidt belongs to the Fagus works, so Mayor Fritz Hesse and the municipal official Ludwig Grote belong to the Bauhaus in Dessau.

APPX. PL. 20

The men and women who figure in the – single – famous photograph of the Bauhaus group are Joseph Albers, Hinnerk Scheper, Georg Muche, Laszlo Moholy-Nagy, Herbert Bayer, Joost Schmidt, Walter Gropius, Marcel Breuer, Wassily Kandinsky, Paul Klee, Lyonel Feininger, Gunda Stölzl and Oskar Schlemmer. To these should be added at any rate Johannes Itten, who had already left the Bauhaus, and Ludwig Mies van der Rohe, who had not yet taken over the leadership. This gathering is quite unparalleled. It is true that there was just as important a collection of famous artists in contemporary Paris, but they met at the most on the boulevards, in a café, at an exhibition or in a studio; they did not live together.

FIG. 11 – *Oskar Schlemmer, Egocentric spatial pattern. Pen and ink drawing, 1924.* $8^1/_2 \times 11^1/_5$ *in.*

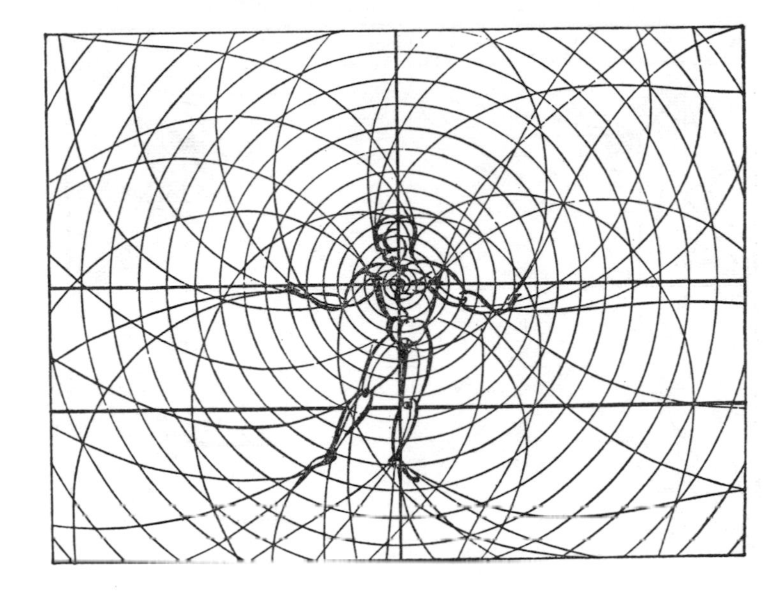

The basic idea of the Bauhaus was precisely that there is no such thing as an art that can be isolated from other things. Therefore the word 'art', which had figured in the titles of the earlier 'Academy of Arts' and 'Commercial Art School', was dropped. There was no longer, they maintained, any painting, sculpture or architecture that could be isolated. It would be like trying to think of economics or scholarship as a separate thing, as if they could exist without man and state and the present day. It is true that the field in which the individual person operates and acquires an expertise, in which his products give him a recognizable identity, threatens to become more and more specialized, but art as such has become something on its own, something separable from the rest of life; it has become an aspect of life itself, a part of it, necessary and undismissible, and, to that extent, life itself. But it is no longer an adornment of life, no longer 'art' in the sense of something added on, a pleasure and refreshment after the working day.
And the reason why the Bauhaus is so fundamental, why its 'idea' is so exemplary and encouraging, is that such a number of important people lived alongside each other. They form a living disproof of assertions about *Vermassung* ('massification'), lack of contact and fateful loneliness in the twentieth century.
The 'old Bauhaus students' (in inverted commas) who meet today in noisy reunions are pupils of the second rank. The real masters are those for whom the Bauhaus formed only one stage, albeit an important one, in a creative life; who did not wish to base their whole existence on their Bauhaus period. No first-class artists grew old in the Bauhaus, and this is not simply a reminder of its political closure: it is implicit in the very idea of the Bauhaus.

OSKAR SCHLEMMER

The real doctrines of the Bauhaus were not formulated by the architects but by the painters, Itten, Klee, Kandinsky and Schlemmer. A discussion of Oskar

FIG. 12 – *Oskar Schlemmer, Figure and spatial pattern. Pen and ink drawing, 1924. $8^2/_5$ in. × $11^1/_5$ in.*

Schlemmer will therefore form a fitting conclusion to our section on architecture; he leads us back to the beginning, to the theatre.

For the present-day theatre is no longer organized round the auditorium, as the great opera-house of the nineteenth century still was; it radiates out from the centre, which for the Greeks was the orchestra; in modern terms this is the stage, the screen, the broadcasting studio, the film studio, to which boxes for the spectators are simply appended; or even completely omitted and replaced by armchairs in the home. For this reason present-day theatre-building is much more expensive, much more difficult to survey; it is much harder to define where the machinery of the theatre begins and where it can be halted so that it does not swamp everything and the performance does not consist only of scraps, of manipulated pieces.

What hovered before the Bauhaus as collaboration, as permeation, as idea, if one were to take the word 'hover' surrealistically and in a literal sense, could only be presented by a dancer. What architects were meanwhile trying to lay their hands on through town and country planning Schlemmer gathered together by renewing it from the dancer-like core of his being. He taught history and the essence of all theatre, all acting, all dancing and staging from the temple to the fair-ground booth, from the priest to the charlatan, from the sermon to the street ballad. He saw man as posed between astrology above him and the magnetism of the earth beneath him, between art and nature; he investigated movement as well as digestion and reproduction. He understood how man is fixed in the dense criss-cross of a given room-space, and at the same time he depicted the emanations issuing from man, a thick cloud of circling waves.

He himself was permeated in this way; otherwise his many changing roles would not have been possible. At one moment he was the teacher for mural painting,

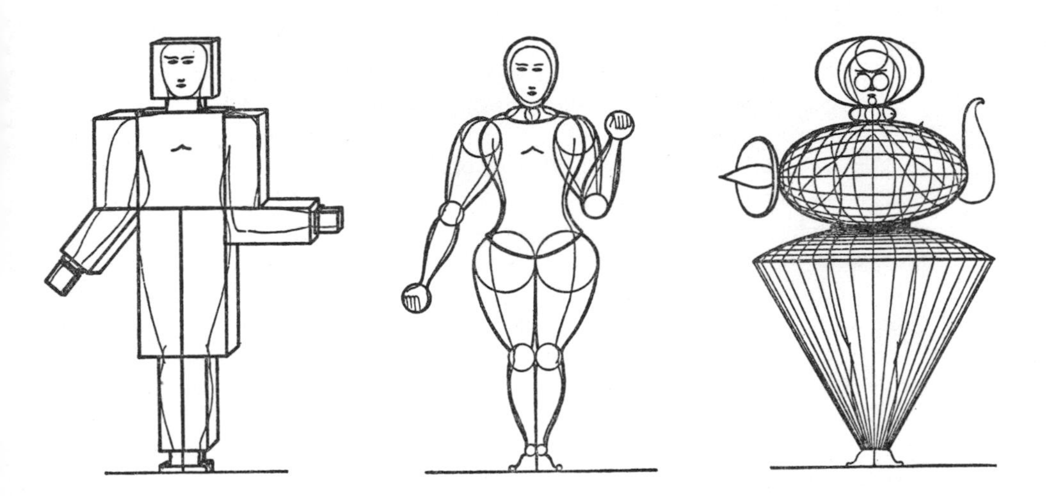

FIG. 13 – *Oskar Schlemmer, Costumes for the Bauhaus stage. Pen and ink drawing, 1924.*

the next he became the chief instructor for wood and stone carving. At one moment he was directing the study of the nude, the next he took over the experimental theatre. It is as if there were a sort of professional Bauhaus teacher, like the professional politician, who moved quite happily from department to department.

He demonstrated systematically the various ways of constructing the figure of a man. First came the assembling of stereometric, right-angled and therefore 'addable' cubes; this is called the domino method of building by the architect (Le Corbusier) and the agglutinative method by the prehistorian (Ernst Heinrich).

Then comes movement on hinges. A Schlemmer drawing represents the process of movement abstractly; it is not the picture of a joint, but resembles a technical blue-print. It also simplifies the possibilities each time to one disc, screw or socket.

Finally the rotation of the human being on his own axis. This gives rise to the basic forms with which we are familiar from the very beginning of art – skittles, chessmen and marionettes – and which today are assuming the space-shape of the satellite. But in the highest sense, where grace returns again, 'so that it appears at the same time in its purest form in that human body which has either no consciousness at all or an infinite one, that is, in the puppet or the god' (Heinrich von Kleist).

An artist like Schlemmer forms a focal point for the abstractions of the arts, so that they acquire a centre, a tiny but dynamic radiating nucleus. Architecture becomes demonstrable in a staircase, in the famous pictures of staircases – but the Bauhaus staircase proper fell a victim to growing reaction as early as October 1931. A staircase not like the one at Herrenchiemsee, stationary for the unfolding of power, but like a place of communication, for hurrying up and down. A place

that brings people together; the reverse of what was broken apart in Edvard Munch's *Totenzimmer (Death Chamber)*. The lines of advance drawn across a public square; the careful piloting-through of the various directions: one is bound to think on the one hand of Alberto Giacometti and on the other of an aerial photograph of a junction point on a motorway – and then one has to reflect again what degree of 'art' is present in such a junction. Schlemmer could have said, like Klee, 'I have long had modern architecture in me.'
Seen from this vantage-point, what a very 'optical' artist is Degas. How very closely bound up he is with the nineteenth century's mode of looking at things from outside, to applying colours to the prepared surface of the picture. How very emphatically the completed picture is a work of art, whereas Schlemmer's dance figure (and consequently all dancing, all 'theatre-in-the-dark' and also present-day kinetics) only comes into being through the use of coloured light and spot-light beams in the darkness. Nor does Schlemmer's figure remain where he put it on paper. It is only the choreographic indication for the movement now to begin, only like a musical notation. One might say (with pardonable exaggeration) that Degas and Schlemmer stand at opposite poles, like a novel by Balzac and a railway guide. One is to be read as an independent, individual action, the other as an intricate but reliable guide to criss-crossing movements that are renewed every day. Or one could read a Schlemmer drawing as a kind of cheque: please pay bearer a space formed in such-and-such a way. Compared with Schlemmer all Degas remains mere painting-and-nothing-more, just pictures to be looked at. This does not mean that the life round Degas was mere life-and-nothing-more; it was just as dense as ours, but the spark and life of art was elsewhere. Or the other way about: compared with Degas Schlemmer is only a theorist, a constructor; he had to renounce looking at man from outside, he could only put on paper 'instructions for use' for 'man-in-space'. Our fellow beings are thus not for their part 'constructed figures'; they are just as warm-blooded as they were a hundred years ago, but the possibilities open to us for giving an account of them are no longer the same.

Since the more detailed discussion of architects and individual works is reserved for the forthcoming volume on twentieth-century architecture, I shall conclude this first chapter by trying to define the basic difference between the nineteenth and twentieth centuries – not so much in actual building, but in conceptions of buildings, in architectural theory, or, to be more accurate, in self-understanding, especially in that part of it of which one is not conscious because it is self-evident. The nineteenth century had ended with the assertion that architecture was an art concerned with space. Space, said to be the only important element in architecture because man himself can only live in a space, eventually met a boundary. The formation of this boundary to space, whether interior or exterior, was the task of those concerned with architecture. As the opposite to bright space they conceived of a dark mass: 'where there is no space there is mass.' This was really not very well considered, for both the architectonic empty space and the architectonic wall are 'volume'. Even the concept 'dead mass' was often employed.

In other words, only the shaped visible surface of wall, column or stone really belonged to architecture.
The opposite of this is the twentieth-century view that the wall contains power and exerts an effect. The very method of manufacture of reinforced concrete contradicts the notion of a 'dead mass', and for every architect it is decisive that the reinforcement inside the wall effects something. He will always regard a slab of concrete as something that strengthens, supports, holds together; and since he has a feeling for dynamic forces this slab will be anything but dead to him – on the contrary it will be living, pre-stressed, dynamic.
The word 'slab' *(Scheibe)* has taken root in architectural language. We must not think of a sausage, from which one also cuts off a slice, but rather of a slab of glass – not of the drop of water that trickles down it, but of the fly that bangs against it, so 'square' stands the glass. One would like to replace the term by 'front' and thus have the same word as in contemporary painting (Munch, Toulouse-Lautrec), which also utilizes the placard effect, the frontal element. However, the concept 'slab' has also proved useful for the storey, that is, for the horizontal. The expression 'front' would be no good for this. This notion of the slab as a basic concept in building unites a number of quite different twentieth-century personalities, while differentiating them all from the nineteenth century:
Frank Lloyd Wright, for he pushes the rooms of his prairie houses out from the fireplace. Here we have a quite literal 'radiation' of the so-called hearth-wall.
Rietveld and Doesburg: from them we can learn that although the slabs are arranged at right angles to each other they need not be joined by a right-angled corner. Rather is the arrangement of the slabs an intellectual structure.
Gropius, whose director's room for the Bauhaus at Weimar consists of such intersections. Neither could the furniture be shaped differently nor could it stand at any spot in the work of art as a whole. FIG. 10
Mies van der Rohe, the outside view of whose Lange house at Krefeld is deceptive. PLATE P. 77 The skin laid around it looks as if it were a spatial boundary in the old sense, but in reality even the Lange house consists of separate but coherent slabs, like (in a much more elementary way) the pavilion in Barcelona and the Tugendhat house.
Le Corbusier, precisely with the extraordinary pilgrimage church of Ronchamp. PLATE P. 78 Anyone who calls the walls of this church hollow is thinking in terms of the obsolete opposition between light space and dead mass, as if the volume embraced in the shells of concrete were empty or not genuine simply because everything is not fully stamped out. In that case a slab of glass would not be genuine, for to a purely optical viewer who only used his eyes it would not be 'there' at all. He could only establish its presence indirectly, by something reflected in it; he would have to stick warning notices on it so that no accident occurred. The slab of glass is very much 'there', but transparent. The walls of Ronchamp could correspondingly be called 'transspatial'.
This church is a far simpler and more comprehensible example of our interpretation of the 'slab' or wall, because the statue of the Madonna is visible from both sides. It can be seen on the inside via the 'sinking' (notice again the ambiguity of a word like this, for on one hand the ground does sink topographically, while

on the other immersion in prayer can be meant); but the same wall and the same statue of the Madonna also dominate the place of pilgrimage in front of the chapel, as façade. The dais, altar and pulpit are also repeated outside as well as inside. The sharp south corner of the external shape is sometimes compared with the bow of a ship; but the chapel is not streamlined, it is not transport architecture. It divides two adjacent outside spaces.

Similarly, before the turn of the century, if a teacher wanted to test the aptitude of a young man for architecture he might make him draw a bunch of asparagus, an antique head or a Renaissance doorway.

The twentieth-century teacher hands him a few lumps of wood, match-boxes for example, and gives him the task of arranging these bodies so as to produce clear intervals, definite angles, fruitful conjunctions. Then he has to draw from it some kind of key. The experienced teacher can find out how gifted the young man is by both methods and give his advice accordingly. For I repeat: neither the architecture nor the people of the twentieth century have changed fundamentally. Essentially they are the same. But the methods we use are different.

II. SCULPTURE

In the case of architecture it is easy to show that art is embedded in a wider context, that the possibility of art having its own laws is one that can be accepted only fleetingly, and even then only if the context is left visible. In the case of sculpture, however, it is difficult to see the products of the nineteenth century within a wider context and to perceive tasks that sculpture alone and no other art could undertake in its place. I shall try to give the reasons why I consider nineteenth-century sculpture just as significant as twentieth-century sculpture, even though it produced few really first-class works and only one genius, Auguste Rodin, who created a world of sculpture that is incomparable. Reluctantly I must begin with a negation; I must begin by eradicating an error, because it is from the error that the enquiry into the positive side follows. I refer to the exaggerated attention paid to the experiments in sculpture of artists whose real place is in painting, to the sculptural work of Carstens, Géricault, Daumier, Böcklin, Degas, Gauguin and Renoir. And, to make sure at once of gaining the help of these artists themselves, let me point out that none of them except Gauguin attributed any real importance to his attempts at sculpture. They were painters; they were what would be called in the twentieth century experimentalists; they were used to trying unusual things. These included the attempt to represent graphic conceptions three-dimensionally. It was not unusual for a painter to make plastic models in preparation for his pictures; Poussin is reported to have done this. Degas handled his wax models quite carelessly; it was only after his death that they were restored from their fragmentary condition and then – to suit the art-dealers – transposed into a work in bronze with a guaranteed limit on the number of casts made. Degas knew only too well that one is not a sculptor just because one has a feeling for three-dimensional relationships; he knew that art – or at any rate what he, Degas, regarded as art – meant a reliable, thoroughly studied craftsmanship based on training, a mastery of the difficulties, a proved capacity to hew stone, handle casting, control the construction of a large piece of sculpture. Little wax models have never made a painter into a sculptor. Degas took his plastic works for what they are: sketches for his paintings, to enable him to understand the complicated balance of dancers. It is not until colour is added that these sketches acquire their real value. As they stand, they are like the animal skeletons which taxidermists have to clothe with the prepared skin. And in fact the only case where Degas exhibited a sculpture in the Salon is connected with an experiment of this sort – clothing a dancer with a skin or, to be more accurate, with a genuine pleated skirt and a real bow for the hair. Mad, brilliant, fascinating, but only tried by Degas on one single occasion. Much the same is true of Daumier's sculptures, which in reality were the reservoir on which the political artist drew, his exercise book, intended to enable him to depict recognizably every member of parliament

from every possible point of view – sideways, from below, from above – as he might be required to do the very next day.
Only Gauguin has a genuine place in sculpture, in connection with Art Nouveau, because with him a new world of art begins in which the home-made cupboard, home-made pottery, home-made South Sea carvings move into a new, re-embracing context – to which Daumier and Degas do not belong.
But if these experiments are not sculpture, what then is sculpture? It is part of bigger whole and a part that can only be represented by sculptural means. When Degas makes a horse, the governing factor is not yet the space-time problem of the twentieth century. Even a slighter twentieth-century work would be more serious, more universal, because it would be connected with a genuine enquiry. The gallop of a horse is not on the same level. Its depiction is a peripheral problem, and it is only in connection with the colours, with the progress of painting during and after Impressionism, that the experiments of Degas acquire their significance.

MONUMENTS

But at the beginning of the nineteenth century as well sculpture did have a universal significance of this sort, or a share in it. Its centre did not lie in the naked figure – the ideas of Hegel or Schelling are deceptive here, emphatically though they place the basis of sculpture in freedom, upright self-determination, the self-awareness of the spirit within the body provided by nature. They did not realize that the sculpture of their age acquired its universal significance rather in the context of a great new task, in the context of monumental sculpture.
Monumental sculpture was state sculpture, and as European states for the most part still had monarchs at their head it might be suspected that monumental sculpture was only a glorification of autocracy, perhaps even of despotism. But states were already filled with new forces. The ruler – if we are to believe sculpture – no longer ruled by divine right; it is an exception that the Albert Memorial in London should emphasize divine favour. Rulers had already been compelled to accept a Napoleon into their own circle. They had already been made to abdicate, even been judged, and compelled to rule through a constitution.
Thus in the apparent honouring of the monarch something else is already really depicted; the monarch is the representative of the state, not the state itself. The monument was in a genuine sense the self-portrait of man, of the citizen who belonged to a state, to a people.
When sculpture represents man standing erect it needs self-determination. It also needs the belief, which we have lost today, that man can determine his own nature. The statue, the self-determining human being, occupies the 'universal point' *(Weltort)*. It orders everything around it. Its attributes surround it: *clementia, justitia, liberalitas, fortitudo*. It defines directions; that there is a front and a back, right and left, is determined by the statue. It stands upright; there is nothing above it; and it is separated from the earth by the base.
So much for the ground-plan of monumental sculpture; now for its elevation. It is one of the age-old perceptions of human art that there is a difference – between what? A difference between writing and picture, between magic formula and statue – it was so even among the Egyptians. A difference between a historical

event and the human character which proves itself in this event or which has provoked the event through its inflexibility. In other words, the human figure represented in the monument is tranquil, raised out of the moment. The text which gives information about the man, reports his name and relates his deeds, belongs on the base, not on the figure itself. It can take the form of text, narrative, exhortation, relief – but it is always on the base, not on the statue itself.

Perhaps we can gain a deeper understanding of this arrangement from Nietzsche's idea, in his *Birth of Tragedy*, that the Apolline dream rises out of the Dionysiac intoxication. Half-way up the memorial to King Maximilian I (Joseph) of Bavaria, by Christian Rauch, in Munich, there is a huge block of bronze with reliefs on all four sides. They are not bounded at the corners by architectural frames. So far as is possible with a rectangular block they go all round, return upon themselves and form a circle, not a directional narrative. Sculptures on bases can make cyclical contexts clear, indeed must do so; painting cannot do this so long as it clings to the self-imposed conditions of the easel picture and does not also develop into a circular picture. The shape of this block is reminiscent of an ancient sarcophagus which tells of death and resurrection, of the cyclical course of life, in the form of the ancient myths. Or it recalls the so-called pulpits on whose sides old Donatello showed the Passion of Christ. Information is given on the four sides of this base; on the front is the dedication of the monument to the king in 1824. It was not King Ludwig I but the citizens of Munich who erected this monument; hence the symbolism of integration in nature, which extends from astronomy to investigation of the interior of the earth. The right-hand side shows the administration of justice (Themis, the goddess of Law, between Strength and Wisdom) and the exploitation of the earth through agriculture: the ox-team in front of the plough, seed-corn, the improvement of trees. On the other side religion and art are shown: the Catholic and Evangelical Churches, united by the angel between them. The clergy are portraits of contemporary persons: the court bishop of the Catholic king and the chaplain of the Evangelical queen. The representatives of art are also portraits of contemporaries: in the middle Peter von Cornelius, in the art of painting one of the pictures in the Glyptothek; on the right the architect Leo von Klenze; on the left the sculptor himself, Christian Rauch, looking up in admiration at Cornelius. The rear shows the bestowal of the constitution on Bavaria: the three estates of the realm, soldiers, teachers and food-providers, represented as youthful noble, earnestly attending citizen and good farmer in boots and storm-cloak.

RAUCH

PLATE P. 95

There can be no question that this is the real centre of the monument. Here the state is presented as it sees itself, as an enlightened constitutional monarchy, as a collaboration of forces; a patriarchal concept, sympathetic to the veneration of the divine providence evident in the annual return of fertility, unsympathetic to the excitement of sudden political or historical revolutions.

When one thus sees the middle of the composition as the most important element, then the pediment-like lines above in the figure of the king and the opposing obliques in the lions of the base converge. We then have here a totality which is probably not just the creation of our own eyes but is thought out in discussions among the artists: the figure of the king would correspond to the pedimental sculpture of a Greek temple and the plinth with reliefs to the frieze of the Ionic temple (or the metope-triglyph zone of a Doric temple), with the architrave below. Further down comes comes the Caryatid zone, the supporting of the heavens above the earth – but between this and the ground are three great steps, corresponding to the crepidoma of the Greek temple. The structure is not simply a matter of proportions, of measurements and lines, but an intellectural entity. As in all the great artistic schemes of earlier times, not only the artist himself but also many other men and minds contributed to the creation of this monument. For example, the arrangement of the Bavarian heraldic lions at the four corners was Klenze's idea, but it was Rauch who first used them in a high relief, like Assyrian gateway-lions (though at that time the Assyrian examples had not yet been excavated). It was also Rauch who first filled the space between the lions with military trophies – thus basing this state too on the power to defend itself. It was Rauch who first inserted the goddess of Plenty, and on the other side a solemn figure of Bavaria, on the base, thus shoring up the great weight and emphasizing the central axis.

This monument is not simply a magnified single figure, raised as high as possible on a tall base. Rather is it a sort of free-standing, outlying cliff, set in the midst of all the architecture around it but itself possessing and displaying all the layers which give architecture, too, its universal significance – the morphologies of roof and base. Nor is the king just a clothed figure; he is the ruler, making the gesture of *adlocutio*, of invocation, healing, blessing. Baron Gros had used this gesture in his picture of Napoleon at the Battle of Eylau; it is the age-old gesture of munificence. The figure is bare-headed, in coronation ermine, modelled with much more accuracy than a head under a helmet would be, yet on the other hand raised above the passing moment.

It is the most beautiful monument, and the richest in content, produced by the nineteenth century. But we must follow up this judgement and justify it by carrying our investigation further in two directions.

First, the monument did not come into being simply through the momentary exertion of one single artist. The collaboration between King Ludwig I, the architect Klenze and the sculptor Rauch was much closer, much longer, much more productive than any that one individual could have secured. The fact that Ludwig I and the citizens of Munich were Bavarians, Klenze was originally a Hanoverian and Rauch a Prussian broadens the cultural base on which the achievement rests. It also rests on the legacy of monumental sculpture, which – so far as knowledge extended at that time – could be traced back to Roman coins and Roman statues and had subsequently been handed down on triumphal arches and sepulchral monuments. Nor was the monument completed all at once. The date 1824 marked the beginning of the communal work, the vow to erect the monument to commemorate the 25th year of the reign. Klenze had already started to make sketches in 1823. The lower part of the base was finished in 1828 and the statue of the king in 1829. Work on the reliefs proceeded from 1831 to 1834. The casting was done in stages – the statue in 1833.

The monument was unveiled on 13 October 1834. It thus took ten years of combined work, combined thinking, combined tenacity to turn the original decision into reality.
To make an express comparison that will remind us where we stand today, just think of a statue erected in front of any state building you like to name – for example, the statue of a recumbent woman outside the provincial assembly building in Stuttgart. The building was completed in 1963, the statue selected from finished works and put up between February and June 1963. There is no question that it is an excellent work by the great English sculptor Henry Moore, but what relation has it to the Württemberg parliament? Who recommended the erection of the statue? How did the artist embark on the task? What does the statue say about the state of Württemberg? It can be predicted that the modern work has very little prospect of enduring alongside the monument of Maximilian Joseph and that the deputies who commissioned it have very little future in comparison with Ludwig I as Maecenases exerting a living influence on art – once another hundred years have passed and the monument in Munich can no longer be classified as 'historicist' or the statue in Stuttgart as 'modern', but both are seen simply as achievements.
Second, consider Rauch himself: apart from his great conscientiousness, which ruled out any botching or evasion, and apart from his genuine links with Goethe and the world of Goethe, he was really a genius in the matter of proportions. The notion that the zone of the relief, of earthly activity, is the real point of genesis for a monument recurs both in his Blücher memorial and above all in the memorial to Frederick II in Berlin.
Third, it is the fundamental thesis of this book that our evaluation of historicism, indeed of the whole nineteenth century, rests on a false assumption and is indeed almost itself conceived in the spirit of the persecuted nineteenth century. It is assumed that something is spurious, questionable and inartistic if we discover through proximity to it that we can detect traces of doubt, criticism, knowledge of earlier achievements and continuation of previous practices in the artist and the patron. From this the conclusion is drawn that the age of historicism is spurious and, together with history, must be buried and forgotten. The 'genuine' periods of history on the other hand, so the story goes, came into being spontaneously, directly; they were homogeneous. The present, so it is asserted (but what 'present' really? That of 1920 or that of 1970?), has no connection with the past; it arose entirely out of itself and moves on progressively. All three views seem to me to be false. To regard the so-called 'genuine' periods of art as homogeneous amounts to romantic glorification of history; every new piece of research brings the complexity of every earlier age more clearly to light. To adduce a tinge of doubt, of self-criticism, even of self-despair, as evidence that something is spurious is just as romantic; it would sound as if we ourselves were above doubt and no longer practised self-criticism. And that the past is buried – who would maintain such a false, indeed such an irresponsible, doctrine?
It was at a dinner in Goethe's native city of Frankfurt am Main on 28 August 1819 in honour of his seventy-first birthday, in the presence of Bertel Thorwaldsen

and Sulpice Boisserée, that the idea of putting up a monument to Goethe was first mentioned. A memorial society was formed and its thoughts turned to a temple in a beautiful position with, inside, a huge bust, possibly by Dannecker, like the one the latter had made of his boyhood friend Schiller, and on the wall perhaps a frieze showing scenes from *Hermann und Dorothea*. Goethe himself, who was informed at Weimar of the plan, suggested Christian Rauch, who had done a powerful portrait in the ancient style and also a lively statuette of the poet in a dressing-grown. In 1821 and 1822 the people in Frankfurt had discussions with Rauch and ordered the statue, either standing or sitting. The question at once arose what kind of dress should be chosen. In 1824 Rauch sent to Weimar a sketch or, to be more accurate, a thoroughly worked-out little model of a seated statue. Goethe's answer, transmitted by his trusted adviser on matters concerning the fine arts, Hofrat Meyer, ran like this: 'Your rejection of truly contemporary dress is most praiseworthy. Nothing satisfying could be achieved in this line; what could be hoped for from such an approach, however carefully it was worked out in marble? To use Minister Goethe's own words: the statue itself as well as the dress would be obsolete in a few years. The ancient mode of dress which you, honoured friend, have chosen for the model is undoubtedly the best. A portrait of this kind remains valid for all ages; so the model you sent can be accepted for the time being as the basis for a large-scale statue.'

There is no need to speak here of the delays and intrigues which led to the result that in Frankfurt neither Rauch's statue nor one suggested by Bettina von Arnim was erected. Instead, a seated statue in ancient dress was put up inside the city library; it was the work of Pompeo Marchesi in Milan (at that time subject to the Emperor of Austria and thus a member of the German League; Marchesi had never seen Goethe). A free-standing statue by Ludwig Schwanthaler was also set up; this is a poor work by this normally creative sculptor, who worked for King Ludwig I of Bavaria.

PLATE P. 96

However, in 1849, the hundredth anniversary of Goethe's birth, an old project (first mooted in Weimar in 1827) was resurrected: that of erecting a combined memorial to the two friends and princes among poets, Goethe and Schiller.

Goethe's views had by this time rebounded against himself; classicism had not proved to be the eternally valid criterion of all art, but simply a style that was affected like others by the lapse of time. A Goethe in ancient dress (which he had never worn) would now have been felt to be old-fashioned, indeed ridiculous. On the other hand Goethe and Schiller in the clothes which they had actually worn would be indissolubly bound up with their age and with the influence they had exerted. Such a memorial would immortalize the realization that all activity, even artistic activity, is bound up with a particular period. Precisely what was historical would remain unalterable, valid and right. King Ludwig I of Bavaria, a great power in the world of art, promised to have the statues cast in his works at Munich, but demanded German dress – 'otherwise he would be contradicting the whole of his artistic activity, for it had been his constant endeavour to make our German manner of dress at home in art and through it to immortalize the period in which great minds had been at work.' But Christian Rauch, who was to undertake the commission and had already done a great deal of preparatory work on it, was too old to dance to King Ludwig's tune. He wrote to the Grand Duke of Weimar: 'The model, which I can well say has been designed to express the highest respect for both the two men concerned and the ruling house under whose aegis they worked, is the product of my innermost being, and I see it as a wreath laid in dedication, after the ancient fashion, at the spot from which I, too, received much encouragement on my difficult path as an artist. It can only cause me deep sorrow that in this particular case I cannot accede to wishes which otherwise would be as commands to me and that I must reluctantly refuse your request. Your Highness will pardon this attitude in a man and artist who in the evening of his life would not like to do anything that was in contradiction with his own ideals.'

RIETSCHEL

Rauch himself named the man who would be in a position to create the group in the desired form without running counter to his own nature. Rauch's nominee was his pupil, Ernst Rietschel. This brings a third German city into the nineteenth-century picture, in addition to Berlin and Munich, for Rietschel was a Saxon and lived and worked in Dresden. His teacher Rauch had introduced him to Goethe a generation earlier. He really did succeed in bringing to fulfilment the efforts and thought of thirty years. We must repeat: the great works of the nineteenth century took a long time and were achieved with the co-operation of the whole people (even the Emperor Napoleon III gave 2,000 francs towards the sum required). This group was 'popular' in the fullest sense of the word; it was the perfect solution to the problem posed; every other Goethe memorial – and there are many – is less effective.

For this kind of monument, too, there was a *kairos*, a particularly opportune moment, when the few really good monuments were created. This moment was round about 1850, a period which produced Monge in France, by François Rude, Lessing in Brunswick, by Rietschel, and this double memorial in Weimar, which was completed in 1857.

A *kairos*? Yes, because in this decade the 'civic' period was most in accord with itself. When it was dealing with a poet it did not attempt to produce an allegory of poetry. This was tried earlier on and it was tried again later – each time to the detriment of the purely civic – with the aid of flights into the unrepresentational. For example, the figures of tragic, epic, lyric and dramatic poetry were placed at the four corners; personifications from the works of the poet (or musician) swarmed around the base; on a monument to Beethoven nine cherubs were said to represent the nine symphonies; and on the base of Schwanthaler's memorial to Goethe, which we have already mentioned, the Bride of Corinth, the Erl King, Hermann and Dorothea and many others all appeared in a mixture of old German, classical and Renaissance dress. Or think of the *Inner Voice* which Rodin essayed for his *Victor Hugo*. The inner emptiness of this grouping made Rodin himself despair, but it was tried again by his successors Max Klinger and Georg Kolbe in monuments to musicians.

In comparison with all these attempts the concentration on the historical appearance of the poet himself, as was possible in the fifties (and in those years alone!),

was an achievement of considerable skill, self-denial and even vision. What was said later – that the genius of a poet does not reside in his tail-coat – is not the whole story. Of course it does not; but nor does it reside in a figure purporting to be his 'inner voice' or in the gown that Rodin's Balzac wears. In each case it is much rather a question of transposing intellectual intensity into the terms of another art. The classicist's toga does not mean that the poet used to dress in the ancient fashion; contemporary dress does not mean that his verses can be equated with a tail-coat or overcoat; and Balzac's gown does not mean that the novelist used to walk amid swirling mists across lonely heaths. The classicist thought that intellect as a whole could not abandon the legacy of Greece; the realist of the middle of the nineteenth century thought that intellect as a whole was not present unless it donned a non-recurring historical form; and Rodin thought that intellect as a whole could only be expressed in sculpture if the artist obeyed his own inborn sense of responsibility. None of these answers is false; none of them can be dispensed with. The conflict arises out of the fact that in each case the living artist represents exclusively his own standpoint and no longer understands the standpoint of his predecessor, the artist no longer living. In reality he himself also shares all other forces and standpoints to some extent: the classicist and Rodin also work partly on a historical basis and Ernst Rietschel is to some extent a strict sculptor obeying his own artistic conscience.
Today we can no longer create memorials, for a number of reasons, among them the fact that we are no longer 'citizens' in the same modest but proud sense, that we no longer believe in personality as a 'highest happiness of the children of earth'. For this reason Rietschel's group remains essentially the clearest, most honourable and thus the best achievement in the line of monumental sculpture that was possible. To this extent the monument is a self-portrait of the 'civic' age, and it is genuine precisely because it contains nothing at all in the way of allegories rising above – or falling below – the civic ideal, not even a 'Dionysiac zone' on the base out of which the 'Apolline sculpture' could rise, nothing but the wreath which Goethe holds firmly in his hand and which Schiller just touches as he steps forward.
It should be emphasized how seriously such a detail as this wreath was taken and how much it was discussed. It was from the wreath above all that Rauch drew his conclusion: if the symbolism of a wreath was necessary, he said, then the symbolism of ancient dress was also necessary. And if there was to be a wreath, then there should be two wreaths. Rauch pointed out that there was no ancient group of two poets by which one could be guided; only allegorical figures such as Sleep and Death had come down to us from ancient times. The problem now was to characterize the tranquil Goethe and the fiery Schiller, to put four men's legs alongside each other without gaps arising, and to give four male arms significant positions – classical sculptors had hidden at least one of the hands in the robe at the breast. That Goethe must stand a little further back, that the difference in height, which in real life was considerable, must be levelled out, that Goethe should be laying an encouraging hand on his younger friend's shoulder, that Schiller should be looking up with a noble glance – these are some of the ideas

Christian Rauch, Monument to Maximilian I of Bavaria in the square in front of the Residenz in Munich. 1829. Bronze. *Cf. p. 89.*

Ernst Rietschel, Goethe-Schiller Memorial in Weimar. 1857. Bronze. *Cf. p. 92.*

that Rauch contributed to the creation of the memorial. There was no statuette of Schiller that reproduced so well the subject's manner of bearing himself as the statuette of Goethe, on which – thirty years before – Rauch himself and the young Rietschel had worked together.
Thirty-five years later, from 1887 to 1892, the great French sculptor Rodin tried to create the figure of a writer, a *Balzac*. The commission was a perfectly conventional one, for in the meantime the idea of honouring a writer in this way had become a cliché. Balzac was not the poet of a whole people, and the monument was not being paid for by the public and the government but by the Société des Gens de Lettres. As Rodin for his part was not a hack sculptor but a genius, obedient to his own laws, he transformed the conventional commission into his own unmistakable work. As an artist he was still obsessed by the notion of working from nature. He considered it impossible to create without reference to nature. Therefore, as Balzac was no longer alive, he looked for the head of another living man in Touraine, the novelist's native district, a man who might perhaps look like the dead Balzac. He worked from a nude model, which might perhaps be able to express the energy, the powerful, broad gait of the novelist.

APPX. PL. 14

But how should the statue be dressed? Instead of the ancient toga, instead of the historical dress of Balzac's day, Rodin essayed a vaguely shaped garment which was to be wound round the naked figure. He called it a gown and justified his choice with the reminder that Balzac had worked by night, drunk innumerable cups of coffee and walked restlessly up and down his room. If this were taken seriously historicism would frankly overreach itself. One would demand the actual cup of coffee that accompanied the nocturnal productivity. Finally, it is interesting to note that statues of poets in the nineteenth century begin with a garment like a toga and end with one like a gown, and that historical dress stands in the middle, possibly only at a historical moment – not before and not after.
Of course, Rodin had not really aimed at a gown. Rather is the figure's grandiose covering the first piece of amorphism, one that reaches out by anticipation far into the twentieth century. It is not smooth silk but rough rock into which Balzac is transformed, and in fact it is as a menhir, rising gigantically against a misty horizon, that Rodin had his statue photographed by Edvard Steichen. In other words, the question of dress, which in the nineteenth century was discussed and solved in terms of historicism, becomes in twentieth-century thinking a conflict between outer space and inner space, a question of dissolving surfaces, of 'de-becoming', de-historicizing. It becomes a sculptural problem in the narrowest sense.
This will be welcomed by all who in any case are on the side of the twentieth century, on the side of Rodin against historicism. That is where I stand, too. But two reservations must be made. First, there is a difference in class between the artistic capabilities concerned. Rietschel is an important sculptor, much more important than is realized at present, but he is not a genius. Rodin on the other hand is a genius, the greatest artist of the nineteenth century. So let us not talk about the difference in ability between Rietschel and Rodin.
But second, it happens that Rodin's importance does not lie in his monuments,

and if we wanted to be pedantically critical we should have to say that Rodin ought not to have accepted any commission that was in conflict with his genius. His *Balzac* is certainly the better piece of sculpture, but it is the poorer monument, for the qualities we see in it are not essentially monumental qualities, but qualities that cause the monument to disintegrate, making it impossible and superfluous. The strength of his sculpture is not that it provides information about a writer but that it speaks of the extent of the extra-human, where form dissolves into the formless. Younger sculptors, who produce no more memorials at all but devote themselves from the start exclusively to these tasks of the twentieth century, can speak of this realm even more accurately and conclusively than Rodin.

I repeat: the two laws of monumental sculpture are that the monument represents a fixed spot in the world and that the figure on the monument is perpendicular, raised above events. Anything necessary in the way of action, text or information must appear on the base, not in the statuary.

PLATE P. 113

Now let us measure by these criteria Rodin's other mighty work, the *Burghers of Calais*. Here, alongside the monument to heroic intellect *(Balzac)*, we have the monument to patriotism, to historical memory. No doubt the Committee wanted a historical scene, comparable with the innumerable battles preserved in the galleries of the Palace of Versailles, comparable with the reliefs on the monuments to the Kings of France. Or else they wanted a hero (in fact they wanted only one out of the horde of medieval victims, just Eustache de St. Pierre), and imagined him in an attitude in the pathos of which they could renew their oaths of loyalty to their country. There were many such pieces of patriotic sculpture in France at that time. Instead of this Rodin produced a group, almost a mass, whose arrangement makes their circular movement round the hero in their midst almost imperceptible; moreover they are going off not to victory but to a sacrificial death. He acted contrary to both laws of monumental sculpture: he did not leave his figures – which are no longer a single form, a perpendicular, but rather, as a group, a horizontal mass – on their fixed site, from which they would be able to define the points of the compass, but on the contrary made them leave the spot, strain away from it. And second: he magnified what was really the relief, the account of action, and turned what according to the rule should have belonged on the base into the monument itself. Naturally Rodin would not have admitted that these two rules of monumental sculpture were in fact rules – he had not heard them formulated as such; but if the whole story of the *Burghers of Calais* has led to a powerful piece of sculpture, though certainly not to a genuine monument, it is precisely because of these contradictions. From historicism (for the whole commission is historicism), from a fourteenth-century scene in Froissart's *Chronicles*, he took a number of isolated details – the hair shirts, for example – but deep down inside himself he had no desire to model historical shirts; he was already

APPX. PL. 14

striving for the cleft exterior form which he achieved ten years later in *Balzac*. Classical shaping, historical accuracy in the surface of sculpture was replaced by his *modelé*, his art of humps and holes, which no longer produced hollow-casting that rang like a bell but held fast by its tattered edges a kind of explosive cloud somewhere on its way from an inner nucleus to an outer infinity.

There can be no question that Rodin lacked the feeling for monuments; the proof of this, if one were needed, is that this group is extant as a museum-piece in six different places. It can be seen to much better advantage in the museums of Basle, Zurich, Tokyo, London and Paris than in Calais, where it never became anything other than an occasional piece. The monument to Maximilian I, on the contrary, is unique and can only be found in Munich; and Goethe and Schiller can be seen only in front of the theatre at Weimar. On the other hand, there can be no question that Rodin produced a splendid piece of sculpture, against the will of those who commissioned it. Nor can there be any question that – this time against his own will – the group does not belong to the rank of historical monuments but alongside the realism of the contemporary labour movement, alongside miners setting off to take help to their comrades underground, alongside Meunier, and above all alongside Vincenzo Vela's great relief commemorating those who died during the construction of the St. Gotthard tunnel, a work which dates from 1882, two years before Rodin began the *Burghers of Calais*.
Rodin's monuments – all his other designs remained fragments – came to grief on the contradiction between the concept 'monument' and his own artistic aims: the monuments are not the works that make him immortal.

RUDE

After the classicistic firmness of the upright human figure standing on its own ground ('Wie schön, o Mensch, mit Deinem Palmenzweige stehst Du an des Jahrhunderts Neige, in edler stolzer Männlichkeit'* – Schiller), but still long before the chaos of the gates of hell in which Rodin's men find themselves, comes the transitional period of Romanticism: sculpture still portrays the individual, but man is no longer the centre, defining the points of the compass; rather is he swept along by his destiny. He hears a summons from without, from another world, and he has to obey this summons. This situation is most clearly portrayed in Rude's *Jeanne d'Arc, écoutant les voix*: the peasant girl from Domrémy hears the voices, uncertainly puts her hand to her ear as if by doing this one could improve the audibility of voices that really come from within, and miraculously there arises beside her a medieval suit of armour, the garb of war which she is summoned to put on. It is almost impossible to convert such an inner summons into an outwardly visible gesture; one could speak of limited gesture as a further characteristic of Romantic sculpture. It is a kind of gesture that does not proceed from man's free will – it is not like the bestowal of a constitution by a ruler with upraised hand – nor yet is it the diametrical opposite of this, the involuntary movement of the marionette. It is a gesture whose spontaneity, whose expression almost, is limited, being the result of a summons from outside this world; yet it is executed all the same by a sentient human being. Whoever hears the summons must leave the spot on which he happens still to be standing – and this too is in characteristic opposition to the 'fixed site' of monumental sculpture.
The same definition can be seen in the deeply romantic element in Rude's most famous work, *The Departure of the Volunteers*, the so-called Marseillaise group on

* 'How finely, O Man, thou standest with thy palm sprig at the turn of the century, in noble, proud humanity'. (Trans.)

the Arc de Triomphe in Paris. The summons is made visible: it is the mighty figure whose open mouth and legs planted wide apart offended two conventions; but the patriotic summons was so unmistakable that the exponents of classicism had to remain silent. Those summoned have already started to leave their previous positions and to move off to battle. And further, two individual figures, a generation apart in origin yet miraculously alike in spirit, Mercury, fastening his winged shoes, in other words already rising, in the direction of his upraised arm, into the invisible, the divine. Nude classical sculpture: Rude always longed, at every new commission, to be able to create the naked figure of a god, for in his theoretical approach he still clung to his classical training, to his conversations with the respected Jacques-Louis David, with whom he had shared the fate of emigration to Belgium after the downfall of Napoleon. He did not realize how 'romantic', even in its physical proportions, its metallic slenderness, his figure of Mercury was. It was made in 1828, but the memorial to Marshal Ney in 1852; yet it is as if the ancient god had been transformed into the tragic hero of the Napoleonic age, with the same upraised arm, with the command which the Marshal gives – it is the last command, 'Fire!', which he hurls at the firing squad, the ultimate in military bravado and in the same moment the summons to death, far further off than the Olympus to which Mercury was about to ascend. And again: Napoleon ascending to immortality – what sculptor except Rude could have hit upon an idea like that?
Can a Romantic of this sort, summoned by history, by science, see anything else in them but once again forces that sweep him away? Surely Rude's statue of the mathematician Gaspard Monge, 1846–1848, renowned at that time as the first piece of sculpture to reproduce with perfect accuracy the dress of the eighteenth century, cannot simply be classified as historicism? For Rude it marks an effort at self-mastery. And the gesture of the two hands – no: the emphatic gap between the two hands – does it not indicate the scientific problem by which the geometer is puzzled?
Contemporary dress shown with careful respect – yet history regarded not as a reality but as a romantic challenge: this description would cover *Marshal Saxe* as well as *Gaspard Monge*. The marshal is shown in accurately-reproduced seventeenth-century dress, yet it does not look as if it is really being worn; it looks tinny, even rattly.

CARPEAUX

The same historicism serves those sculptors, indeed those people in general, who do not want to be romantic as a means of defence against a supernatural summons. They know perfectly well that there are situations which are beyond comprehension, but their sense of reality then produces the result that they prefer to concern themselves with the recognizable, scientifically ascertainable facts of the story rather than with feelings. Historicism is then employed as a defence against the chaos of the emotions.
Jean-Baptiste Carpeaux corresponded with the nineteenth century's picture of an artist's life; today we can see archetypal features in him. He grew up in straitened circumstances, the son of a lace-maker and of a mason who emigrated to America

when his son was a child to make money there and returned at once when he sensed that his son had meanwhile become famous and was the better source of money. He created an impression early in life in the provincial French town of Valenciennes, was given assistance and soon achieved fame with patrons and his fellow citizens. Haunted by the same sort of obsession that later caused Max Beckmann to say, 'I would crawl through all the sewers in the world in order to be able to paint', Carpeaux followed Napoleon III from town to town to show him an obtrusive piece of flattery, a relief of the subjugation of Abd el-Kader, so as to be able to step forward and say 'I made it', to have the work commissioned in marble, and to gain access to high society. To what extent was he genuinely an artist of the Second Empire? How far could this be true of anyone who would have pressed his service on any other régime in just the same way?
Grand Prix de Rome, sojourn in Rome and then the ambitious, grandly executed but basically stiff and empty *Ugolino* group: Ugolino in his hunger-tower, whose children offer themselves to him in order to prolong his life with their own flesh. If one attempts to treat a theme like this by academic methods, that is, with athletic, muscular bodies, the result is bound to be cramped; it needed a Rodin to portray hunger, to venture on the step from the human world to the animal world, to an Ugolino who can think of nothing else but eating, who lunges forward on all fours like an animal over its prey. (Perhaps one of the more equivocal aspects of Carpeaux's Ugolino is the fact that he is gnawing at his own knuckles.) Then came the return to Paris, fame and glory at the imperial court. The same Rodin recalled in his old age: 'How can I describe the emotions which stirred us poor pupils of the drawing-school when Carpeaux walked past and corrected the work of the best of us. Unforgettable memory! Oh, the respect we felt for him!' The radiant moment when General de Montfort's beautiful daughter became his bride and wife – to suffer what a martyrdom! She had no idea that already the father and the good-for-nothing brother had returned from America, that already they had fastened on to the successful brother, and were monopolizing the fame, the income, the daily life, the interest of the defenceless artist, stifling him – a man quite incapable of freeing himself from the vicious circle of his early life, and of believing in love. There was strife between the family to which he no longer belonged and the family into which he had married, and which – the courage of his wife notwithstanding – confronted the artist in him with all the alien characteristics of the conventional bourgeoisie.
In Carpeaux there developed what we today would call the archetypal element, certain realms which sought physical expression, three-dimensional conceptions which no longer came from patriarchal thinking or historical accuracy but from personal experience, foreboding – in other words, the need for personal expression. This is true even though the themes can at first be given names, as if they were obvious: portraits first, the individual as a personality, no longer built up out of classical forms but to all appearances fleetingly sketched, on the principle that there is a nucleus of humanity which cannot be portrayed and does not need to be portrayed, that over this nucleus hovers the ephemeral part – the Emperor's bonhomie, the indescribable charm of his bride – already decked with flowers.

These flowers form the second set of themes; they should be equated with the animals which Barye introduced into nineteenth-century sculpture. It was not because the ornamentation of the Pavilion of Flora demanded flowery ideas but *vice versa*, because Carpeaux had a special interest in flowers, that the ornamentation of the newly-erected pavilion became a 'Flora' scheme. Flora also occurs in Italian sculpture of this period, the antecedents of which have not yet been investigated; it is a noteworthy moment in nineteenth-century art, this connection with the Jardin des Plantes.

As for the upright figure with arms spread wide as a real archetype – it appears in Carpeaux's earliest important relief as a naked figure of peace above the body of the man stretched out on the ground, above a figure of Charity – it would have needed a man like Munch to make a free artistic creation out of this central element; in the work of the twenty-year-old provincial Carpeaux it suffocated among the subsidiary details. But he returned again and again like a somnambulist to this upward straining figure with the outstretched arms.

In Carpeaux's life, the story of which outwardly resembles a novel by Balzac, there is a genuine artistic centre, the moment of fulfilment. This was when he was commissioned to execute the *Dance* group for the façade of the new Opéra. A *Dance* – but no longer the timid movements which sculptors before Carpeaux had employed to indicate dancing, and indeed not the sort of dancing that is expressed in postures and ballet steps. At that time the minuet was being replaced by the waltz, and ceaseless, insatiable circling is one of the movements predominant in Carpeaux's *Dance*. However, it is not the circling of the waltz, which is a dance for couples, with no central figure; it is a round dance, which grows closer and closer, swifter and swifter, until the spinning top stands erect; how different this erectness is from the logical erectness of the monument! The central figure is not the beginning of the group; it is a consequence – a furious vortex in the midst of which there shoots up a driving force, a virile power. That was also the impression it created. It was not the nudity that made people furious – nudity in an allegory of the dance would not have caused offence – but nudity heightened by movement. Nudity neither as coquetry nor as pose, but as ecstasy – that was it. Ecstasy has something exclusive about it; whoever does not accept it from the start – whoever is not born to it, one might almost say – will never be swept into it; it is a demonstration of the doctrine of predestination.

People were furious; but here, at this central point in his creative career, Carpeaux was magnificent, free at last, inexorable, never yielding for a moment, while the director of the Opéra collapsed, the architect withdrew, the minister ordered the removal of the group, a successor to produce a replacement was already named and his model already delivered (it had even been depicted in illustrations). Carpeaux, who had broken through his own taboos, found a form that cannot perish, dared to make the leap and gambled everything – honour, connections, family – was saved by an act of vandalism on the part of the objectors (they threw a bottle of ink at the white marble group), by the sudden death of the replacement sculptor and by the Franco-Prussian war. The group ceased to be a focus of interest; it remained quietly where it was and gradually became – although

Carpeaux did not live to enjoy his fame – the greatest, the only work of art on the new Opéra. Today it has been moved to a museum – the embalming seal of immortality – to protect it from the inclemency of the weather. It has been replaced on the Opéra by a copy.

It represents, in place of the gesture which permits a literary interpretation, frenzy which escapes control; in other words, a completely new kind of sculpture which does not arise out of dignity, validity, history but wells up from the emotions, from the involuntary side of the artist.

Yet here too, amid the wealth of nineteenth-century French art, one can find the roots, the possible stimuli: the high altar of the Madeleine church, by Carlo Marochetti, with a saint who feels herself carried up out of a chaste circle of angels.

Carpeaux's days ended in worry, pessimism and gloom; he died at the age of forty-eight.

RODIN

What is a genius? A man who has been trained as a craftsman; who displays ceaseless fertility; who fulfils an age; who carries a world in himself; who is all mind. All these requirements must be satisfied. Rodin is the genius of the nineteenth century.

His ability as a craftsman has been graphically described by Judith Cladel; he was just as capable of delivering designs for porcelain groups in the taste of his patron Carrier-Belleuse as of hewing out pedimental groups and caryatids under the balconies of Parisian avenues. This period of his life shows how wrong it is to classify Rodin as a 'modelleur', as the school of Hildebrand tried to do for a time in an attempt to protect itself against undue influence; Rodin would have made the marble-cutters of Carrara sweat.

As for ceaseless fertility, how quickly one comes to an end when one enumerates the works of Carpeaux; it is almost impossible, on the other hand, to list all Rodin's works, however well one is acquainted with them, because there are too many of them and because they continually overlap one another. The best evidence for this would be an attempt to give a detailed description of the *Gate of Hell*, which is not a work comparable with old church doors but a work that gives an account of the artist's own path through life; it is rightly called the *Gate of Hell*, for the Inferno in Dante's *Divine Comedy* is the only thing that can be compared with it. It is the reflection of all life in the mind of one single man, the reproduction of every figure in such a way that we know it only through him.

A world in himself; I do not know how one could imagine Dante's figures, whether they would exist outside his verses; whether they did not originally circle round simply as fates, as characters in the inferno of his heart and only retrospectively, during the work, acquire actual names and destinies; whether Paolo and Francesca were first themselves and then were noticed retrospectively by Dante or whether the whirling of a fatally intertwined pair of lovers had long been alive in him before he heard the names Paolo and Francesca.

At any rate, it is so with Rodin. All the titles of his works (we except the works executed as commissions – the monuments, the architectural sculpture, the portraits; they do not appear in the *Gate of Hell* either) come not from him but from his literary friends. From Rodin come the basic tensions which are expressed in sculptural terms – the human conflicts, the happiness and despair. What is sculpture for Rodin? It is no longer the monument, which would have to have its own fixed site. To that extent all his work on the so-called monuments is a struggle with a task that was not his – yet for which, because he was such a towering genius, he created in his failures better, more important sculpture than others who trod along well-worn paths.

Nor is sculpture for Rodin just the human figure with its bone structure and network of muscles; it involves the play of the muscles down to every detail and goes even further in this direction than Michelangelo did. Naturally the nineteenth-century genius was able to outdo the sixteenth-century genius in anatomy, in the accuracy with which each individual strand of muscle is shown, in sheer, dogged work. But how could people be so superficial as to say that Rodin's *Thinker* thinks not with the head but with the muscles, and therefore does not think at all? As if the sculptor were an anatomist, as if he had to register the position of the brain-cells being used for thought. The sculptor's job is rather to convey mental intensity in his own material. With poets and philosophers, who make use of words, the thought is not in the words themselves, whether printed or spoken; thought is the intensity which can be conveyed by means of words. It is the same with the sculptor: thought is the intensity which can be conveyed by his modelling. There is more thought in a foot by Rodin than in a head by another sculptor.

And gesture? Are not Rodin's figures, even the *Thinker*, nevertheless intense because of their gestures? What is the difference between the pose of classicism (contrapposto), the summons-from-outside in Rude and gesture in Rodin? Rodin has no summons from outside, no 'reality' providing a support. He has no history, in spite of the *Burghers of Calais*, no animals, in spite of an occasional lion, no furniture, no objects, as Magni or van Gogh do, no dress, in spite of penitent's shirt and gown. Yet in spite of this he always remains close to nature, uses it as a support, corrective, lodestar. He has stone as his material, anticipating the twentieth century and following the many millennia in which stone has been a living, fertile substance. What is gesture in Rodin? It is a kind of cramp, despair. It does not happen to man as a single individual but to man as a pair of beings, an unhappy pair.

What is gesture in Robin? It is physical sensation, clash, warmth, repulsion. It is not like this in Rude. In front of a figure by Rude, could one ever deduce the odour of the body, fancy one was breathing it? Thus Rodin, knowing much more about the body, also knows much more about the heart, about destiny. Then there is the chaotic state of human culture. Whereas in Rubens Antiquity and Christianity are still firmly established realms with an ascertainable content, for Rodin they are ruined worlds, fascinating and amorphous – in spite of his enthusiasm for cathedrals. What did he see in the latter? Surely not scholasticism, the unity of a divinely ordered world? How much Christian imagery occurs with him? A madonna? No, for there is no mother-figure at all among his works. A genuine

Christ? No, only ideal figures for Magdalens. A Christian saint? Yes, John the Baptist; but even he turns into *l'homme qui marche*.
Ovid's *Metamorphoses*, on the other hand, do provide him with themes. Not because he was familiar with this poem in Latin but because in his world fates mingled, one tension changed into another; for Rodin himself they needed no names, they formed their own bodies. But for catalogues and sales they needed names, and they received them from these mythological stories – harmless names that acted as a disguise and provided a cover for sexual themes which could not have been named directly.
While Rodin was no longer a central figure in the history of the monument – he did more to destroy the form than to perfect it – he was at the centre of another universal moment in art, a moment that falls in our century.
Everyone knows, of course, that art is connected with erotic, indeed sexual tensions; that it ceases to be possible, either in the artist who creates it or in society as a whole, if it does not allude to and make use of the world of sensuality. Even in prehistoric times fertility, the womb, the element that generates and gives birth, had been one of the seeds of all art. French art, French society was for centuries rich, gifted, favoured because in every period the French took the erotic side of life seriously; they tolerated neither repressed violence nor the reserve which the erotic element as a vital energy encountered in the public life of the Nordic nations. The salon, gallant conversation, intellectual frivolity, the seduction of wit – the French had always been accustomed to walking amid thousands of naked bosoms. The only thing was that they had to be gilded, they had to have the abstraction of verse, of witty conventionality, like the tights worn by the ballet dancers in grand opera.
Just as Richard Wagner with his total work of art had to fight a bitter battle against the 'routine of the theatre which I detest from the bottom of my heart', so in Rodin (and before him already in Carpeaux) sexuality sprang up as a primitive force and broke through the conventions. Here lies one of the great possibilities for our own century. While beauty, maidenhood, maternity, religiosity are all explored territories, sexuality is not. There is an equivocal background to the fact that this territory is still virgin (paradoxical phrase!), although art and fertility have always been connected; for at this spot the very strongest taboos were in operation, permitting allusions by and agreement among those in the know but not a real investigation, a real examination of what goes on and how. In the course of the nineteenth and twentieth centuries these taboos have been infringed. In a world which allows medicine to practise depth psychology and geneticists to investigate genes it is no longer possible to exclude artists from the field of sexuality, for they must have fresh ground to investigate, not ground that has been cleansed and levelled with the rollers of convention.
But how superior Rodin is to present-day artists, who have to work, in documentary films and opinion polls, with sexual symbols, descriptions of coition, sadism and homosexuality, and have to discover a whole new arsenal of disguises. Even if bold spirits are necessarily attracted by the unknown, the untried – no 'Legion of Decency' will ever alter this – that does not mean to say that the angles

from which we investigate sexuality in the twentieth century are the happiest ones; perhaps indeed they are very unhappy ones, for they have to make use of keys, of surrealism, of amorphous or mechanistic symbols, of complicated couplings and curiosities that are half-way between the incomprehensible and the pornographic.

How different it was for Rodin, who still had the female body to himself, who could still discover the undiscovered in it, and who had at his disposal the whole world of French *amour*, the accumulated flood-waters of many centuries. The French had been the masters of the graceful love-story, of the frivolous engraving, of the *Contes drôlatiques*. What had become, especially in the Second Empire – the age of Nana, of the Marquise de Paiva – a society pastime, with no danger of its being taken too seriously, for it was deliberately left playful (naturally the French were masters of this too – *La Maison Tellier*), was transposed by Rodin into a quite different and much deeper dimension. Perhaps the depth was already present in the fights between animals depicted by Delacroix and Barye, but it was still so heavily veiled that it did not really make its presence felt. In Rodin it is no longer veiled, but so transformed, so suddenly and so thoroughly converted into something artistic, that one no longer notices either the sexuality or the depth even when they are there right before one's eyes. In the first few moments one feels that one is simply looking at a piece of sculpture, an abstraction. But anyone who has not seen the sexual act in Rodin's groups, the special 'position' on which they are based, must grow more mature in order to see it; it is just as certainly there as the colour in an early Renoir. Rodin is infallible; and he is rich and many-sided. With him, too, sex turns into the tragic, the perverse, the unrestrained, the cheerful, but before one can be shocked it is sculpture again, a pure artistic form. Form, in so far as form is spirit. It is a question of sex turning into spirit, not of eroticism being purified into love, which would have pleased the moralists at any rate. Spirit as something eminently male. There is no happy love in Rodin, no maternal love. Nor is there any connection with prehistoric sex, which is always a vegetation rite. Rodin's fertility takes the form of pure spirit, not of children or flowers. When children occur at all they are half-grown persons already caught up by fate, or brothers beside sisters from whom they are already separated, from whom they are already striving to part, pushing each other away – *Fugit Amor*.

There is the arresting realization that to him the female body – pressed together in the attitude of the '*Crouching Woman*', so that a classicist would describe it as ugly, withdrawn in the stress of overflow, rigid in masturbation – appears as beauty petrified, not to be released from its rigidity by any desire or love; for on this piece of sculpture he wrote Baudelaire's lines:

> Je suis belle ô mortels comme un rêve de pierre
> Et mon sein où chacun s'est meurtri tour à tour
> Est fait pour inspirer au poète un amour
> Eternel et muet ainsi que la matière.

('I am as fair, O mortals, as a dream of stone
And my bosom on which each has bruised himself in turn
Is made to inspire in the poet a love
As everlasting and dumb as matter itself.')

There what is depicted is the in-comprehensibility, the un-touchability of beauty. To many people, there may be something frightening in the thought that beauty is meant to be depicted here, where otherwise they would have discovered at best an aspect of truth.

Baudelaire is the nearest parallel to Rodin; not artists like Courbet or even the late Renoir, with their possibly strong but certainly primitive sensuality.

Love that passes on; time that tears lovers apart, the hopelessness of ever being able to hold anything fast: Rodin was the first to depict all these things, and in a language that does not need to be enciphered, that has turned so thoroughly into form, into what he called 'modelé', that he is in a position to say everything. Any weaker artist who uses this method soon degenerates into insufferable tawdriness; there is nothing so empty as Rodin-like ideas depicted by weaker artists; for example, a kiss by Sinding or a ride on a cloud by Kolbe.

Rodin created the world of half-size figures and also re-created it as an artistic form, for previously nineteenth-century sculpture had been either monumental or miniature sculpture on the scale of the mantelpiece clock. Rodin produces the sort of sculpture that can pass into the possession of the collector; it does not need to stand in a public place or in a museum. In it, like Rubens, he reshapes the whole world of ancient mythology to fit contemporary ideas. And the eroticism – but the word is too weak; sexuality is the term required – of Rodin's groups reacts on his large-scale work, even on his official work. It is the horror inspired by life that makes his big figures like *Eve* shudder. It is the weightlessness of the ascent that causes the torso of his *Iris* to hover – *Iris*, because it is the tidings of divinity that reach us in no other moment but this; torso, because when a statue is built round the female bosom the head becomes blind. It is the hopelessness of ever managing to fill the vessel of desire that makes his *Danaïd* collapse – and immediately watch again for the next ride, with transparent shoulders and trembling hips. The impossibility of holding on to the moment, an impossibility which allows only a just-before and a just-after, never unconsciousness itself – if it could be represented it would mean the end of life and art. From the *Danaïd* develops the *Perseus:* the back of the woman, of the repulsed beloved, and over her the triumph of the man rising into the air, carrying off some precious part of the woman he has abandoned, her head as a trophy – but he knows that he cannot look at it without turning to stone: the mythology of old legends transformed into the rending violence of the present.

Marriage does not appear in Rodin, which sometimes makes his work almost unbearable. The *Hand of God* – which is often wrongly positioned in museums and wrongly illustrated, as if the hand stretched upward, whereas in reality it is held quietly straight out – the *Hand of God* is a self-portrait of Rodin's hand, in which he holds reflectively a tiny statue, just as the figure of God the Creator in Michelangelo's ceiling is a self-portrait of the painter apportioning the different areas of the Sistine ceiling. And this question of position is a detail of supreme importance. For we repeat: monumental sculpture was perpendicular. It originated in man's experience of upright existence, in a pride that was five thousand years old. Rodin's sculpture does not set aside gravity. Once again, before quite different abstractions become effective, sculpture conforms to the – apparently always valid – context of gravitational force. But Rodin's figures acknowledge the validity of this force not by standing erect but by lying down; and the lying gives rise to a hovering – or rather the hovering is the prior assumption, the experience, and from it is retrospectively deduced the conclusion that there are conceivable situations, conditions, expressions in which man feels that he is hovering.

If Rodin's figures are weightless and rear up, they are always based on the assumption of weight. Rodin is the last of the really great sculptors who can portray weightlessness in the context of weight, and dares to do so. The sculptors of the twentieth century, on the other hand, have lost the aid of gravity in their work.

Egyptian sculpture was dense, but not heavy. In Greek sculpture we find weight borne by its own strength. In Rodin, weightlessness within weight, unconsciousness, almost anaesthesia. The vortex that Blake tried to represent by means of Art Nouveau lines, that appears in graphic art as sheaves of lines, occurs in Rodin as the shortest, though well stretched, link in an endless chain, a cross-section through the endless space modelled thirty years later by Brancusi. Such is the vortex that drives Paolo and Francesca round the nucleus of movement. Such is the vortex, the wreath, that the unconscious woman lays round the neck, round the face, of the man in the *Hand of God.*

These figures are half life-size and so not really doll-like but big enough to exist for themselves, to express everything. But they are not life-size; here too we see the wisdom of the sculptor, his enviable freedom to model what could not be expressed in words. A half life-size world, really an endless world of sculpture that with another artist would be relief.

Rude's figures are by their nature life-size and therefore individual, never to be united in a *Frieze of Life*. Rodin chooses half life-size because in this way there can be a whole. The individual figure would make this impossible.

There is a way out for museums that want to have individual pieces of sculpture: the *Man with the Broken Nose*. A life-size head, so strongly modelled that it is no longer a portrait; a self-portrait, a link with Michelangelo's shattered face: a way out for museums, so that they do not have to miss all contact with the universal genius of Rodin.

Then there are the other experiments of Rodin's late period, very extensive in their scope, giving rough indications of what was bound to be created during the twentieth century both in France and outside it. In importance and intensity they still surpass all the work done before and after him. He is the only sculptor who has created a whole world.

There are some touching photographs of Rodin as an old man drawing dancing girls from Cambodia. Artists before him struggled with the difficulty that one cannot see and set down at the same time, that one can never really draw from nature (except with a *camera obscura* and on a screen), but only in recollection of nature, of what has just been seen, which is pushed as far away by the process of looking down at white paper as love is when the act is interrupted. Rodin is not looking down; he lets the pencil hang from his hand while he follows the movements with his eyes. He produces the drawing by oscillation. And in his drawings one can see more and more the lines of this oscillation; it is precisely these which become the ghostly traces of an incredible capacity for creation.

AFTER RODIN

Rodin is often placed beside the Impressionists; this means no more than that he lived at the same time. He was neither personally acquainted with them (in John Rewald's history of Impressionism Rodin occurs only once, as a subscriber to the purchase of Manet's *Olympia*) nor had he anything in common with them in his artistic tendencies and aims. If one wished to find sculptors corresponding to the Impressionists one would have to look for men who sought in a comparable way for a new arrangement and consolidation of artistic form (and thus of plastic compactness); men who were convinced that this was the decisive factor, who were not bothered about content but rather stuck to pleasing subjects – the painters to landscape, sculptors to the human body; men to whom other themes – death, love, fertility, the organization of the state – were unimportant. In other words, one would end up with artists who might possibly be called archaizers or artists of the Arts-and-Crafts idea: in Germany Adolf von Hildebrand, in France Maillol, Bourdelle, Despiau and others. The distance that seems to separate them from each other is only apparent; in reality only fifteen years divide the birth of Hildebrand (1847) from that of Maillol (1861), though it is true that a generation separates their periods of activity, for Hildebrand began to sculpt right away, while Maillol did not start until he was nearly forty.

Hildebrand strove for a renewal through nobility of form; this was modern because art was identified with form and content was put almost completely to one side, but also historical in a very emphatic sense because it was a second return to the early Florentine Renaissance; the first, a generation earlier, had been led by Lorenzo Bartolini. From Michelangelo Hildebrand took over the idea that a piece of sculpture comes into being out of its block of stone as if water were being let away and the shape already resting in the water then emerged like an island. Michelangelo can only have said this because, like every medieval craftsman, he had the block in a horizontal position while he was working on it. Hildebrand, on the other hand, who had the block standing up in front of him, made out of it a main-view, a wall which was hollowed out optically, not by craftsmanship. Behind this was his friendship with Hans von Marées and Konrad Fiedler, with their 'perception aesthetic', which achieved a great clarification in the field of art criticism, of aesthetic conceptions, but could say little about the significance of an artistic achievement.

Hildebrand's best known early work was a standing male figure. His literary friends did not quite dare to turn it into a piece of mythology, but they wanted at any rate to christen it *Alone*. However, Hildebrand stood firm and insisted that even in the catalogue nothing more should be said than just 'a standing male figure, carved from stone by the sculptor himself'. Both details indicated a kind of revolution. Today it is difficult to know whether we should see here the beginnings of Art Nouveau, whose adherents wished to make things themselves, or an early form of modern experimentation with materials and the details of craftsmanship. But if Hildebrand (and his disciples) meant that he was the sculptor in stone, while Rodin only modelled and had not carved stone, then they were wrong. Hildebrand, just like Rodin, also tried to produce monuments. When, already a famous artist, he took part in the competition for the Kaiser Wilhelm monument in Berlin he was granted an audience by Wilhelm II. The Kaiser expressed the view that in the design his grandfather was not recognizable enough. To which Hildebrand replied: 'Your Majesty, in fifty years' time no one will ask any longer what he looked like but only whether the sculpture is good.' He was surprised that he did not receive the commission. We are inclined on this occasion (but only on this occasion) to admit that Wilhelm II was right for once: anyone who does not wish to produce a memorial but only 'good sculpture' should not want to win a competition for a memorial. We are also of the opinion that the *Bismarck* commissioned in Bremen is an indifferent piece of sculpture; a poor translation – not even a good one – of *Colleoni* from Venice to Bremen.

In Munich the connection with Italian art widened to include the Baroque style. It is difficult to have an unequivocal opinion about this, since on the one hand at this same time, from 1880 onwards, the first and very influential critical works on Baroque were beginning to appear and historicism took up this previously neglected style, while on the other hand it seems questionable whether such a stylistic classification, which may be convenient for the history of art, corresponds in fact with reality. It seems more likely that one should speak – especially in Munich – of a continuously existing Baroque style, and that one should oppose the doctrine that a distinct style has to come to an end where the art historians draw the line between eras. In that case Munich, for example, would have to be an 'abstract' city from 1911 onwards, the date of Kandinsky's *Blauer Reiter (Blue Rider)*. But things aren't like that, as Bertold Brecht was saying even in those days, and sometimes one cannot help feeling irritated at the arrogance which assumes that only one style and only one view – to wit, the speaker's own – are possible in any given period, whereas the merest glance at the facts reveals that all kinds of things are possible in the same year. Indeed, 'everything is possible in every period'; or at any rate this assertion is as well justified – because it is just as one-sided and exaggerated – as the opposite one, which was also formulated at that time by Heinrich Wölfflin, namely that at any given moment only one contemporary style is possible.

Anyway, it is Hildebrand's later Baroque period that produced the two Munich fountains – the Wittelsbach fountain, beautifully designed as the end of one square and the start of another, and the Hubertus fountain, architecture almost too delicate to make its mark in a public square. The *Father Rhine* fountain in Strasbourg was removed in 1919, when the city became French. Regarded in Strasbourg as undesirable and too far away from the allegorical tradition, this fountain too found its way to Munich.

While these architectonic forms certainly have nothing to do with the archaizers or the Impressionists, the four huntsmen on the four diagonals of the Hubertus fountain can undoubtedly be mentioned in connection with them; the figure of Diana could take its place beside Despiau's statue of a maiden. Hildebrand has the ability to raise the female body, without emaciating it, to a springing position just clear of the ground, and to make the powerful male body stand in motion outside the contrapposto. The value of this ability depends, as he would have said himself, on whether the sculpture is good, not on whether it was produced at the right moment in the view of art historians.

PLATE P. 114

The great influence exerted for a time by Hildebrand was confined on the whole, it is true, to Munich. His leading disciple was Hermann Hahn, who acted as a kind of deputy for the master (Hildebrand never accepted a professorial chair and gave no classes). Alongside Hahn there was Bernhard Bleeker. Hildebrand's grandsons, for example Toni Stadler, are still alive and at work among us.

If the next sculptor we name is Maillol, it is certainly not because he was a disciple of Hildebrand. Maillol's connections were much rather with Rodin, though he spent more time in Rodin's studio than in his classes. But our fundamental conception of what sculpture is permits us to bring in Maillol at this point. He too lived a 'Mediterranean' life, that is, he would not abandon the link with the beautiful (female) body. He wanted to substitute the firmly cohering outer surface of his own sculpture for the allegedly rugged surface of Rodin's. This notion affected many sculptors at that time, especially German ones, like a sudden flash of illumination; through Hildebrand the Germans were accustomed to such ideas and now found a good example quite unconnected with historicism. Yet even then it was also an archaism; that is, it was a possible form for modern sculpture but not the obligatory one. Brancusi was already experimenting with quite different forms, no news of which reached Germany. Naturally it was not a question of really archaic form, though artists were not unaware of contemporary archaeological discoveries. The generation which had been indignant at the idea of using neo-Gothic forms was ready without any further ado to recognize similarities of form in Egyptian or Negro art. Or, in the case of Greece, to go back to the Archaic period. Although Maillol, on a trip to Greece, described the *Hermes* of Praxiteles at Olympia as 'soap', he was prepared to learn from the severely classical figures on the pediment of the temple of Zeus. A generation earlier it would have been the other way about.

Since Bourdelle is scarcely known outside France, we illustrate, as an example of these new archaizers, the figure of a girl *(Assia)* by Charles Despiau. We have no desire to conduct one-sided propaganda; works like these could be passed over. It is not academic – none of these men sat in an academy – but it does belong to a stream of art that runs parallel to the so-called 'avant-garde'. It is not intellectual, but certainly to a high degree artistic. It solves the problem of satisfying the tensions of sculpture without driving the sensuousness out of a woman's body, without in fact becoming 'soap'. Statuary of this sort is like a kind of re-

PLATE P. 114

insurance. There must always be people who in spite of the existence of typewriters can write in their own hand as well, and people who can grasp and portray heaviness and charm in the human figure in equal proportions; artistic production must always be kept rich, many-sided and comprehensive – otherwise we shall soon be lost. The twentieth-century cult of the body must be given its chance in art. Otherwise, as is demonstrated by the film industry, roads divide and 'art' becomes a more and more arid path. It cannot be denied that in the twentieth century a young girl can move about naked in a quite unembarrassed way – something which she could not do in the nineteenth century. Consequently the photograph of this statue amid the trees is quite natural and right. The statue can stand for generations of well-developed sporting girls. It is a garden figure, not a museum piece. Maillol's statues always have a touch of the public square or the war memorial about them. What is the difference between the cylinders on which the torso of this statue by Despiau stands and the legs of a Greek ephebe? The Greek sculptor, with the aid of the colour of marble and the way it absorbs the light, can get much nearer to the warmth of human skin. The present-day sculptor, even Despiau, makes cylinders, and is therefore always nearer to an artist like Léger or Wotruba than to the Greeks. What he models is an abstraction that has become sensuous, not the reverse: sensuousness become abstraction. Really it is incorrect to call such a statue 'a young girl'.

Or again take Wilhelm Lehmbruck. A miner's son, like Henry Moore, tied to the artistic tradition of the end of the last century, an earnest pupil of the Düsseldorf Academy, he began to awaken slowly and steadily – one might also say very quickly – through contact with Paris, became independent, overhauled his teachers and ventured on into the unknown – until he could no longer bear the tension and took his own life.

His very first impressions of Rodin gave rise to a ponderous poem on the *Kiss*. Then came charming etchings, a bit studied, in the style of Modigliani, just about as sensuous as traditional modes of expression permitted. He cannot have seen Rodin's late drawings.

The sculpture which Lehmbruck produced at the same time surprises us by a capacity to put more into one particular view than really belongs to this view, in other words to evoke the adjacent forms so distinctly that they are equally expressive. If it were possible to photograph the phenomenon, it would emerge even more strikingly: there is a space-content as well, not just an outline.

Then there is the influence of Brancusi, which must have been very strong. Part of this influence consisted in an intellectualization of sculpture, a growing aridity almost, a continual impoverishment, so that it became thinner and finally almost metallic. But not only that; he learned how to work with intervening spaces, how to realize negative spaces, the tensions between a hand and a breast or a head. In Lehmbruck's work there is not just a tendency to wiriness or a fining down to stereometric forms (as practised at the same period by Rudolf Belling in a famous *Triple Tone:* originally three women dancing like a dance group by Matisse, developed in space instead of on canvas; the corresponding nineteenth-century groups, by Marochetti or Carpeaux, were richer), but limbs and joints that remain limbs

Auguste Rodin, *The Burghers of Calais*. 1884–1886. Bronze. *Height 6 ft. 10 in., width 7 ft. 10 in., depth 6 ft. 2 in., height of base 10 in. Kunstmuseum, Basle.* *Cf. p. 98.*

Charles Despiau, Figure of a girl (*Assia*). 1937. Bronze. *Height 6 ft. 4 in. Middelheim, Open Air Museum. Cf. pp. 111, 112.*

Valle de los Caídos (Valley of the Fallen) in the Guadarrama Mountains near Madrid. *Height of cross about 520 ft., length of cross-piece 156 ft. Cf. p. 118.*

Constantin Brancusi, *The Kiss.* 1908. Stone. *Height 4 ft. 2 in. Montparnasse Cemetery, Paris.* *Cf. pp. 120, 121.*

and joints, only very earnestly so, reduced to bones – certainly not to a play of humps and holes, but more like dead bones in leather bags. Later, these limbs are bent in sad gestures, into a great *Kneeling Woman*, a great *Seated Youth*, *The Fallen* erected as a war memorial in the First World War, which had been raging in the meantime. The limbs became architectonic and formed a bridge on four pillars, spanning space: probably the most impressive thing that could be achieved in sculpture under the influence of iron construction without sculpture actually employing iron as a material. These works were the product of an almost unbearable seriousness, which was by no means a general melancholy, for a wife and little children lived with him. We cannot say where Lehmbruck would have ended up: whether he would have given way to complete abstraction, whether he would have found a no man's land like Klee, or whether he would have successfully combated abstraction. What is certain is that he would not have taken the easy path; he was the strictest of the German sculptors and the one most directly concerned with the intellectual use of forms.

COLOSSAL SCULPTURE

The impulse to alterations of scale, like those represented by Lilliput and Brobdignag, is obviously innate in man; indeed all living creatures nourish the impulse towards excessive growth. Nations and churches, tyrants, democrats and private dreamers are all fascinated by it. The earlier examples of colossal sculpture were to be found in Egypt, India and Afghanistan, in the Hellenistic period and in the Roman imperial age; it was the colossal statue of Nero that gave the name and concept of the colossal to the neighbouring Colosseum. In the Middle Ages it was architecture, not sculpture, that was colossal. Today the essence of the colossal is difficult to define. Parade grounds may be colossal for mass meetings but not the launching pads for space rockets. Are bridges and dams colossal? Or only appropriate in size? Or even, measured in relation to their functions, only modest in size? The colossal must be measured by an illuminating standard of comparison; this is what makes it colossal. The most obvious one is the human figure. It is not without reason that the concept 'life-size' is immediately comprehensible and is immediately referred to the size of a man, although an ant is life-size too. Possibly for architecture as well the proper criterion is the human figure, in comparison with which anything becomes colossal.
The nineteenth century offered colossal sculpture a certain opportunity, since the human figure was still taken seriously (though the twentieth century has not lagged behind; there is the huge figure of Christ above Rio de Janeiro and that of Kwannon over Tokyo, in 1960). Bronze casting, copper chasing and steel skeletons offered the technical means; it was only a question of finding the money.
In accordance with King Ludwig I's peaceful temperament Ludwig Schwanthaler's statue of *Bavaria* was a motherly figure, a patroness of the October festival, redolent more of folklore than of patriotism. Even her lion has something pleasantly friendly about it; there is no hint of an aggressive attitude towards any adversary. The *Lion of Belfort*, on the other hand, reared up roaring: against the Germans, as it thought; it could not know in advance that Max Ernst would adopt the roaring line and offer resistance with the book *Une semaine de bonté*.

FIG. 21

Patriotism apart, the *Lion of Belfort* is a good piece of sculpture. And since the same sculptor, Bartholdi, also succeeded in producing the statue of *Liberty*, which illumines the world as a gift from the French nation to the Americans, he is the most important example of a private obsession with the creation of large statues. How big would the large-scale sculpture of a man like Antoine Wiertz have been when even his normal pictures needed a height of thirty feet?
The corresponding German 'private sculpture' created by one individual, who stuck to his idea for more than a generation, through the choice of site, through the foundation of the many necessary societies, through the mastery of the technical difficulties, until finally a newly-won war made the conclusion possible – was the *Hermannsdenkmal* in the Teutoburger Wald, by Ernst von Bandel. (Examples of private sculpture on this scale in the twentieth century are the heads of American presidents at Mount Rushmore, U.S.A., 1929–1941, by Gutzon Borglum.)
What contemporaries questioned in Bandel was the merit of his work: neither the figure nor the base is historicist; they do not belong to a datable style, unless it be Romanticism. They are born of the necessity that the bigger a piece of art is, the simpler it must be in its details. The five-sided pillars, the tori, the tall shape of the round plinth are slightly reminiscent of some kind of Gothic, or of Theodoric's tomb at Ravenna – but in what style is Theodoric's tomb built? In reality the base is not in any one style but thought out in its own forms. And the figure itself, clearly distinguished in colour by the patina of the chased copper: it is just one single figure, holding a sword up high in a thoroughly 'romantic' gesture, but the iron skeleton is thereby simplified, the projection is reduced – in other words, the figure is arranged according to laws connected with architecture, although up to then Bandel had naturally been a sculptor working with classicistic attitudes and curves. In just the same way the figures of Chartres were retrospectively inscribed in their fluted forms when they had to obey an architectonic law. The tense, yet quite tubby figure, the narrow hips and thighs, the quite unhistorical armour – could it be scaled down into a mantelpiece ornament? No more and no less so than the Eiffel Tower. It is the best big monument of the nineteenth century, while the Niederwald memorial is the worst.

PLATE P. 115
APPX. PL. 8

Of the huge monuments of the twentieth century, Spain's monument in the Valley of the Fallen is shown here. Innumerable monuments have been erected to the wars of the twentieth century. If it were called 'Valley of Heroes' I should not have included it in this book. The term 'heroes' would mean that death was being treated more or less as something to be celebrated instead of as a sacrifice, not to mention the fact that perhaps only the warriors of one side would have been heroes while the other side's dead would have fallen in error. The Spanish memorial is called simply 'Valle de los Caídos', a conciliatory name. If it is argued that the cross on the mountain top is a party emblem, that here too a victorious party has erected its emblem over the fallen – so let it be. Even if we admit that at the present day the possibility of living without Christianity is being tested, even if as an art historian I cannot be Christian to the extent of taking the view that artistic 'truth' only came into the world with Christianity, that the religious

basis of the Pyramids, of Greek temples is 'false', while that of the cathedrals is 'correct', if we go further and remember that most – no, really all – of what has been shown in the previous volumes in this series was religious, if not Christian; if we thus see the human world as a world in which life is always based on religion, if not everywhere on the Christian religion; the fact remains that the premises of atheist thinking still come from Christianity itself. Let us say that this cross stands on the slope of the West, just as it stands on the slope of the Sierra de Guadarrama, a mountain range away from the Escorial Palace, from which Philip II supervised a Christian, if in many places a very cruel, régime.
The fittings of the basilica in the mountain, its ornamentation, the marble facing, the neo-classical transverse arches and domed vaults, the Stations of the Cross after graphics by Albrecht Dürer – all this we shall pass over rapidly. Nor shall we do more than glance with respect at the huge angels and Evangelists (no illustration can give any idea of their size), the latter with their appropriate lions, eagle, bull and angel – these granite mosaics are only made possible by the honest reinforced concrete underneath them – and at the cross, whose shaft is 520 feet high and whose cross-piece projects 78 feet on each side. But the granite cliff itself is a different matter. So is the cavern in it (it is surely difficult to regard this real cave as unreal, and the unreal vault of the pilgrimage church at Ronchamp as real?), and the monastery, and the services for the dead, which go on continually. And the symbol over the site, pointing from earth to heaven! Both Christianity and the present are embedded in continual emotion. Only those who will not admit that emotion must find a means of expression can renounce the use of these forms, which are more than five thousand years old. I should not like to live in an age of which people would have to say afterwards that it no longer knew any service for the dead.

BRANCUSI

The question whether an artist is intelligible to us because he is himself or because he represents a transformation in art, or has even brought one about, provokes in the case of Barlach the reply that it is because he is himself. If he had not created his work we should not know that it was possible in this form. With Brancusi, on the other hand, it is different. It is not just the other way about, as if Brancusi were simply the executor of a command given by the world-spirit (to use Hegelian terminology). No, the work and figure of Brancusi are quite personal. But the transformation recognizable in this work was bound to take place. If Brancusi had never existed we should today still have sculpture that was different from nineteenth-century sculpture. The only thing is that the difference would not have been so striking as it is in the work of Brancusi.
It may be that we feel the change more strongly in sculpture than we do in architecture or painting. There was town-planning in the nineteenth century as there is in the twentieth. Paintings were hung on walls and sold at exhibitions in the nineteenth century as they are in the twentieth. Paintings have remained panels, as they have for five hundred years. The fact that the framed rectangular panel contains themes different from those of a century ago is not so revolutionary, when seen from Sesostris, as we ourselves think. But what about sculpture, or

what we still call sculpture? Is it just a question of the objective being replaced by the abstract? Can we classify twentieth-century sculpture, too, according to themes, and reduce all the themes to the same principle: namely, that through the human figure human concerns can be expressed? For it is always a question of human themes; pure technology or pure science, portrayed through itself, is not art, even today. The answer is that we cannot classify modern sculpture in this way. What does remain true is that sculpture is still handled even today by art dealers; though this in itself almost differentiates it from monumental sculpture. But otherwise even the factual definition of painting – that it is produced by means of colours – can no longer be applied, *mutatis mutandis*, to sculpture. Even today sculpture *can* be the same warm-blooded thing that it was in days gone by; it is still this in the case of Moore, Marini, Zadkine and others. But Naum Gabo, Calder, Bertoia, Lippold and Kricke are also classified as sculptors, and one can scarcely call their work a continuation of the nineteenth-century tradition.

Perhaps the general term 'sculptor' should be abandoned; even in the nineteenth century attempts were made to distinguish between stone-carvers and modellers. Perhaps one should look for a new name for artists who think in terms of shapes in the third dimension or in movement and distinguish them from sculptors who think in terms of the human figure.

Human motives and human concerns are common to both kinds of artist.

When one takes into account Brancusi's peasant origins, when one reads how he lived in Paris, how he dressed (though it has already been pointed out that it was part of his peasant cunning to know the precise effect of his patriarchal beard and peasant food on urban intellectuals), one can see him as a man who came from even further afield than Roumania, namely from a still existing primitive age. But Roumania is far enough, even though one does not need to visualize his training by the Academy there as very different from a training by a Parisian academy. At any rate, he was still a product of the nineteenth century; he had learned that art must arise out of the comparison between what is seen and what is made. His path to Paris, via Munich and Zurich, and his swift transformation in Paris were genuine, as one would expect with a completely independent genius. He attached himself to Rodin but declined to work in his studio: 'nothing can flourish under big trees.' The archaizers could not teach him anything; the Fauves and Cubists worked alongside him. His flair was for a hardening, an ever increasing economy of form, for intensity in the use of materials (metal as well as stone and wood), for a symbolic idiom to express human thoughts (Brancusi always clung to human ideas; he never thought in abstract or technical terms). The stereometric approach, the conversion of shapes into block-like forms, which in architecture can so easily be confused with classicism, is quite spontaneous with Brancusi. In no earlier phase of classicism could one find the transformation of a loving couple into a rectangular block; on the contrary, in the last 'classical' period but one, that of Jacques-Louis David, architecture that was cubic formed the background to quite rounded, naturally-shaped human figures. Indeed, Brancusi is the principal witness, superior to all other sculptors in his irrefutability, to the fact that this move into the stereometric was a necessary process. Twenty years had gone by since

PLATE P. 116

Rodin's *Kiss*, ten years since Rodin's *Balzac* (of which Brancusi said, 'Indubitably the point of departure of modern sculpture'). It would still be true to say of Rodin's *Kiss* that it was intended to portray two people. We could not say the same of Peter Behrens's woodcut; the important thing there is that a sheet of paper should be turned into a graphic design, a quadrangle divided into two, entwined as if with ribbons, more of an indentation than a kiss. Shaped according to Art Nouveau's law that the objective fact should be placed first. Brancusi adopts the same line, and although, following Rodin, he may call his sculpture *Kiss*, the important thing is not the representation of the kiss but the erection of the menhir. That is how it can come to be used as a stone over a grave.

Just as genuine is the transformation of a girl's head, of a Medusa head on a dish, into an egg-like form. It originates from the ancient Medusa, the horrifying head that expresses the petrifying sadness of the world, separated from the torso by Perseus, frightening no longer because of the threat it implies or the horror of its snake-locks but through its glance into the abyss of sorrow associated with the human figure, even the fairest. Rodin would have expressed the suffering in the bearing and look, for example in the head of his *Crouching Woman*. Here Brancusi is much more decidedly opposed to the master than any other disciple of Rodin's. The sorrow, the human element, does not disappear but is turned – no, perverted or concentrated – into stone; it acquires different outlines, it becomes stereometric; the basic formulas are discovered which embrace sorrow and much else too, for naturally when the head of Medusa approximates to the shape of an egg it comes to resemble not only the death of life but also its beginning – the egg. This is the knife-edge along which the artist must tread: on one side the warmth of life, which he does not wish to abandon, on the other side the stereometric figure, which is as seductive as a sphere or a cube but would be artistically dead were it polished not by the artist's thoughts but by mere formulas.

A similar path of development was followed by the worried bowed-down head of *Mademoiselle Pogany*, from preliminary sketches still reminiscent of Art Nouveau to gleaming metals which look similar to the chrome parts of a car – but only similar, not identical, for they are alive. Nevertheless, this brings up the problem of 'chroming', of optical reflection on a metal, in other words the problem how far Brancusi's sculpture is controlled by eye and appearance. It abolishes the outline, on which older sculpture lived, but not just in order to produce reflection (which has played its part in Western art since the old Dutch painters, since the picture of the *Battle of Alexander* discovered at Pompeii, in other words since Hellenistic painting). No, the aim is to harden the plastic object until it acquires a polish, so that not only metal but every material gives a reflection. The optical element is only a subsidiary phenomenon; the important factor is extreme compression. Such extreme precision of the surface can only be produced with the hand and it can only be felt with the hand. But the hand, by its warmth and breathing, clouds the surface again. This antinomy is present in all art, but only here is it carried to extremes.

Animal sculpture, which had not really been developed any further since Barye, though Frémiet had certainly introduced the element of excitement, while Gaul and Pompon had led it back again to the forms of the 'archaizers', was at any rate the representation of warm-blooded living creatures. Brancusi cautiously extended its repertoire of themes so as to include fish, sea-lions, tortoises and birds, though not yet insects and bacteria; in other words, so as to include creatures which are exceptionally 'streamlined'. These creatures are also very close to man: for example, that skilful and playful animal the sea-lion, with its mastery of the art of balancing. It was not until after Brancusi's death that scientists began conversing with dolphins. As for Brancusi's interest in birds, this certainly has atavistic roots; it reflects some kind of prehistoric, Icarian dream; there is no connection with contemporary aeronautical engineering. It is certainly a piece of anthropomorphism at the limit of what is credible today when he attributes to birds the sensations of 'up' and 'high' and 'radiance'. All these expressions are to be found in his papers and conversations (conversations drawn out of him by interrogation, for in himself Brancusi was not a literary person), but far more often implied in his photographs. For Brancusi phtographed his sculptures himself – with a technically not very sophisticated camera – and thereby provided his own explanation of himself, a wordless but perfectly clear key to his work.

It is not surprising if artists of the twentieth century who have become perplexed with man in general, and who can no longer perceive any possibility of expressing what they want to by means of man's outward form, should fancy that they see in animals a natural existence free from the trammels of the intellect. Marc, for example, and other artists of the early twentieth century sought this assumed 'wholeness' in animals, just as Gauguin sought wholeness in Tahiti. Now, in the middle of the twentieth century, we know that even animals are not free of reflection and are consequently not so 'whole' as was assumed at that time.

In Brancusi's wood carving we find once again links with prehistory, with ethnology. He chooses symbolic themes which cannot be explained 'formally'; these themes are christened with titles like *Adam and Eve*, which again are symbolic; the mere words 'man and woman' would not be adequate. For centuries artists had put Adam and Eve side by side. Brancusi puts them on top of each other – as tricksters had already done in the case of Rodin and were to do again with Calder – as if Adam were a 'stand' (symbolic term) on which the 'female screw' (symbolic term) is fastened by a 'thread' (symbolic term). The curious thing, and it is characteristic of artists of this generation, is the primitive state in which these symbolic subjects are left. The same artist who, when working in metal, aims at attaining the highest polish, as if it were a question of engineering something to one-thousandth of a millimetre, leaves his blocks of wood in the rough condition which the axe can produce; he renounces all the delicate tools which the woodwork industry could put at his disposal. He feels an indispensable need, and assumes that others do too, to have a direct link, in a mechanized world, with a rootstock that has grown naturally. The link is, of course, illusory – but as illusory, in other words as fundamental, as art in general.

That life consists of breathing in and breathing out, that it contains returns to earlier points and not just simple progress forward, as historians assume, that the returns are similar to each other but also just as different from each other as the individual, hand-carved sections of an *Endless Column* – this basic idea was symbolically represented by Brancusi in a tree-trunk which stands in Edvard Steichen's garden in Paris. The same concept exists in the form of a hundred-foot-high piece of cast steel in Roumania. The ancient world had symbolized this eternal return by means of a snake forming a circle. Infinity may stand upright and point to another world but it is not like a bird soaring upward on its own impetus; it is infinite through the possible, haphazard, continuous return of the once-discovered form.

Brancusi did not create many works if one counts the symbols. To have created one single symbol would fill a lifetime. But he played on them, varied them, modelled the same symbol many times, as well as transposing it into different materials. As a result his works are not exactly commercialized, but at any rate not so unique as they were when they were conceived.

A great deal must come from the few real artists – more than they could create themselves. The necessary consequence is diffusion, reproduction, repetition in thousands – hundreds of thousands – of copies.

III. PAINTING

REALISM
Courbet, Millet, Menzel

Over the entrance to the special pavilion which he felt obliged to organize at the Paris Exhibition of 1855 Courbet had this inscribed: 'Realism'. The word remained the riddle of the whole century. Courbet certainly felt much nearer to understanding it, and also the term 'socialism', so often used at the same time, than we do. He interpreted it to mean renunciation of idealistic subjects, renunciation of academic techniques of painting, renunciation of conventional bourgeois privileges, and in place of these things realism, actuality.

Realism from a sociological point of view? In so far as Courbet went from a semi-peasant background straight to the extreme individualism of an artist's life he always kept firmly away from the mass fate of the proletariat. It is true that he painted a large-scale picture of a stone-breaker at work. In this he repeated the step taken three hundred years earlier by Caravaggio and Jordaens, who for the first time had recognized the sacred figures of the Bible, the respected figures of the ancient world, as the publicans and beggars of their own time. But what was realistic about this picture of Courbet's? In the figures one could sense the efforts of models to maintain their poses. Pick-axe, basket and wheelbarrow became equally important actors and were treated like parts of a monument; there was really no difference from the way in which Rietschel had treated Lessing and his dress. It was a glorification of simple work and thus really the opposite of what we today would understand by proletarian work, which cannot be glorified. Where was the road for which the stones were being broken? And where were the railways, modern means of transport built by modern methods? It would never have occurred to Courbet to paint industry.

Realism in form? It is here that our conception of realism is nearest to that of Courbet. He used colour in a 'real' way; he applied it with a palette knife. Even though the tint of the colour was what he was really after, not a thick impasto, nevertheless we are used to looking at the texture of a painting's surface and to seeing the great difference between Courbet's approach and that of academic painters.

Realism of subject matter? Courbet produced the *Artist's Studio: a Real Allegory of Seven Years of my Life* and it was precisely because this huge picture and the equally big *Burial at Ornans* were not accepted by the jury that he had opened his separate pavilion. He thus showed that he wanted to think in mythical (or allegorical) terms; it was the same with François Millet, who painted the *Angelus*. How did it come about, then, that they could speak in the same breath of realism and that they and their pictures were rejected by the jury of academicians?

PLATE P. 133

PLATE P. 134

The depiction of a studio in a big picture was not something completely new. The special thing about Courbet's picture was the juxtaposition of the realistic and the allegorical.

The architecture of the room depicted remains vague; it recalls the wings of a theatre or the side walls in Leonardo's *Last Supper*, and then seems to change again into a barn. The group of people on the right consists of friends of the art of realism, looking at Courbet, their creator, and understanding reality through the medium of realism. The conception as a whole does not by any means stand outside the European tradition; one has only to think of Rubens's so-called *Festival of Love*. There, too, a young couple are introduced and an Arcadian, 'super-real' existence comes into being. There is something similar in Courbet's picture: so-called realism is not identified with battles for wages or political systems or industrial production but is depicted as the reality which comes into being through art. The loving couple, as in Rubens, signify the heightened state of consciousness in which men are nearest to 'super-reality', to art. Naturally among the friends is Alfred Bruyas of Montpellier, who had made the erection of the pavilion possible. Outside the group, on the extreme right, sits Baudelaire, who played an important part in Parisian artistic circles at that time but did not wish to be identified with realism, with Courbet's individual utterances or with social sympathy for the proletariat. Baudelaire built his own world of ideas and is thus portrayed in the picture not really as a friend but at a noteworthy distance from the rest of the group. Beside him there was originally a mulatto woman, but Courbet painted her out after a complaint from Baudelaire.

The group on the left consists of representatives of human life; they are not really present in the flesh but stand for ideas, for types behind realism. We know from letters of Courbet's who the figures are among them: one is a Jew whom he had once seen ten years earlier in London holding fast to his purse – an incident which had subsequently taken root in the artist's mind. Another figure is a priest, yet another a disabled veteran from pre-Napoleonic times, an incredibly old, fossilized man. Then come a huntsman, a Hercules from a fair-ground booth, a second-hand dealer offering old clothes for sale, then a Spanish hat, a mandoline, a weapon – things which lie beyond realism. Just to the left of the easel is a phlegmatic woman who has sunk to the ground and is feeding her child; next to her is a skull lying on a newspaper. Then there is a figure which according to Courbet is a puppet, though it is positioned fairly close to a real figure, a thief. Naturally birth and death, mother's milk and death on the cross, are intended in their turn to signify something mythical, something cosmic.

The central section of the picture hangs firmly together: the painter, the canvas on which a landscape has been painted, the naked woman and the little boy, who represents something like 'admiring posterity' or 'the child's voice is the voice of God'. That there exists a modelled photograph of the naked figure – it was in the possession of M. Bruyas – may not have been an embarrassment to Courbet but even welcome to him – as a proof of reality? Since only a landscape has been painted, perhaps one is supposed to draw the conclusion that life is like this in an artist's studio, but this is only a guess. The female figure is placed on her dress as if on a podium and becomes a kind of Muse; she is a 'realistic allegory'. The other allegory of reality is the landscape. Between the female model and the landscape sits the painter and, together with these subjects which he is about to convert

into reality, he is the creator of allegorical realism, the centre of a world now coming into being.
In his – to us – somewhat unpractical enthusiasm for realism, socialism, communism, Courbet allowed himself to be persuaded, in the political confusion of 1870, after Napoleon III's defeat at Sedan and during the siege of Paris by the German armies, to become President of the Commission for Fine Arts, and after the suppression of the Commune he narrowly escaped being shot. On the basis of a photograph of Napoleon's statue, torn down from the Vendôme Column, in which the prosecution pointed to Courbet's head – juries did not yet know in those days that photographs could be touched up – he was sentenced to pay for the reconstruction of the Vendôme Column and his fortune was confiscated. In 1873 he was able to slip away to Switzerland and lived on there as an émigré until 1878.

MENZEL

In order to see clearly how variously the question of realism can be posed let us put alongside Courbet's tripartite *Artist's Studio* the likewise tripartite *Iron Rolling Mill* by Adolf Menzel. It is a good deal bigger than one would guess from reproductions, more of a mural than an easel picture, but the figures are still less than life-size. It is in fact not a picture of people but a documentary painting of a centre of production. It was painted between 1869 and 1875 on Menzel's own initiative; we know of no commission. It seems most likely that the artist's point of departure was the illustrated magazines which aimed at informing their readers about new developments in industry. There are woodcuts of similar subjects, but in the world of art this painting remains the first of its kind. Almost sixty drawings have been preserved and these make it clear what extraordinary care Menzel devoted to his task.

PLATE P. 133
PLATE P. 133

To what extent is the *Iron Rolling Mill* realistic? In it is depicted the industrial revolution, the transition from an agrarian state to an industrial state, speeded up in Germany after the war of 1870–71 with the help of the five thousand millions which France had to pay by way of reparations. A transitional period, therefore, and a picture that could be compared with the *Fighting Téméraire*. Technical processes are here accurately portrayed; by means of working drawings, plans and elevations, Menzel made himself thoroughly familiar with every press, every machine before putting them into his picture. He also made a plan of the layout of the picture as a whole and inserted on this plan the positions of the individual machines; for he followed accurately and functionally the whole process of production from the arrival of the glowing ingot to the completion of the rolled rail. Thus the preparatory drawings come somewhere between Leonardo's designs for machines and the production schedules at the disposal of an industrial architect. The painting contains just as accurate a picture of the daily life of the workman, who does not cease to be an individual person even when his lunch is a hasty one (bottom right-hand corner) and his clean-up after the end of the shift pretty superficial (extreme left); both meal and clean-up take place in the machine shop itself, for there are as yet no welfare rooms for the workers.

PLATE P. 35

How should Menzel's exactness be judged in the context of the nineteenth century? His father had moved from Silesia to Berlin and set up a lithographic press in order to develop and make use of his son's talent, which became apparent quite early on. He died when Menzel was sixteen. The son had to take on the task of feeding the whole family. He was and remained self-taught in the fullest sense of the term; it is true that he possessed quite exceptional talent, but he had to try out and assimilate everything for himself. As a result, in many points he lacked simple instruction in the workshop tradition but in many others he was superior to the trained artist precisely because he had to discover things for himself. A publishing house wanted to bring out a popular life of Frederick the Great. The historian Franz Kugler, who was responsible for the text, suggested Menzel as the illustrator; 'he is only twenty-four', Kugler said, 'but none the less the right man'. He knew that Menzel had already published a book on uniforms which contained the most accurate illustrations of every regiment and every rank in Frederick's army. How should we classify this trustworthiness of Menzel's, which was applied indifferently to the historical uniforms of a hundred years earlier and the rolling process in contemporary industry? Is it historicism? Is it realism?

PLATE P. 23
PLATE P. 133

When one compares Monet's *Gare Saint Lazare* with the *Iron Rolling Mill*, painted in approximately the same year, and when one reads Jean Renoir's words, one becomes sharply aware of the lack of seriousness in the Impressionist, who is only interested in the narrowest specialities of his own profession and is trying to outplay his fellow painters; he is not in the least concerned to make himself familiar with the world of technology. Compare with this the quiet seriousness with which Menzel goes to work; he does not interrupt the technical process with extraneous demands but seeks to understand it and wins artistic form from it. The comparison cannot be sidestepped by introducing the question of artistic quality. Obviously the Frenchman is the better painter, but on the other hand Menzel is the better draughtsman. It is a question of the relationship between reality and art, a question that was still posed in approximately the same way for people of this generation, since after all Courbet and Monet did not wish to produce abstract art either. It is a question of these pictures' sequels, which have caused two different worlds to develop in our own day. It is too simple to look only at the Western half, to ignore the fact that in the other, Eastern half of the world the questions posed in the *Iron Rolling Mill* are still at the centre of art. If we do no more than recognize the co-existence of the question – and that is surely worth a moment's reflection – then Menzel's picture becomes a work of the very first importance.

Menzel's brushwork is a sort of curly mass, an interlaced pattern of strips of colour reminiscent of a light yet transparent skein of wool, in contrast to Monet's colour, which lies like gleaming quartz on a hard background. Menzel uses a great deal of 'non-colour', a great deal of grey and brown. No need is felt for everything to be highly coloured; on the contrary the view taken is that there is a sort of colourless background, of dull 'material' into which the colour only shines, to which it is applied, in contrast to the independent glow of the white-hot block of iron. This indirect, reflected light is relatively simply produced; it differs from the cold daylight, but neither is very strongly emphasized and certainly not transformed into a fresh 'mass of colour', for that would nullify the picture and its meaning. The mistaken view of the pure artist in colour that anything and everything can be expressed artistically is not accepted. Only certain aspects of life can be expressed artistically – and again and again new men demand to speak out about other aspects of life which cannot be expressed by the old artistic methods (for example, Impressionism), or only in such a complicated, diluted, intellectualized way that one day they have to yield before a more elemental mode of expression.

So if we call Menzel one of the first artists of the industrial age we must at the same time recognize that he was a man with a thorough historical training and one who made use of this historical approach. In his work too, not only in Courbet's *Real Allegory*, the concepts with which we are dealing become confused. What is realism? What is historicism?

It is true that in Menzel's case his concern for realism led to the Order of the Black Eagle, to decorations and titles, to public marks of respect from the German Empire.

PHOTOGRAPHY

After being ignored for a century photography has today been admitted to the history of art. It is at last mentioned, and its early products are shown in exhibitions. So few of them have been preserved that they could be reproduced in one album, like the early stamps of Mauritius and Thurn-and-Taxis. However, if the history of art is a history of seeing, and cultural history a history of the facts by which the consciousness of mankind is shaped, then photography may demand not just a mention at the beginning or end of a book on nineteenth-century art but the middle of the whole book.

We are not going to discuss here whether photography can be art; it is a question of no importance. Photography was developed by men who were painters – landscape-painters, scenery painters, portrait-painters. And in so far as these specialities played a role in painting then replacement by photography constitutes a complete revolution. It would be idle to estimate how many times today in the course of his life a person is photographed and how seldom he is painted, or how many snaps of landscapes there are to one painted one, not to mention the replacement of the visit to the theatre by films and television.

On the night of 19 August 1839, when the process announced by Daguerre was described at the Paris Academy by Arago, thousands of Parisians waited in front of the Palais des Quatre Nations and photography was already recognized as a vehicle of information by which none, literally none, of the ensuing political, artistic, technical and scientific developments could fail to be affected and changed.

How could it have been otherwise? Man is man through the collaboration of mind, eye and hand; the replacement of seeing by photography was bound to alter us all to the same extent as we were all altered by the replacement of the hand by the machine. None of us is any longer capable of saying how he would see things, what he would know about the world, if the picture had not been pre-formed for him by the sight of a hundred thousand photographs since he first opened his eyes. No one could claim to know how knowledge as a whole – not just artistic

knowledge – would have developed without photography and the dissemination of knowledge which it has made possible.
Consequently it is not very interesting to know whether a painter was influenced in some picture by an already existing photograph, or whether *vice versa* photographers rang technical changes on a new way of seeing created by the artist: both occurrences are attested. What is much more important is that the present-day artist is already surrounded by photographs before his infant hand can hold a pencil; that the visible world in which he begins to think, to feel, to model would be a different one without photography; that even the mythological situation – and we know how powerful that remains even in our century – is influenced by photography. There is no longer any 'pure' well of consciousness, that is, one not infiltrated by photography.
Of all the means by which a unified world opinion, an informed view comprehensible in all countries, could be created, photography is the most effective. So far it is the only one that almost all men understand.
All this must be said in order to define the bounds of photography in general. It, too, would have to be allowed a 'limited infinity' in the nineteenth century, and one might wonder whether or not in the present day its realm has become boundless.
Its special contribution in the nineteenth century, the thing with which it influenced the fine arts as a whole and painting in particular, was its relationship to reality. That this 'reality' was a central word in the nineteenth century, and likewise the concepts subordinate to it – realism, naturalism, objectivity, absence of prejudice, sound common sense and so on – is no part of art history's task to explain or deduce; nor can the other branches of knowledge deduce it either – they can only investigate and describe its consequences in their own fields. One can say that for us, who with one part of our being have turned away from a fanatical enthusiasm for reality, this faith in reality is the really enigmatic thing about the nineteenth century, the thing that divides us from it most sharply.
In this faith, which did not involve abolition of the old myths but rather added a new one to them, the peoples of Europe felt themselves raised to a completely new plane by photography. They felt not just strengthened and supported, but that their faith had been proved true in an irrefutable, scientific way. How can it be made sufficiently clear to men today what such a conviction was bound to mean to the men of the nineteenth century! What it was bound to mean for a painter that there was a *correct* view of the world he saw before him, beside which any other view became capricious and false!

The everlasting antinomy still present in photography was contained right from the start in the first exposures; subsequent simplifications of procedure have not resolved it, but simply carried it further. This antinomy resides in the belief on the one hand that photography is a procedure which, without any possibility of falsification by human interference, provides genuine and authoritative pictures of reality; and in the belief on the other hand that photography is a procedure for fixing images observed by the human eye, in other words for enabling individuals, for human beings, actively to see and assimilate as much as possible. Both views are so strong and evoke so much enthusiasm that they pass beyond the realm of things attested by the intellect and reach down to the emotions, the unconscious urges.

And when we immediately add that the whole disposition of human beings, animals, landscapes, objects are bathed in light, converted into rays and form a world of light – are then gathered in a more and more finely ground system of lenses, pass through the incomprehensible transformation of the object glass, and in a world of darkness, a *camera obscura*, are fanned out again, caught, developed, eternalized – that this whole disposition contains so many of the basic human ideas about a world of light and darkness, day and night, fleeting appearance and enduring retention, death and rebirth – then in my view the truth is just the opposite from what is usually asserted in 'artistic' quarters, namely that photography is a soulless, mechanical process which liberates no inner forces in man, while the use of the words 'artist's eye' and 'artist's hand' guarantees in itself that everything drawn by hand is imbued with soul. No, a great deal on the 'art' side can be mere empty activity which is just passed on from one person to another, while photography involves processes and arrangements which, even when man is unaware of them – indeed especially then – stir forces and memories in his unconscious, so that he is capable of faith.

In the first place, the argument for the belief that photography reproduces reality unchanged was precisely that photographic information registers itself. I should like to call it the 'frieze arrangement' of photography: the subject, then the object glass, then the receptive photographic layer of emulsion on the plate stand in a row beside each other, all equally far removed from man, merely put into a certain order by him and not influenced by him in any other way. The basic principle of the *camera obscura* was really not much more complicated than is here implied; it may have been known in the ancient world and was certainly known by the time of the Renaissance. What was difficult, difficult enough to need a whole generation of research, was the optical, chemical and technical application of the principle: the invention of lens-grinders, cameras, emulsions, vehicles for the layer of emulsion, and fixatives. But now all this had been accomplished. The light inscribed itself on the plate; and man (who was always inclined, even in the nineteenth century, to suffer in himself, to say 'the world is perfect wherever man does not reach with his torment') – man had no occasion, no chance to interfere by importing his own falsifying ideas. Precisely what the plate showed was therefore 'reality'. The whole credibility of the procedure rested on the fact that the process took place uninfluenced by man. This arrangement – I repeat the expression 'frieze arrangement' for it – is still today the basis where photographic procedures are employed as a source of information for science and scholarship.

In the second place, from the start people coupled, or to be more accurate confused, with this photographic arrangement the 'frontal arrangement', that is, they believed that the camera is directed at the world in the same way as man looks at his environment with his own eyes – out of his ego at the non-ego, to borrow an expression from Romantic philosophy. In other words, it was supposed that the photographic camera corresponded to the human eye, was modelled on it, was a substitute for it (either a superior substitute through its technical precision or an infinitely inferior substitute because of its soullessness, according to one's point of view), an apparatus which for the purposes of reflection could be equated with our eyes. The same attitude still prevails today with the snapshot camera which is put up to the eye: someone ought to invent a camera that would hang in front of one's eyes all the time like spectacles: we should certainly get used to people with camera-spectacles of this sort – as if the snapshot were really as good as our own sight. And now the adjurations begin: it is difficult, people assert, to see why the application of technology to what our eye sees cannot be art just as much as art results from the application of technology, in organ pipes and piano keys, to notes sung previously by our voices.

Much in the discussion of photography can be traced back to this lack of clarity, this mental cleavage, right at the start of photography.

The snapshot, the photograph from *Life* which aims at the 'illumination of reality', today confirms the view that the desired reality is not directly recognizable and photographable. As a result the nineteenth century's belief in the real has in the twentieth century turned into its opposite. In the nineteenth century what scientific photography captured was regarded as real; but what the twentieth century would like to call reality cannot be reached by scientific photography. That is, the scientific side of human life can still be studied with the help of photographic evidence, but 'interhuman reality', 'life itself' cannot. Things have gone so far now that the seamless 'photographability' of life, striven for and indeed already almost attained by Cinerama and similar devices, is no longer regarded as reality, but on the contrary as concealment and delusion. Only through holes in the curtain, through snapshots, can the gaze be directed at a realm lying behind reality. What is visible there in flashes has to be pieced together; the reading of photographs from *Life* assumes active co-operation on the part of man, makes him almost creative: but all this again hangs together with contemporary experiences in art and is unthinkable without Dada, collages, the *objet trouvé*, and all these various methods of piecing together a new reality out of what were formerly torn scraps.

Thus it can be seen that the relation between photography and art is not so simple that one can always assert that one has influenced the other. It must not be thought that in our century the mutual influence works in such a way that the influence of art is necessarily reflected in things that look like art or that the influence of photography must be reflected in works that look like photography.

The 'frieze arrangement' in photography permits comparison: the 'reality' offered to man by his previous, primitive method of seeing is compared with the 'objective' picture obtained by photography. The reflective intellect with its capacity for

Above: Gustave Courbet, *The Artist's Studio.* 1855. Oil on canvas. *Height 12 ft., width 20 ft. Paris, Louvre. Cf. pp. 125, 129, 161.*

Below: Adolf Menzel, *The Iron Rolling Mill.* 1875. Oil on canvas. *Height 5 ft. 1 in., length 8 ft. 5 in. Berlin, Nationalgalerie der Staatlichen Museen. Cf. pp. 127, 128.*

François Millet, *The Angelus*. 1858–1859. Oil on canvas. *Height 1 ft. 10 in., width 2 ft. 4 in. Paris, Louvre.* *Cf. p. 125.*

Arnold Böcklin, *Odysseus and Calypso*, 1883. Tempera on wood. *Height 3 ft. 4½ in., width 4 ft. 10 in. Basle, Kunstmuseum. Cf. pp. 149, 150.*

Anselm Feuerbach, *Plato's Symposium*, 1873. Oil on canvas. *Height 13 ft., length 24 ft. 4 in. Berlin, Nationalgalerie der Staatlichen Museen.* *Cf. pp. 151, 152, 194.*

making comparisons stands at an equal distance from both, and distance from the object is the essence of the scientific approach. The ability to control distance, the lens, the illuminated subject and the picture taken make it possible for this 'reality' to be grasped and demonstrated by the photographer. The 'frontal arrangement', on the other hand, the identification of the camera with the forward-concentrated gaze of both eyes, inspires no desire to check the difference and even destroys the wish to recognize its existence. The working hypothesis (it is known that the goal cannot be attained, but the fiction is that it can be) is that the difference does not exist, that what is photographed is identical with what is seen. It is precisely on the abolition of distance from subject that the theory of photography in *Life* is based; it is at this that the *Life* reporter's technique is aimed. As part of the bargain he has to accept among his results a considerable number of photographs in which the eyes of the frightened subject stare at the camera like the eyes of a wild animal frightened by a flashlight. The reaction of the person photographed is to clown: he makes some grimace or other. It is all a question of reality.

Again and again photography activates forces tending to cool off emotion, to secure the maximum distance from the subject and to suppress personal involvement; but then it proceeds to awaken an emotional, almost chaotic surge of respect for reality signifying the opposite of distance. Photography first makes comparison possible, then prevents it; is first supposed to prove that the picture is objective, then that it is subjective; first that the picture is equivalent to reality, then that it is much more like our own sudden glances. Thus photography is continually cancelling itself out. It is continually making fresh aspects possible.

The nineteenth century's view was that everything real could be captured by photography. People would not have been surprised if patriotism or piety had turned out to be photographable. In photography is concentrated whatever new outward form reality may take. In Courbet this reality appears as social milieu. In Pietro Magni or in van Gogh as cane chair, farmer's boot, sunflower. In Schwitters as 'Merz', in Duchamp as *Ready Made*, in present-day sculpture as scrap metal – it is always the 'real' that fascinates artists.

Daguerre, who became very articulate as scene-painter, as inventor of the diorama and perfecter of the panorama, and also in his achievement as inventor or, better, organizer of photography, is less articulate as a photographer himself. Perhaps because photography, once discovered, did not lend itself so quickly to conversion into those large decorative expanses to which he was accustomed.

David Octavius Hill charms us with his early portraits, which are, it is true, only transpositions of very sensitive Biedermeier painting. The giant photograph of the Scottish estates of the realm would be more important if the collection of four hundred individual heads had really coalesced into a group picture – and even in that case he would have been a successor of the Dutch group portrait-painters of the seventeenth century. He is a real photographer, no longer to be confused with a painter, in his late portraits: for example, that of the actress Ellen Terry.

Nadar, who raised photography 'to the height of art', as Honoré Daumier wrote bitingly under a lithograph of 'Nadar, the first man to photograph Paris from the gondola of a balloon' – is remembered for an irreplaceable series of portraits of the great Frenchmen of his time, including Manet and Baudelaire.

Portraiture in general was undoubtedly the first victory of photography. The profession of miniaturist died out, or rather its practitioners re-trained as photographers. It is not photography's fault that portrait-painting was later shattered by uncertainty about the nature and significance of personality, with the result that it almost disappeared in the first half of the twentieth century and is not much in evidence even today. The residue of individuality still to be traced in oneself and others can be more quickly photographed than painted, with less fuss and sometimes with more illuminating effect.

Landscape-painting as practised by the early nineteenth century, that is, partly as a report from distant lands, has been completely replaced by photography and now by the documentary film. The exceptional success of the Impressionists becomes all the greater when one views it in the context of the otherwise dominant landscape photography. They created a landscape of the Ile de France. On the other hand, only a little later, Gauguin did not succeed in creating a 'landscape' of the South Seas – assuming that one expects the same thing of him as of the seventeenth-century Dutch painters or even the Impressionists.

Victor Hugo was the first surrealist in photography, and not by mistake, but from insight into its possibilities.

During the nineteenth century photography remained a European achievement. Important contributions from other continents have so far not come to light. It is only around the turn of the century that the overseas masters appear: Alfred Stieglitz, Edvard Steichen. Today photography is truly international.

Another important feature of nineteenth-century photography is its black-and-white character. Naturally efforts to produce colour photographs as well were made right from the start. That a hundred years went by before this obvious wish was fulfilled (as late as 1891 the physicist Émile Du Bois-Reymond considered colour photography a technical impossibility) shows what difficult technical problems were involved in photography as a whole, and therefore how highly the inventive genius of the first generation is to be regarded. The absence of colour photography had far-reaching if unintentional effects. During the classical period the ancient world had been seen in the white of plaster or marble, not in colour; this was a genuine piece of self-expression on the part of classicism. But if the later nineteenth century saw – and thought of – its 'reality' to an increasing extent without colours, although aniline dyes had already been discovered, this was due to the influence of black-and-white photography and the information it provided. In return, the achievements and triumphs of those great masters of colour, the Impressionists, should be seen in the context of the increasing distance between their pictures and the colourless mental world of their contemporaries. Here too is the background to the passion and success of the Fauves.

But this restriction to the black-and-white spectrum also had a certain value. It not only taught people to distinguish the valuable graphic possibilities available, just as Dürer's woodcuts and Rembrandt's etchings had become valuable in the period when printed graphic art was regarded, as it was originally, as a cheap substitute for the rich illuminations in manuscripts; it also brought the advantage of a genuine if involuntary abstraction, of a limitation to homogeneous, concentrated, less diverting reproductions, into which variety had to be read by intensified comparison, by a synoptic view which encouraged analytical investigation. Black-and-white photography educated people to look more intently. If colour photography had been achieved too early, the nineteenth century's view of the world would have disintegrated far more than it did. For could one assert that today the colour photograph really makes our view of the world more colourful?

ACADEMIES

The verdict which we are supposed to pass on academic art is that it is official art, against which the opposition – and hence the good – has successfully asserted itself. Theodore Duret said (or, to be accurate, Alice B. Toklas thinks she remembers, according to Gertrude Stein, hearing Duret say): 'My dear young friend, there is art and there is officially recognized art; so it has always been and so it always will be.' To pass over the last part of this assertion, without pausing to reflect whether it was like this in the time of Raphael, Bernini and Rubens and whether it is so today, Duret is speaking in the first sentence – and Gertrude Stein in her whole book – almost exclusively of painting, and this is the first objection we must raise to this schematic view of academic art. We shall put forward the grounds for this objection in the next chapter.
Academies? The shrewd Picasso complains (or, to be accurate, the shrewd Françoise Gilot thinks she remembers hearing Picasso complain):'. . . We have no strong, powerful academic art worth fighting against.'
In fact, the assertion that in the nineteenth century there was only a backward bourgeoisic on the one hand and the progressive painter on the other; that the Academy was always bad, always wrong, and the opposing painters always right: this assertion, repeated *ad nauseam* for a century, is not an adequate summary of the situation. If it were, the 'opposition painters' would be the worst winners known to history. After they had triumphed and were able to dictate their own terms to art dealers, they would not have understood the one great virtue of victory, that of being reconciled with the defeated adversary. They went on hurling insults at him and continue to do so today. They had moved into the academicians' chairs – posthumously – but as they did not know what an academy was they could not continue to give positive leadership. The Academy was not so childish as it is painted in books on Impressionism. On the contrary it was full of strength, not just because it had possession and tradition on its side, but also because it also had intelligence on its side.
According to the 'opposition painters', academic art is 'trivial' painting. Today 'trivial' art is being very carefully investigated by all the historical disciplines (music, literature, fine art) because it has been realized that it contains one of the keys to the understanding of our century. One must distinguish between popular art, trivial art and academic art. Popular art is often defined today as 'high art in decline', and the decline is understood either as a decline from a more artistic structure, in which case the result can be simpler but also more intensive, thereby making up for its distance from the model (thus a simple folk-song can be worth

more than the artificially-wrought air of a master-singer); or it can be a temporal decline, that is, the work may follow some earlier style. This view, which rests on the art historian's assumption of a succession of styles and which – whether justified or not – is dependent on the belief in progress, can be left to fend for itself.
Trivial art is a by-product of civilization; it belongs to the big city and mass production. It shares a 'decline' with popular art, but has sunk from a rigorous intellectual level; it has been simplified and trivialized into premature emotion, imprecise form, unmotivated excitement and too facile identification. Trivial art lacks the strictness of the intellect; it lacks the capacity to stand away from itself, to check itself.
What is an academy? We are told that it is a collection of average people, of 'John Bulls'. But among the Forty Immortals – to confine ourselves for the moment to the French Academy alone – do we not rather find incisive intelligence, far-ranging thought, wide professional experience and a high level of education? And is that not because these are the qualities that go to make an academician? The relationship between the academician and the 'opposition artist' cannot be described as one between trivial people on the Academy side and highly cultivated people on the opposition side. It tends to be the other way about. The characteristics of triviality are more likely to be found on the opposition side than in the Academy. People do the Impressionists no good by writing about their women and publishing all their letters; on the whole it is a world of such banality – the actual business of painting always excepted – that one is glad to be able to return to Delacroix's diary, to Baudelaire's intelligence and to the noble scholarship of Viollet-le-Duc. What is it about academies that is rejected? Again it is amazing to see how simple the theory of 'opposition art' turns out to be: everything has just got to be social, modern, progressive, and then life is perfect. There is no trace in this theory of the forces that maintain and conserve; anyone would think that art must be everlasting rather than brand new. Even the work of an artist's old age is either accepted because the name is respected (as with Renoir) or else (as with Monet) searched for 'modern features' – as if the result of a long life must be modernity, as if the aged Titian or the aged Rembrandt had been modern.
If even in the nineteenth century mythical forces were preserved, if with modernity alone one swiftly becomes unmodern, where were these forces to be found? Only in the 'opposition painters'? Is not the reflection on the patriarchal order behind Christian Rauch's monuments anchored in the mythical? Are only freedom and progress mythical passions?
It is impossible to give an account of the nineteenth century, or even an account of Impressionism, without a proper evaluation of the Academy. John Rewald's admirable work will have to be supplemented because there is no trace in it of an opposing force, because only the same old anecdotes about domineering professors without any insight are repeated, professors who were wrong in the anecdote and continue to be wrong throughout the book. If only art historians had read just one scene of Schiller or Shakespeare, just one scene by a real dramatist, and learned from it that one must fill the opponent's arguments with life if one wants to depict one's own heroes as real, live people. At the moment the history of

nineteenth-century painting is written as the history of a clique that wants to keep itself to itself, that does not want to talk to other people but just to hear the rightness of its own views confirmed.

Who in fact are the academicians? In the history of architecture people have come to see that the great engineers are the 'modern artists' of the nineteenth century, upon whom the twentieth century is based: men like Telford, Stephenson, Brunel, Paxton, Gerber, Röbling, Eiffel, Dutert, Contamin, to name only a few. Have their lives been so thoroughly investigated that we know what pictures hung on their walls? The Impressionists, as in the case of the finance official Caillebotte? Should it not have been perhaps the purest academic paintings? Even the engineers of today are not always on the side of 'opposition' art; many buy Impressionist pictures, which today means the art of the day before the day before yesterday.

Is a proper estimate of the Academy possible? It is certain that one does not exist at the moment; there are hardly even any up-to-date studies of individual academicians who were well thought of in their own day. Where is the biography of Ary Scheffer? Of Piloty? Of Couture? (We are not talking only of occupants of actual seats in the Academy; for Delacroix competed for a seat and yet is regarded as an 'opposition artist'). No, a proper estimate of the academicians is simply not possible. Their pictures are no longer to be seen; even the keepers of art galleries no longer know how many of them are preserved and how many lost. The directors of German galleries are in the process of trying to find out when their predecessors sold the academic pictures bought for the galleries during the nineteenth century. They may have been thrown out in hundreds in order to finance the purchase of one single van Gogh. Were the hundred other pictures really so bad? And was the one van Gogh really so good?

In the present state of research one can only indicate the existence of this gap. It is impossible to write a balanced account of the nineteenth century until the gap is filled. In particular, any account of painting is bound to be distorted. We can see the distortion but at the moment we are not in a position to put it right.

Unlike the absolute rulers, the nineteenth-century bourgeoisie had a double task to accomplish. Men like Charlemagne, Harun al-Rashid and Philip IV met little opposition. The nineteenth-century bourgeoisie was always meeting opposition, or rather it was always criticising itself. It had the double strength to keep itself under control and at the same time to meet the improbable demands put on it – for this western bourgeoisie changed the culture of the whole world. For this reason it is in the long run false to describe Impressionist painting as 'opposition'. This would mean retaining the narrow outlook of the parties of that period and impeding the development of a detached, genuinely historical view. Today it is a greater service to Impressionism to see it as one of the achievements of the loyal bourgeoisie, to compare it, not contrast it, with the Paris Opéra. It is inappropriate to talk of Impressionism as revolutionary art. It does not revolutionize; it attaches the greatest importance to quality, and this is a characteristic of the solid middle class. Goya's *Shooting of the Hostages* is revolutionary; the *Raft of the Medusa* is revolutionary; Munch's *Puberty* is revolutionary – even today. But what is revolutionary about the *Gare Saint Lazare?* It would be a curious kind of

PLATE P. 176
PLATE P. 23

revolution that had to be explained historically by the statement that in those days it was revolutionary to use ochre for locomotive smoke.

Did the academic painters possess no good quality at all? The academician Léon Bonnat assembled a collection of drawings which now forms the Musée Bonnat in Bayonne and is one of the treasure-houses of western graphic art. He had no means of knowing that one of the Baroque drawings he acquired would be attributed today to the early period of Rubens; so could he have been devoid of any feeling for quality when he bought the drawing? Could he have only recognized quality in others, while remaining quite uncritical towards his own work? The drawings of the academicians are now gradually beginning to appear in art dealers' shops and at auctions. It could be that many of their successors will find themselves a bit short of breath when it comes to competing with this kind of quality, this skilled craftsmanship, this masterly ability acquired by learning. It may well be that the historicists' big pictures will cause us difficulties even in the future, always assuming that we get a sight of them. But their drawings are a different matter. The strictness of academic instruction was not without effect. A man like Odilon Redon, who opposed this strictness with a determination all his own because he carried within himself the vision of a sensitive, untouchable art that was his alone, was an exception; he proved that it can be right to oppose training by the academy.

POSTAGE STAMPS

Stamps: the happy idea of collecting things. What does the pursuit require? An object that can be collected. There must be no serious deviations from the standard pattern. How irritating to the stamp-collector are postcards with the stamp printed on them and the franked envelopes used for bulk postings, for they cannot be accommodated in his albums. The object must not be so small that it easily vanishes. That it should have the traditional format and thinness of a postage stamp, so that even big collections can be kept without any difficulty in a private house, is in itself a tremendous advantage. The object must be pleasing to the eye, and a stamp is certainly that. The stamps in any given series can vary in design as well as colour and are thus gay-coloured things. Their graphic design is settled by competition among artists. They also fulfil the demand for instruction in geography and history, unobtrusively but so vigorously that there can be no scepticism about the educational value of stamps. The advertising experts of big firms have often tried to build up a history of art, a natural history or a collection of tales with series of cards, but they have never been able to achieve the success of the postage stamp; they have not managed in the long run to establish a market. The object must be available in almost unlimited yet controllable numbers. An object that cannot be obtained is not much good for a popular hobby. Here postal ministries have an economic, educational and sometimes also artistic task to perform. They are the big regulating hand behind the small-scale market. The lesson of the famous tulip crash of 1637 – the need for a cautious bulb-exchange conscious of its duty – has been well learned, through natural human shrewdness and for other reasons, by the postal ministries; they know that they must keep the number and frequency of new series under their own control, under an international control, so that the number of objects continues to correspond with the number of possible philatelists. In the nineteenth century postmasters-general only changed their issues when a new monarch ascended the throne, and that did not happen frequently enough.

The object must be worth something, and here the postage stamp's good fortune borders on genius. It is actually worth something and can effect something: to wit, the despatch of a letter to its destination. Stamps can be bought, and at such reasonable prices that the value of a purchase can vary from a few pennies to any sum you like. This basic link with a real value and with a purpose quite unconnected with collecting is unbeatable; tulip bulbs did not have this advantage, nor do cigarette coupons, which can only promise rewards for reaching certain target numbers.

However, the real value of the stamp does not reside in the fact that it can be licked and despatched, but in the fact that it can be traded, that it has a market value, not a subjective, random, unmeasured value, but an honest one that can be checked. Any philatelist can check for himself what his collection is worth at any given moment.

In all these respects the stamp cannot be beaten as an object to collect: a great piece of luck, as we have already said. However, its origin as an emblem of a postal charge was not luck but a purposeful idea of the nineteenth century, and its present status is again not luck but the result of sound control.

The resemblances with the trade in paintings and graphic art are numerous and important enough to justify this mention of the stamp, which can be allowed to have the same importance as an individual example in the sphere of graphic art as the individual railway line in architecture. First of all, it is only with paintings that a serious art trade is possible. As is well known, it is impossible with architecture; it remains to be seen what the modern building industry will accomplish in this field: whether it will succeed in building up a collector's trade, so that the playboys of the future, in order to express their individuality, will have to have a bungalow of one brand but a swimming-pool made by some other firm. They already have a Cadillac and a Volkswagen alongside each other, or arm-chairs designed by Rietveld, Mies van der Rohe and Eiermann. There can be only a limited trade in sculpture too. The objects are too cumbersome and the collectors not numerous enough; the museums alone hardly form a popular movement yet. It has not come to a real investment, a real market, which must always remain independent of love for an object and have some element of quotation.

One can deal in paintings because the objects are flat. This advantage should not be underestimated, and it is as well to adopt a reserved attitude to contemporary attempts to turn paintings into exaggerated statements difficult to store. When one remembers that besides paintings there are prints and drawings, which are almost as important and indeed often more valuable, it is clear that the collector comes close to enjoying the advantages of philately.

One can deal in paintings because the production and number are controlled by a well-meaning art trade. The painter cannot please himself and paint something quite different from what has become connected with his name, for it is his previous product that the art trade has made marketable. Nor can one paint just as many or just as few pictures as one fancies; both courses of action would irritate the trade.

However, all these advantages, which make paintings comparable with stamps (even though the comparison may be rejected with fury), form only one of the reasons why painting is at the centre of histories of art written in this century.

The history of painting has been written by individualists about individualists for individualists. The need for individuality is more compulsive in the nineteenth and twentieth centuries than it has ever been before. For it is just as clear that important areas of life in this period are governed not by individuality but by the communal approach, by the mass, by industrialization, by potted education. By its very nature painting can give answers to individual questions; but it can give no answers, indeed by its very nature it cannot even pose questions, in the mass field. It can answer the question about the life and death of the individual, but it can scarcely find a reply to the housing estate or the big city, unless one thinks that the painting of boulevards is an answer to the problem of traffic. It has absolutely nothing to say in the realm of mechanization and industrialization, which are fundamental problems of our existence. The further we advance into the twentieth century, the more urgently traditional painting is compelled to adapt itself to the methods, means and modes of thought of the other so-called branches of art. The breakthrough to this kind of creation – it is dubious whether it should still be called painting – occurred with the Dada movement and the collage. It became impossible to depict the world with the means hitherto employed by painting; things belonging to other worlds were fitted in, stuck in, hung in, either as they were found or after undergoing conversion; we shall return later to this subject.

As the questions which concern the single individual are felt by him to be the most pressing ones, it is understandable if someone deeply occupied with the answers provided by painting poses no other questions. More: painters' work embody impressions of the world around them. Attitudes to the contemporary world can be read from pictures: we learn about railways and iron bridges through pictures by Monet, about war and its aftermath through Dix and Grosz and Picasso, and we fancy we learn something about atomic physics through abstract painting. Painting has already achieved a view of the chaotic, mass life or of mathematical science; it has already created order. Even when painting seems to be abstract it provides attitudes to knowledge; it simplifies, provides information and light. In a word, the impression arises that painting is the most informative, the basic art of the nineteenth and twentieth centuries. In reality it is the *biblia pauperum*, as it was in the Middle Ages. It may be fair to say – modifying the original assertion – that painting has produced the greatest individuals (apart from Rodin). But even this is only true of that part of the nineteenth century which left room for individ-

Edouard Manet, *A Bar at the Folies-Bergère*, 1882. Oil on canvas. *Height 3 ft. 2 in., width 4 ft. 4 in. London, Courtauld Institute. Cf. p. 155.*

ualism. For the rest of the nineteenth and twentieth centuries architecture is the basic art, as it was in every other century too.

Every other century – with exceptions. In the seventeenth century painting is the central art in the Low Countries. Whether the same can be said of the rest of western Europe is dubious. But if we take just this one exceptional example, it is clear how slight building activity was in Belgium and Holland during the seventeenth century and how enormous it is, changing the look of everything, in the nineteenth and twentieth centuries. For all the volume of painting that exists today, its influence is restricted to the world of collecting, exhibitions, galleries, reproductions and books on art history. It hardly has a share in the transformation of the earth's surface. This is one of the reasons for its depth, its inward-directed intensity.

The art trade plays a quite inevitable, necessary and beneficial role. But for art dealers, painting and the arts not dependent on industrialization would be unable to exist and we writers on art would be unable to ponder them. The art trade not only takes over the role of the exchange – and even the wildest social theorists cannot manage without an exchange or market – but is also much more humane; its most estimable representatives have been the friends and helpers of artists to the point of unselfishess and often, as with Père Tanguy, beyond. The changeover from the mid-nineteenth century's method of bringing art to the attention of the public by means of the Salons, the annual exhibitions (this is why it was so important for artists to have their work accepted by the Salon), to the fostering of art by the art trade was again due to the Impressionists, and was quite consciously willed at that time by artists and dealers. The names of Durand-Ruel and later of Vollard, Kahnweiler and others are indissolubly bound up with the history of art. Today the role of the art trade is a decisive one. Not only does the art dealer give the artist commissions; he advises him, influences him, defines him. The only people who speak of the art trade in unfriendly terms are those who do not enjoy its support. If the art trade were abolished it would be succeeded only by art produced to order, not by a free, individual exchange of views between artist and art lover.

The uniformity of this social relationship throughout the period from historicism to functionalism is an important reason for regarding this period of a hundred years as an artistic unity as well, not a contrast between opposites. A really new artistic situation would express itself first and foremost in a change in the way in which art comes into being.

Of course, the desire for the existence of a personal relationship between artist and art lover has something wistfully attractive about it, and as an individual one can try to be friends, not with as many artists as possible, but with just a few – only as many as one can help by sharing their worries. Unfortunately one of the

Edouard Manet, *Le Déjeuner sur l'herbe*, 1863. Oil on canvas. *Height 7 ft., width 9 ft. Paris, Louvre, Galerie du Jeu de Paume.* *Cf. pp. 152, 154, 155.*

results of having an informed public is that attention is concentrated on a few stars, who through books, newspapers and television receive more publicity than is their due and above all more than they can cope with. Everyone wants to have something by Picasso, even though the simplest calculation makes it clear that there cannot be more than a few thousand Picassos in existence and that therefore, if ten million people living now all want to have a Picasso, they cannot obtain a genuine work but only one of a large number of reproductions. We are not talking here of colour prints (which would suffice even for nine million) but so far only of numbered prints. No one takes kindly to the idea that a picture by an artist whom one knows personally should be more precious than a print by Picasso whom one does not know personally. And there is also the serious argument that the mere breath, the tiniest particle of the saint's body guarantees the proximity of the divine, and that thus even with the tiniest sketch of Picasso's one can be sure of standing on holy ground. The artist whom one knows personally, on the other hand, may later on have been a friend but not a saint. This would involve a risk which we try as far as possible to avoid. Yet art is always a risk. In other words, we are deeply entangled in myths; the art trade resembles the trade in relics carried on in the late Middle Ages.

P.S. The cheque forged, or rather manufactured, by Marcel Duchamp and given in payment instead of a picture.
P.P.S. Seven engravings by Rembrandt and a Dürer from the mail-order firm of Sears Roebuck & Co; the Maeght Gallery in the Corvette Discount House, Long Island.

BÖCKLIN When Böcklin died, Hugo von Hofmannsthal wrote: 'Those who are like the Master go their way, and there is beauty and meaning wherever they look.' But besides those who were in enthusiastic agreement there was just as obstinate a body of people who rejected his work, people prejudiced from his first picture onwards to his death and beyond it, right up until today. His pictures were not only rejected; they filled people with fury and contempt. A critic wrote in 1869: 'As for the nymphs and fauns, the sight of them tempted us to put the psychiatric question how long anyone shut up in a room furnished with nothing but pictures like these could last without losing his reason.' These may be only the sort of words that could be cited from any year about any artist, but the following assertions are unmistakable and aimed deliberately at Böcklin. Adolf Menzel said, 'This man Böcklin is responsible for all the mischief now going on in painting'; Wilhelm Leibl said, 'Yes, how can one paint things that do not exist?'; and Émile Du Bois-Reymond (in a speech to the Berlin Academy of Sciences on 3 July 1890) said, 'We are inwardly infuriated when a celebrated contemporary artist paints crassly realistic pictures of male and female monsters whose bodies taper off into fat, silvery salmon, with the seam between human skin and scales barely veiled, rolling about on cliffs and splashing about in the sea.' And these views can be grouped together, for the resolute scientist, Du Bois-Reymond, unwilling to admit that anything could be done in the fine arts that natural science did not recognize as correct, said much the same thing as Menzel and Leibl.

The sharpest attack on Böcklin, one from a third quarter and by far the cleverest, was made by Julius Meier-Graefe. In 1905, four years after Böcklin's death, he published a whole book entitled *Der Fall Böcklin* ('The Case of Böcklin'). It was at this same time that he also unfolded 'the case of Menzel'. He refused to allow Böcklin any artistic or moral integrity at all: 'Böcklin interrupts the sole health-giving stream of art.' He stamped him as an outsider, an adversary, in a period when all art should finally flow for its salvation into the stream of French Impressionism.

Meier-Graefe succeeded in his immediate aim, that of making French painting known in Germany. Menzel and Böcklin have long outlived praise and blame. The only thing that still concerns us now is the thesis that there is 'one sole health-giving stream of art', for we are always coming up against this view that in any one period only one kind of art can be the right one, and that this one kind forms 'the style of the period'. So it was in earlier centuries, we are told, and so it must be today as well. It is almost enough to make one laugh if it were not serious. When we ask what 'the style of the period' really was in the Florentine Quattrocento, for how many months, for how many square yards of ground it was valid and binding at any one time, and what was being produced in the same year – say 1450 – in Florence itself, in Rome, Brussels, Nuremberg, Granada, Cairo, and also in Sinkiang, Teotihuacán, Ife – for all these places are part of the frame within which we are now supposed to accept a contemporaneous 'world-wide style' – when we do this it must surely be clear that any so-called unity of style has only ever been valid for a very limited period of time and a very limited geographical area; and that very similar human and artistic demands can be met at the same time and even in the same place with very different styles. At the same time as Meier-Graefe was refusing to tolerate Menzel and Böcklin, and preaching Impressionism as the art of the age, Matisse was creating Fauvism, Picasso was creating Cubism, Kirchner was creating Expressionism, Wright was creating prairie houses and Gaudí the Güell Park – almost all without the knowledge, or at any rate without the approval, of Meier-Graefe.

Böcklin has links with his predecessors, with the German Romantic school, with pre-1848 Paris, and in the last analysis with Italian realism. It is more important to see the transformation which, at the end of the century, made him an ancestor of the coming apocalyptic movement, Surrealism. In between, or already towards the end, comes the picture *Odysseus and Calypso*, alongside which we place Rodin's *Balzac*, the dates being Böcklin 1883 and Rodin early 1892.

PLATE P. 135

When I said that *Balzac* moved over into the amorphous I was speaking of form as opposed to content. I could also have said that he turned back to the mythical; Edvard Steichen's photograph, which was approved by Rodin, shows the plunge into Nordic, Scottish, misty prehistory. Böcklin's picture, on the other hand, shows the Mediterranean, not the pleasant, lush shores of Maillol, but the scorched, treeless Mediterranean of Dali. This picture too goes back to the mythical, to the relationship between man and woman, or between task and obstacle, or between longing and possession; it can still be shaped in terms of the old Mycenean legends. The return to the mythical is present in both artists' methods, and I repeat my

APPX. PL. 14

repudiation of the assertion that in the nineteenth and twentieth centuries the use of myth cannot be regarded as valid. But the paths by which the two artists achieve self-expression are different. One path involves an amorphous surface, the re-arrangement of the hitherto continuous and rounded forms of sculpture into a porous intermediate layer in the roughnesses of which the mists can hang, so that the resulting work is no longer recognizable as an articulated human figure but as just a block. That was the Frenchman's path.

Now let us turn to the Swiss, in whose 'method of creation' there was just as much amorphism, who used to pull threads of wool from his coat pocket as he talked and experiment with their colours, who with almost every picture made a fresh effort to see if the problem could be solved in a new way. The group *Odysseus and Calypso* belongs to a process of fermentation which affects the theme just as much as the making of the picture: this Odysseus does not fit in anywhere; he is not transformed by mist into a natural monument but is a human form in opposition to nature, manufactured form as opposed to form that has grown naturally.

PLATE P. 135

For, paradoxically, the really living element in the whole picture is provided by the rocks, with their brown colouring, their stratification, their arrangement. In comparison with the warmth of the rocks it is the human beings who are the alien bodies, not the other way about. They are the elements capable of a spiritual hardening which does not exist in nature. They are like aniline dyes, not natural, earthy colours. They do not merge with nature but remain in sharp contrast to it. Neither the red beneath Calypso nor the blue round Odysseus is a colour that occurs in nature; they are the product only of the questing, sundering (analytical) mind of man. The female figure is not simply drawn but distorted, disturbed in her physical harmony, the fragment of a group which would only become a symbol of marriage through close union with the male figure. The other (right-hand) outline of Calypso is hardened too and the lyre has a new, abstract form – no longer historicism but Art Nouveau *(Jugendstil)*.

The motif of the picture first appears in Böcklin's work with the early *Grotto of Amaryllis*, in front of which a childlike youth seeks to approach the beloved goddess beyond with an air on the flute. In the *Sea Serpent* (1873), now in Munich, we already meet the renunciation of the man and the woman's attempt to reach him still, in vain, in spite of the spitting, in spite of her occupation – intended as a threat – with the serpent. In the present picture we have the extreme alienation of the man, who grows through longing, not longing for another woman – Calypso is herself already the other woman – nor even longing for home (as in the Greek legend, but not in this picture), but introspective longing in itself, centred on something distant, a task, a vocation. It is the motif of man's loneliness, a motif taken further by Kokoschka in the picture *Tempest*.

But why did Böcklin not remain a landscape painter? Surely he was one? Why did he not remain content with rendering landscapes by means of local detail; with the silvery quality of the Seine valley, for example, or the theatrical scenery of the Italian Romagna? Was landscape not enough for him, or too much? For him it had no geographical element; it was connected with growth; equated with birth and death; against the religion of redemption, for the religion of nature.

The musical element: we cannot judge how deep the musical element goes in nature; it is certainly there, as we know scientifically, since not only the song of the nightingale but also the language of dolphins has been investigated. Other painters may think they are being logical in concentrating on the optical aspects of landscape, but this does not necessarily make Böcklin illogical when he pays a great deal of attention to cross-links, analogies and correspondences. When he thinks of the idea of 'returning' he sees a lost son returning home and at the same time he sees the reflection that returns on the surface of a stretch of water. In this Böcklin is genuinely related to the Surrealists. It is the same with musicality. His landscapes are filled with noises and sounds. Pan does not just put his pipes to his mouth, he really blows them.

The possibilities of combination, the cross-links, are taken as far as they can be without breaking through certain taboos. Böcklin never used sexuality as a source for his art, in spite of his clear insight into this forbidden territory, forbidden because of a marriage concluded when he was still young with a jealous Italian woman. Böcklin was a prude; he had to be. How much opposition he aroused even with his 'cautious' work is shown by his clash with Jakob Burckhardt. In 1868/9 he had painted the frescoes on the staircase of the museum at Basle – a Flora with a cloak full of childrens' souls over a human couple. Burckhardt remonstrated with him, whereupon Böcklin said, 'Am I the painter or are you?' He crossed over to the other side of the street and friends were never able to heal the breach. We can see now why Burckhardt was unwilling to accept these frescoes; it was not, as with Meier-Graefe later, because they lacked any Impressionistic element but because the Renaissance element was missing. Böcklin felt – and he was one of the first to do so – that there are artistic idioms which at a certain moment are played out, and which must therefore be, so to speak, blocked off if anything is to come of them again.

On the other hand the human couple already foreshadow the couple in Rodin's *Kiss* fourteen years later. Or a more striking example: as part of the same commission (1868/9), Böcklin produced for the same museum some coping-stones with comical faces larger than life. The citizens of Basle did not care for them; they may have thought that they themselves were represented, and they wanted to have the heads taken down. Just at the critical moment they heard that Strasbourg was showing interest and wanted to buy the heads; whereupon they were left on the building. Today they have been taken down and are in the museum; it could be maintained that they mark the beginning, even before Gauguin, of Art Nouveau *(Jugendstil)* or Expressionism.

This brings us to the importance of Italy for historicism. Why is it that for the twentieth century Italy has faded into insignificance as a model in cultural history? Is it because the Italian Renaissance is identified with scientific accuracy, with the age of perspective? The vision based on perspective is discarded, with it the Renaissance conception of the world is discarded, and not even Michelangelo can halt the change: is that it? Does the world of cultural history collapse, but not the world of myths?

Plato's Symposium, by Feuerbach, can be cited as an example of the picture in the PLATE P. 136

cultural–historical tradition. It is true that it also belongs to the Belgian school. One would have to study Belgian as well as French historical painting in order to see where it fits in. Then there is the frame, a highly literary element but at the same time also a harbinger of Art Nouveau. A frame created by the painter himself; it is no longer a question of a design for a room decoration but of a self-contained picture.
The *Symposium* deals expressly with the erotic, but not with the sexual; it does not infringe the taboo. It is concerned with conversation, not intercourse.

MANET
PLATE P. 146

Art historians have known since the publication of an essay by Gustav Pauli in 1898 that the group of figures in Manet's *Déjeuner sur l'herbe* goes back to a group of river gods in an engraving by Marcantonio Raimondi, beyond that to Raphael, and still further beyond that to reliefs on ancient sarcophagi. Pauli added at the time, 'Manet's gift was not for composition. . . . How fortunate that his contemporaries in 1863 were not aware of this connection; otherwise they would have attacked the artist even more severely than they did.' Our verdict today differs from Pauli's. In face of Manet's work as a whole, the view that he could not compose is untenable. But he need not have feared that the connection between his picture and a Renaissance composition could become known. He should rather have desired it, for then he could have pointed emphatically to Giorgione's *Rustic Feast* in the Louvre, a picture that he had copied earlier on, and could have explained that he had no desire to break with the old artistic tradition but simply wished to transpose it into contemporary terms. He might have been able to kindle a discussion about historicism, which – contrary to the current view that it was a sign of weakness and purely imitative – was much rather the mark of a critical and inquisitive attitude, an attitude of critical experimentation. The incorporation of the earlier mode of composition in the structure of the contemporary picture did not mean that the same sort of thing was to be repeated, but that it seemed worth while to find out how the old principles worked in new surroundings.
But no discussion of this sort came about. The Emperor Napoleon III, who had stopped in front of the picture with his retinue, finally turned away with a gesture of displeasure – he had only looked at the contours of the naked woman and found them unattractive. His retinue saw the combination of a naked woman and two fully dressed men as if it were a suggestion about how to spend the next Sunday afternoon. And the art critics saw the changed mode of painting – which made them feel baffled and hostile. Manet had wanted his name to be on everyone's lips as a result of the picture. It was, but people were criticizing him, not praising him.
As a matter of fact, the bourgeoisie's critical attitude to Manet was the greatest error made in the nineteenth century. For Manet, who himself was of patrician origin – his father was a high official in the ministry of justice and his mother the daughter of a Swedish diplomat – was always striving for recognition by the middle classes, for a seat in the Academy, for the Légion d'honneur; he never lapsed into the self-satisfaction of the revolutionary. This provoked Edgar de

Gas – himself of noble birth, always rich and independent, but less clear in his own attitude – to utter the embittered remark, 'I knew that you were a bourgeois.' This was obviously meant to be a reproach, but it was simply a statement of fact.
Manet, the purest embodiment in nineteenth-century society of the irreconcilability of the genuine artist and the academician who has 'arrived' – a distinction attained precisely because he tried to elude the antithesis altogether – Manet was in his own way once again a comprehensive artist, in that he really wanted to depict the content of big-city life. Before him there had been the historicists, the great thinkers of the historical age, such as Delacroix; there had been Balzac with his *Comédie humaine*, which was to unite all possible destinies and characters round the great opera-house of Paris as if these lives were really lived in the boxes of the Opéra and were only followed to other settings elsewhere in France for the sake of completeness. After him came Rodin, who assembled his figures at the gates of hell. Between them comes Manet, with his very worldly series of paintings which combine to form an educated upper middle-class Parisian picture of the whole world. As he was a Parisian, to him the Boulevards were equivalent to the world as a whole.
To his painter friends – among whom were soon counted the Impressionists-to-be – he was, it is true, essentially the absolute painter, who captured with his brush both colour and content, who never painted over but stripped the colours twenty times from the canvas if the fragrance of the first stroke of the brush was not a convincing success. A man who did not wish to be a revolutionary but was one. An admirable, chivalrous, honourable person; that is how George Moore describes him. He had grown up with Thomas Couture and was thus one of the many so-called 'opposition' painters who nevertheless owed their training to the so-called fashionable painter, the historicist, whose studio he frequented for six years. Obviously Manet was also influenced by Courbet. It may be that Courbet was able to show him even more clearly than Couture what French painting really was: a build-up of colour on the surface of the canvas, a build-up that even with Delacroix had become independent of the demand to produce something 'recognizable'. (We need this expression, and sometimes also the expression 'to compare nature', in order to avoid the term 'to imitate', which at present is discredited.)
This concern with the actual paint, with 'painting' in general, was carried so far by Manet that it is the key to his disagreements with the art critics. For when it is a question of comparing or recognizing (for example, a face or a tree) but not of imitating something, then the construction of the comparable object (namely the work of art) becomes fairly independent of the thing with which it is to be compared (namely so-called 'nature'). Or at any rate within the totality of colours, the total phenomenon, of which the comparable object must consist in order to 'agree', there remains a large area of decision as to how these colours are to be arranged. It is possible to combine them in clearer, more illuminating groups than would be possible if the object of the exercise were 'identity' or 'imitation'. It is possible to keep the grey tones together, the blue tones together, to employ each individual shade only in a certain place, yet to have in the picture as a whole a similar variety to that contained in the comparable piece of reality. While the

main areas of Manet's pictures are very uniform and intensive, almost monochrome in each case, there is nearly always a spot where all the colours are employed in a very bright combination: on a picnic basket in *Le Déjeuner sur l'herbe*, on a bouquet of flowers in *Olympia*, on a little basket of wool in the picture of his parents. In comparison with the disorder of 'nature', the combination of colours in a Manet picture is wonderfully clear and distinct. This method of work has its own rules, applied but not much talked of either then or now, but they are very strict, and Manet's famed honesty consisted largely in the fact that he followed these rules of the game with complete if quite unconscious consistency and fidelity.

PLATE P. 146

The manufacture of a quite separate entity, which is only to be compared with nature but does not imitate it, is in fact one of the features that makes the nineteenth century into the foundation of the twentieth century, which seeks to elude even the comparison and to replace it with a completely separate creation.

For a comparison to be fruitful, for it to be recognized by others, it had to be incontestable. During the preceding centuries the outward look of nature had been the court of last instance (with the one important exception of Leonardo); it had been a question of checking that the superficial appearance was optically correct. Now, in the nineteenth century, the demand was increasingly for scientific accuracy, which made possible an intellectual check independent of the optical appearance. The physiologist Du Bois-Reymond had criticized Böcklin's tritons because, as a scientist, he knew only too well from comparative anatomy that inside legs there are tubular bones and inside fishes' bodies vertebral bones. Moreover, as well as scientific accuracy, historical accuracy was required, which was just as big and just as hard a demand. Scientific historicism contained facts, fixed scenery which could have just as 'crystallizing' an effect (Stendhal, *De l'amour*) as a cane chair or a boot for realists. The scenery could be and was cited against the artist: it was not a case of good or bad painting, but of correct or false insertion.

It now becomes clear how exceptionally bold it was of Manet to incorporate and at the same time to remodel just such a 'fact' in his *Déjeuner sur l'herbe*. He dislocated the arrangement of the Raimondi engraving in just the same way as he dislocated the moral – the one in the other. For as sea gods with a female companion the group would have been accepted without any reservations; it would have been one of the facts of art history. The first dislocation was that in contrast to the general nudity of ancient art two of the figures were clothed, and in contemporary costume to boot. The second dislocation was the woman's gaze. Or, to be more accurate, it may be this gaze that explains the whole fascination of this engraving for Manet. For this gaze directed at us, which was certainly present in the old engraving but did not strike the eye, was now given an intensity which made it independent, caused it to become an essential feature of all Manet's painting.

PLATE P. 146

We know that any such gaze at us is at the same time a self-portrait. One cannot depict any strange pair of eyes looking at one without setting in motion this mirror effect. We know from a whole series of pictures that Manet kept returning again and again to these reflections, these concealed self-portraits. It was almost his mark, his style of painting. Round these portraits he would then paint an environment, retrospectively, parallel to us and at a tangent to the person depicted, who stands in the middle of it and looks at us. Already in *Le Déjeuner sur l'herbe* the intensity is so marked that once one is under the spell of the young woman's gaze everything else, starting with her naked body, is felt only as a tapestry surrounding her. For us this face contains something of the quality of a reflection seen in a mirror, of a self-portrait. Reality is reversed; it is not we who look at the picture, but the woman's head that looks at us out of the picture. There is no trace of coquetry in her gaze. And Manet's contemporaries were sensitive on this point, for to them it was no self-portrait, no occasion for self-examination, but the picture of an undressed woman in the company of men wearing clothes, and if this arrangement was to be credible it had to give clear expression to the piquancy of such a situation. Here for them lay the falsity, the impropriety of the picture. If the young woman had been smiling roguishly it would have made up for a great deal. (That Napoleon was incapable of appreciating the subtle surrounding tints of blue, white and grey by which the flesh-colour of the female body was, as it were, washed clean need cause us no surprise.)

Manet returned twenty years later in his last big picture to this mirror effect, this self-portrait, to the identity of the male element in himself and of the female element before him. He painted the *A Bar at the Folies Bergère* – that is the title of the picture and the girl is in fact standing behind the bar. In the amusement district of the city: this in itself is in the last analysis a self-portrait, for the artist of the late nineteenth century felt more and more that he was exiled from the genteel drawing-rooms of the middle class to this fringe world.

PLATE P. 145

This apparently voluntary but in reality compulsory departure, this fateful farewell, is contained in the picture. It is not a clinging to the past – nothing in the picture is older than now – but a summary of Manet's whole life. In the pictures *Astruc*, *Railway*, *Waitress* he had thought out the combination of front view and rear view; in *Nana*, *Astruc*, *Café* he had investigated mirror effects; and in *Lola*, the *Execution of Maximilian*, the *Opera Ball* and the *Café Singer* he had depicted the moving, shadowy crowd behind the individual. What did the portrait mean to him? Was it an individual personality that stood before him, outside him even though as closely related to him as his own son? In that case *Luncheon in the Studio* was the real stepping-stone to the *Bar*. Or was the portrait also always a self-portrait? Does the element of reflection alternate between Manet and the girl so intensively that one must say that in painting the girl Manet is painting himself? In that case Nana, painting herself with her own means, standing in front of her mirror, was already a self-portrait of this kind.

However that may be, the expanse of mirror behind the barmaid is precisely indicated; it begins on a level with the wrist propped on the marble slab. Apart from the girl herself, the counter and the things standing on it, the narrow strip of red wall and the gold frame are the only parts of the picture that are not reflections. Thus by far the greatest area of the picture is mirror – one of the profoundest representations of a mirror ever painted; the only predecessors that rival Manet's *Bar* are Jan van Eyck's portrait of the Arnolfinis and Velázquez's *Las Meninas (Maids of Honour)*.

The establishment has a downstairs hall which is encircled by a balcony. We look down from the level of these rows of seats above. Right in front sit the ladies, following with opera-glass events on the stage, which is presumably to the left. In the top left-hand corner a trapeze with an acrobat on it swings down into the hall. In those day ladies wore their hats, and gentlemen their top-hats, inside music-halls. The chandeliers are reflected endlessly into the distance.

But the parapet which we see over there, the balcony with all the people, is not in front of us but behind us, for we see it in the mirror. The marble counter and the bottles on it are the first things to recur, but at a curiously oblique angle; surely the mirror cannot alter their position so much, for it is painted parallel to the edge of the picture? The corner of the table, on the other hand, has been moved over sharply to the right in the reflection. The bottles too, to judge by the colours of their contents. And the back view of the girl as well. Where do we stand ourselves? We feel like groping behind ourselves; surely there must be a parapet which prevents us from falling, yet it ought to be visible in the mirror. We begin to feel giddy, or rather uneasy. In this picture, which is based on reflection, we ourselves have no place. We are like people without shadows, without reflections. Even the marble counter hovers in a sort of no man's land. It is only beyond us, through us, that the glittering, indifferent world over there of fashionable women and chandeliers begins.

Or else the girl reflects us. And who again is her reflection? Over to the extreme right, where the picture ends, looms the cavalier who is meeting her. In the sketch for the picture, now in Amsterdam, the dislocation of the reflection to the right was already planned, but the man – her gallant, we ourselves – was still small, shorter and more distant than the girl. That would be right from the point of view of perspective. Now he grows before her, the conversation is in progress – the seduction, the taking possession, the destruction of the mirror image. It is the same as in Cocteau's film on the Orpheus theme: the mirror says 'I am thy death.' When Manet painted this picture (he painted it in his studio, not in the music hall) he was no longer able to stand; the gangrenous leg was amputated and in the next year he died, at the age of fifty-two.

(A link between Manet and Cocteau, between painting and film, is Max Klinger's etching in the cycles *Of Death* (1910): a youth looking at himself in the mirror over the body of a woman lying in between. Illustrated in Hans H. Hofstätter's *Symbolismus*, Plate 94).

IMPRESSIONISM

'For this relief much thanks.' 'To be or not to be.' Who would dispute that these phrases and others like them have passed into everyday usage, and rightly so, because they sum up a standard situation. And who would doubt that Shakespeare, the author of these phrases, was a great poet?

It is the same with the pictures of the French Impressionists. They have become popular in such a disarming way, and so many millions of postcards of them have been sold, that they have become as hackneyed as 'hit' tunes. Yet who could doubt that the Impressionists were great artists?

When the Impressionists were young they did not belong to the Academy. They are pained by this, they laughed at it, and in many cases they waited to become members of the Academy, as is implied by the photograph of Degas in the pose of the beloved Homer, after the picture by Ingres. By 'Academy' they understood hope of artistic recognition, financial success, fame. At the bottom of their hearts ninety-nine out of a hundred contemptuous young artists would like eventually to belong to an Academy of this sort. I know only a few cases in the last hundred years of first-rank artists ceasing to write, build or paint because they could no longer bear the questionable nature of artistic activity; examples that spring to mind are Arthur Rimbaud, Max Berg, Marcel Duchamp. The relationship between recognized and revolutionary art cannot be decided so simply; the proposition that one is good art and the other bad art will not do, nor even will the formula 'revolutionary art is the art which will subsequently become academic art.' Formulations of this sort are dictated by the assumption that the world can be divided into a number of 'either . . . or' situations. In reality the world is rich and has room for many different things.

When a generation has passed, the hitherto revolutionary artists are provided by the new crop of art historians with detailed biographies, in which the artists themselves co-operate if they live long enough. On Manet, Renoir, Pissarro, Sisley (to name the real Impressionists) we possess a comprehensive literature which tells us all they did, down to every detail on every day of the week. Does the artist's prejudice against historicism only last as long, then, as history is not concerned with him?

As for the Impressionists' style of painting, an angry critic wrote in 1874: 'Just look at Mademoiselle Morisot. The young lady does not waste her time on superfluous details. When she paints a hand she just paints as many longish brush-strokes as there are fingers. And that's that. The idiots who carefully paint all the details in a hand do not understand anything about impressionistic art and the great Manet would banish them from his kingdom.' Today we should describe the same procedure in more positive terms: Impressionism replaced the accuracy of detailed observation with a concentration that makes possible the cohesion of the work as a whole, not just of the hand. This should lead to the conclusion that comparisons between an impressionistic work and nature are of no significance. Yet in books on Impressionism we find reproductions of landscapes, with the painting of the actual spot on the left and a photograph on the right. There was a whole exhibition organized on these lines.

Does this mean that while painters of the ages before Impressionism 'composed' their landscapes, so that their models could not be traced in the real world, the Impressionists' first achievement consisted in finding the 'motif' and then remaining so committed to it that the actual spot can be identified by photography? This would correspond with the advice of the Italian sculptor Giovanni Dupré (1882): 'The most important thing is to find a well-developed model.' Or is the connection between photograph and picture, between reality and art, a good deal more subtle than people think?

The final overwhelming victory of the Impressionist school was due to a combination of factors. First of all, of course, these men were extremely talented. On their own territory they are infallible: if at a surprising place in an early Renoir there is a blue (or any other colour) that one would not expect at all, one can take it on trust that here there was or is blue; colour photography would prove it even if hitherto one has not seen it oneself. The second realization, that here there must be blue because of the structure of the picture, arises only during the maturity of Impressionism itself.

Great honesty, unshakeable intensity, a cheerfulness proceeding from the artist's character are further attributes of the Impressionists. The extraordinary concentration with which they work towards this particular artistic goal, indeed the whole notion of an artistic goal: this is to a certain extent the creation of the Impressionists. The replacement of content in painting by the 'manufacture' of the painting, the transformation from a strictly defined end-product which is painted once and for all to a never-ending state of being painted, so that everyone who stands before the picture has a share in the painting of it – advances which have become self-evident to us in the twentieth century but had to be made at some time or other during the nineteenth century, advances which presupposed honesty, toughness, concentration: all this is Impressionism. It is easy to say that a picture is first of all a piece of wood or canvas adorned with colours and only secondarily a war horse or a nude, but it was the Impressionists who first saw this and secured its acceptance. To that extent it is with them that abstract, 'content-less' painting begins.

But 'content-lessness' was not recognized in a single generation; it was not recognized by the Impressionists themselves. Thus the limitations of Impressionism, its vulnerability to attack, lie precisely in the fact that it has too little content but has not yet defined 'content-lessness' as an artistic aim, as a possibility. These limitations were felt and expressed at once most sharply by the following generation of artists, who did not equal the Impressionists in ability and were therefore all the more deficient. To put it quite simply: no God, no love, no death, no myth, no history; or, to look at it another way, no smelling, no hearing, no tasting, no feeling; only seeing.

These limitations undoubtedly made an important contribution to the great, century-long success of the Impressionists. Anyone who buys an impressionistic picture or finds one beautiful does not need to exert himself. Within quite a short period Impressionism, so recently attacked, became the most easily comprehensible, the least off-putting, the most generally appreciated kind of art that the last hundred years have produced.

A quite unproblematical landscape, not romantic, avoiding any kind of greatness, tangible, in broad daylight: did any Impressionist ever paint a moon landscape? Or mountains, or a sea with a demonic element in it, like the seas of Caspar David Friedrich or even Courbet's waves?

Then there are the fairly similar variations on the same theme – Monet's famous haystacks, the façade of Rouen cathedral in various different lights; they are all glorious expanses of colour, but the combinations of colours employed are reminiscent of Second Empire brocades; they are backward-facing harmonies. Look on the other hand at Hokusai's thirty-two views of Fujiyama, already known in Europe and to the Impressionists, with their incomparably more far-reaching links with human mood, fate and activity, with storms, reflections, seasons, crafts, myths. Who today then owns a collection of Impressionist paintings? The man who wants to avoid becoming involved with contemporary art and yet would like to be known as an art connoisseur. Impressionism does both for him.

But were the Impressionists always suited to this kind of aim? Let us repeat the thesis: every kind of art meets lack of understanding in its own age and needs a waiting period; after thirty years have elapsed the previously criticized art is accepted as valid. In the case of Impressionism this is only superficially true. For there is a corollary to the thesis, namely that after another thirty years the accepted art, having been outlived, slips into obscurity and is no longer seen, or at any rate no longer looked at. So far Impressionism has not obeyed this law. The scandals of the early years are well known; in any history of art you can find those incredibly imperceptive critics quoted – these quotations are the only words of theirs that have been preserved. But you do not find quotations showing that the Impressionists have maintained their position long beyond their 'period', and still do. This is not due to their quality, or only partly so, but mainly to the fact that the view of the world held by the well-to-do middle-class citizen, the educated capitalist, corresponds with that of the Impressionists in a way that will never be repeated. Really they are identical; really it was a grotesque misunderstanding that the middle class did not realize this forthwith. This limited holiday landscape, streaming with light (Werner Hofmann calls it 'the earthly paradise'), this limited mental horizon, this harmlessness of theme combined with attested craftsmanship, this flowery feminine existence (Renoir) combined with strict avoidance of the sexual (Rodin) is just what the 'bourgeois' needs. Can Impressionism be justly accused of any social unruliness? Surely not. The authorities for their part never felt called upon to interfere with them, though they did with Daumier, Wagner and Semper.

In what kind of frames do the Impressionists' pictures hang today? They themselves used simple, monochrome borders. But it is only the pictures of the following generation, that of Art Nouveau *(Jugendstil)*, that still demand the frames with which they were originally provided. The overwhelming majority of Impressionist pictures hang today in historical, Baroque-type frames. How would that be possible if they did not contain a fair proportion of 'historicism' in them? One must therefore consider seriously what the really revolutionary thing about Impressionism was, for it can no longer be discovered. It has to be reconstructed out of the objections raised against it at the time. What we arrive at then – if one dismisses the accusation of madness as something not to be taken seriously – is 'inadequate execution', 'inadequate composition', 'inadequate content', in other words a series of objections which indicate disappointed expectations. Then we come to 'too bright', 'not enough shadow', 'nothing but colour' – and with this characterization we are quite content today, for we see in it the concentration on the 'purely artistic'. But the Impressionists themselves were still so very much children of the nineteenth century that they sought support and found it – in the discovery that the idea of 'nothing but colour' could be proved scientifically correct. The theory elaborated by Seurat and Signac, a logical development of the preceding Impressionism proper, actually aimed at the creation of a scientific mode of painting.

Why is Impressionism no longer classified as 'Realism', although the Impressionist demonstrably painted from nature, in the open air, not in the studio? Did the difficulty in accepting his picture lie in the fact that people were reluctant to give up 'reality' and no longer found it? In that case there must have been some foreknown, preconceived element in realism, something that was already characteristic, that corresponded with a definite choice, so that it could be recognized as 'landscape', 'portrait', 'Italy' or 'Switzerland'. In comparison with this desirable, sought-after characteristic element an Impressionist picture had something vague, different, indefinite about it, just as the silvery landscape depicted was indefinite in comparison with the geographical scene.

The Impressionists for their part were proud that they saw 'correctly', in accordance, so they thought, with the teachings of scientific optics. But this was a piece of self-deception. In reality, what they wished to reproduce was something that lay before them in the future, something that did not yet exist; it was the first time in art that artists had sought after the 'unknown', which they carried within themselves as a vision, a mental picture. Does the principle of 'the unknown in art' (Willy Baumeister) occur in any earlier theory of art? While asserting that they stuck to the object, and claiming to paint a Thames bridge, a railway station or a cornfield, in reality they painted something resembling not the bridge or the station but an 'impression' of it, their own mental picture of it. They therefore had to try to distinguish verbally, too, what they were doing from what (as they discovered) people expected and missed in their pictures. It was only at this moment that the word 'imitation' acquired a negative sense that it had not possessed before and certainly did not possess for the Greeks.

An impressionistic picture was not an imitation but a new creation, an 'impression', in fact. Its reference to nature, to the 'motif', was only apparent; in reality the artist was concerned only with the painting to be created. The slogan *l'art pour l'art* which came into existence at that time should not be translated as 'art for artists only' but as 'art concerned only with art'.

This self-absorption, this refusal to make concessions was felt very keenly by their opponents. Delacroix, Courbet and Manet had been unyielding, but they had been isolated individuals. Now there appeared for the first time a whole group armed with this resolve. It is a decisive event in the history of painting: for the first time an epoch of art must be described and dated in terms of collective exhibitions; and exhibitions that were no longer the Salon but a secession movement, even if they were not yet so described. Since then the history of modern art has proceeded by exhibitions. Even present-day art has not outgrown this arrangement; it still needs exhibitions to be organized and to be discussed in the papers; it still needs the journalist as friend or foe, and in any case as a publicity agent. There had been discussions about the Salon in France for a hundred years, but now the emphasis had moved from the official Salon to private initiative.

Just as important, as we have already pointed out, was the intervention of the art dealer, who in the end makes a profit on the products but for a considerable time before that supports 'his' artists, so enabling them to live and work. That is why the pictures have to be relatively uniform. The Impressionists could not have altered their pictures very much even if they had wanted to do so; Durand-Ruel would not have taken them off their hands. (It is inconceivable that anyone would have taken 'on contract' Delacroix's great Salon pictures: *Dante's Barque*, *Massacre at Chios*, *Death of Sardanapalus*, *Liberty Guiding the People*.)

This new self-awareness on the part of a group of painters was accompanied by a new kind of painting, the studio picture. It came into being in the precise form it took without any preconceived plan, and was limited to a certain period, like the Dutch group portrait three hundred years before. Gatherings of artists in studios had previously given rise to drawings, isolated individual studies and then lithographs: David in his studio, Courbet in the studio, and also Courbet's *Real Allegory*. Now suddenly 1863 saw Henri Fantin-Latour's big composition *Homage to Delacroix*. Delacroix, who had just died, was shown as a picture in a gold frame; in his shadow stood Fantin-Latour himself, Manet, Baudelaire and others – critics who had championed Delacroix and painters who were on the side of the 'Romantics' against the 'Classicists', whose patron was Ingres. As was usual in Paris, caricatures appeared at once in which the idea that inspired the picture was extended further. For example, the artistic legacy of Delacroix was shared out: Fantin-Latour got a sack of white, the English painter Whistler got a coal-sack, as if to wear, and one of the critics got a shoe many sizes too big for him.

The *Studio at Batignolles* (1871) had Manet as the central figure; the group included, among others, Émile Zola, Renoir and Monet. This picture too immediately provoked a caricature, which showed Manet with a halo and the text, 'Verily, verily I say unto you, whoever uses this brush-stroke will be a good painter. And you shall illumine the world and your tubes shall be like lamps.' The *Table Corner* by Fantin-Latour was painted in 1872. It would be a relatively uninteresting picture if it did not show in one corner Verlaine and Rimbaud, two more Frenchmen whose names are household words, figures famous both for their genius and for the scandals in which they were involved. Verlaine described Rimbaud as possessing 'the pale face of an angel', and added 'with the hands of a killer'. Rimbaud's poems were written between his fourteenth and twentieth birthdays; his relationship with Verlaine was notorious. He went to Africa and started on a totally different career instead of using his indescribable artistic genius – the first writer to seek self-realization in a totally different aspect of 'reality' instead of in artistic activity. After men like Rimbaud or van Gogh, how can one tell the life story of an Impressionist? There would be nothing to tell. Pissarro? His Jewishness was of no significance at all. The same is true of Sisley and his English passport. Anyway, Pissarro had a Cuban passport throughout his life. Renoir? One would incur the embarrassment of having to speak about his later pictures. The forty years from 1871 to 1911 were a very empty period for the individual middle-class European; he could think that the world – his own middle-class world, that is – was not changing, or else that it was involved in swift progress, which came to almost the same thing. Progress in which one could move about almost as comfortably as in a well-sprung express railway carriage.

As for Monet, the two extreme limits of his creativity are on the one hand the highly talented caricatures of his schooldays with which he delighted his native city of Rouen and gained his family's approval to become a painter, and on the other the *Nymphéas*, the huge pictures of his pond at Giverny which were hung after his death, at the instigation of his friend Clemenceau but in accordance with his own intentions, in the Jeu de Paume in the Tuileries Gardens. They form a truly surrealistic end to Impressionism, a ghostly kind of monomania.

For in ancient mythical times the different quarters of the globe had also been cosmic divisions arranged by God and named by his priests; Michael had come from the east and the dragon from the west; but in the course of the eighteenth and nineteenth centuries the panorama had become a very worldly scene to be viewed. One walked along a subterranean passage and emerged on a circular platform. Round the balustrade began the 'genuine' scenery – the soldiers' arms, the dune grass, the bare rocks; these led on to the huge circular picture, over forty yards in circumference, of the battle of Waterloo, the shore at Scheveningen, or, at Altötting, the Crucifixion on Calvary (to name three of these once numerous panoramas, three that can still be viewed today). For all their incontestable verve these panoramas were at the same time basically banal and illusory; they depended for their effect on blurring the distinction between reality and unreality.

And now – what could Monet, the old Impressionist, achieve in the way of skilful illusion? The play of light upon the surface of water, all around, mingled with drooping branches, all reflected back from the water. Yet only partly reflected from the surface; partly also mingled with the broken rays of light which come up from the much denser substance of the muddy, coloured water. What an overwhelming wealth of interwoven facets of perception! And at the same time how intolerably mundane and banal the subject of the painting is! What has become of the heavenly ocean across which Aton's barque sails; what has become of the world in which the Saviour dies, in which the great battles of history are fought? How much world is left for the man shut up in this aquarium? And if it were an aquarium, an 'underwater garden', on what a tiny sheet of paper Paul Klee was painting it at the same time!

It is no use applying the usual kind of analysis to these pictures; the areas are simply too big. There is very little 'art' to the square yard; it is the situation, fifty years in advance, that we meet at a considerable number of exhibitions today, where we need some means of concentrating our gaze. Or it could be described as the nineteenth century's situation with its railway lines, its postage stamps and their 'art'.

But then these pictures also contain the details which are always cited when people want to find forerunners of Tachisme, when – with good or evil intent – they point out how abstract these clots of colour are, which from the representational angle would be water-lilies. They do indeed possess the inexplicable intensity of strong handwriting, of the transformation into the significant, like the huge characters with which modern Japanese calligraphers travel through the world and dance across paper. They are 'art-work' of the first rank, and let it not be thought that the word 'work' here implies the slightest limitation. Work is what is 'made', and

Claude Monet, *Water-lilies*, 1906. Oil on canvas. *Height 3 ft., width 3 ft. 3 in. Formerly in the Durand-Ruel Collection, Paris.*

Henri de Toulouse-Lautrec, Poster for the Moulin Rouge, 1891. Coloured lithograph. *Height 5 ft. 7 in., width 4 ft. 3 in. Albi Museum.* *Cf. p. 166.*

it is in fact the case with art in the twentieth century that it is not built or modelled or painted, but 'made'. A fanatical impulse to make things himself has seized the artist: he must fashion something, as protection, redemption, in face of the prefabricated article that leaves him no further possibility of any 'genuine' activity. In this spot the walls are as productive as art can ever be.

After the panorama of the nineteenth century, after Monet's *Nymphéas*, comes Circarama, Frank Lloyd Wright's Guggenheim Museum – and the circling radar scanner.

ON THE FRINGES OF IMPRESSIONISM

Among the 'fringe' Impressionists Degas and Toulouse-Lautrec have several things in common. They were both aristocrats (though very different in character); they were both always independent (and hence have left no grumbling letters; on the contrary, Degas once said to Ambroise Vollard, when his pictures were already fetching a hundred thousand francs, 'In my time it was not the done thing to become rich'); they were both completely tied to Paris, and they both consorted with dancers and the entertainment industry in general.

The sketch of the content of Degas's work which we essayed above in connection with the Opéra must be complemented by a description of the formal side of it. Every year the colours are endowed with a brighter, more brittle tension; the individual colouring – the spectrum of colour, so to speak, out of which a picture is built up (a great deal of pastel, often grey or brown cardboard as the background, which shines through and grows coarser and coarser) – increasingly acquires the character of a confection, a frilly look, in violet, rose and yellow hues. The picture becomes increasingly shallower – though not the spatial indications, which on the contrary become as steep as cliffs, making you feel giddy; the room no longer has any boundary; it slides away from a piece of wall which is sited eccentrically, though at the only expressive place on the surface of the picture. The figures become correspondingly more uniform and stiffer. It is no longer three girls with quite different gestures and physical sensations, as in the right foreground of the early picture, but the same step, drill – like the raised arms in the middle of the same picture. A similar change can be traced in the work of almost all the great masters of the turn of the century.

Count Henri Toulouse-Lautrec – chivalrous, warm-hearted, sensitive – did not live in the Opéra milieu but in the much freer, more relaxed atmosphere of the cabarets, music halls and brothels. Lautrec and van Gogh: these two will probably remain the great examples of the tragic clash, the tragic personal destruction which the artist's vocation can involve. There is nothing anywhere near so clear-cut in previous periods, even though artists have always been sensitive and threatened with destruction. It is unlikely that the twentieth century will produce anything so typical, in spite of Pollock and Wols. We shall not see another man like Toulouse-Lautrec, the scion of one of the oldest princely families of western Europe, a man who was almost still a hereditary ruler himself, a man whose father had to play a role like that of Ludwig II of Bavaria, only not such a tragic one, almost a clown's role, because there was no princely role for him to play in a mass society. On top of this there was the son's physical deformity: he was a little man with a big body and crippled legs. His life cannot be summarized in a few sentences; it seems like a collection of witty stories, but in fact it was more genuine that most of that otherwise sham fin-de-siècle. His pictures display the grandiose instability of near-genius – not a genius like Rodin, for Lautrec's world is not one created by himself but one in which he lives, to which he adapts himself – without letting one forget that he is the count, the artist; and also without abolishing the distinction between the artist who paints, who reports something and preserves it for posterity, and the artist who dances and earns her bread by appearing on the stage. And he almost makes even the girls from the brothels into artists.

Dancing seen as a profession – the light tripping in the glare of the footlights seen as heavy, tiring work. The stars who let him draw them, who put up with his posters, must either have loved him or have been convinced of his trustworthiness. Compared with the tired, clumsily raised leg of Jane Avril, Degas's dancers seem prettified; compared with Lautrec's *Salon*, Maupassant's *La Maison Tellier* seems roguish. There is no self-reflection in Lautrec; he has a warm level-headed quality.

PLATE P. 164

The poster, previously a job for hacks, was raised by him to the level of art; the few originals that have been preserved are today among the most valuable examples of graphic art in the world. It is impossible to convey the essence of the poster for the Moulin Rouge in words, in the mere statement that it is all surface, that the colours are pure, that it has the quality of a real object. At the same time it is like the outline of a billiard-table; the balls bang against the lines of the edging, from the yellow balls on the left across the behind of La Goulue to the tip of the boneless man's nose, or rather to the massive kick at his nose. But these yellow balls are also lamps; they link up with the yellow lamps in the background. One cannot simply pass over this violent foreshortening; the nearest parallel today would be the intersection of a motorway. Then there is the motionless mass of spectators on each side, and over them the writing, like banners on the balustrade of a balcony. All graphics were originally the other way round, drawn in a mirror; so that suddenly it becomes clear that it is not a rebounding left hand but a right hand lifted to give a firm shove that Valentine holds ready as a reaction. This is the high-water mark of lithography, the whole history of which would fall within the nineteenth century, alongside photography.

With van Gogh and Gauguin the history of art breaks up into the personal, if typical, stories of individual destinies. If it can be said of any of the great artists of the nineteenth century that nothing compelled him to be a painter this is true of van Gogh. (Just as Barlach was not compelled to be a sculptor, but was indeed compelled to express himself; the art of these two men is the result of a compulsion to communicate, not of a concern with form.) Before van Gogh became a painter he was a sort of prophet, an apostle of the poor, a lay St. Francis; in a different century he might perhaps have become a saint. In his own age, and because of his exceptional talent, he became a painter. One can see from the correspondence with his brother Theo (which resembles in this respect the correspondence between Philipp Otto Runge and his brother Daniel) that on Theo's side there was no real perception of his brother's achievement and position in the history of art, but simply a sort of deep-lying presentiment that he was living with one of the elect. This makes the brothers fellow-workers, fellow-sufferers. I have already said that I regard even our own century as capable of producing myths; consequently the expression 'his disciple' seems to me more appropriate for Theo van Gogh than 'his art dealer' or 'his brother'. In the middle of the nineteenth century realism meant for some people renunciation of bourgeois, patriarchal modes of thought, recognition of social tensions, with the self-evident assumption that one must combat poverty, raise the standard of living. To the scientist, realism meant the basis of facts from which one could analyse the surrounding world. To van Gogh, things – chairs, potatoes, boots and sunflowers too – were real in another sense: they were God's brothers. To encounter them did not mean to improve them or to investigate them, or to use their testimony as the basis for some indictment. Nor did it mean assembling unconnected details to produce a shock effect (as does the woven chair in Pietro Magni's *Reader*); it meant seeking access to a life that is whole, sharing in God, in accordance with the saying in the Bible, 'Inasmuch as ye have done it unto one of the least of these my brothers, ye have done it unto me.' That is why the sunflowers – painted by an already sick man in intervals of lucidity completely occupied by work – are for us so inexplicably beautiful. Not only because they are bright, because they have surprising colours, because this and that background structure is employed. Nor because they 'mean' something – van Gogh wanted to make them the background of an artists' club; one can read all this in his own letters.

PLATE P. 173

The sunflower is different from other flowers; it is a unique botanical phenomenon, not an umbel, panicle or cluster but a plate in which the many blossoms are co-ordinate, flowering and forming seeds at the same time. At least since the Mannerist period, perhaps earlier, perhaps even in antiquity, it has been used in literature as an emblem signifying a season of the year, time, and many other things. It appears in a big self-portrait by van Dyck and it overshadows or outshines Runge's *Hülsenbeck Children*. Yet it is as if all the other sunflowers painted down the centuries stood on one side and van Gogh's alone on the other; and as if only the latter were really sunflowers – or, to use the French name with its much wider implications, the *tourne-sol*, the sun-wheel, symbol of the oldest human tradition. Only van Gogh's sunflowers have a religious rather than a merely aesthetic or intellectual quality.

Here it can be said in the strictest sense that if van Gogh had not been the man he was, if he had not lived and painted, the gap could not be filled by any old 'phase in the history of art'. On the contrary his work would not exist. Since it does exist, its influence on posterity has been enormous; not so much on artists who could be influenced by it as in the incalculable depth of the excitement it provoked in the people who learned through van Gogh that religion could be revealed through art even in the nineteenth century. Van Gogh reaches out beyond the artist's studio down to the ground-swell of life.

Paul Gauguin, who played a part in van Gogh's mental collapse at Arles in the winter of 1888, considered himself much the more important figure. Certainly he too was a man of destiny. He was at first a man of the world, a successful banker who one day stopped doing his painting on Sundays and staked his profession, his health, his very life on art. Certainly he too had a prophetic nature which needed a band of followers that 'lay close to his heart'. He transferred the Christianity that he came to know as folklore in Brittany to the totem poles of the South Seas: *Ja Orana Maria.* The whole flight to the South Sea islands is interpreted by Mircea Eliade *(Ewige Bilder und Sinnbilder*, Olten, 1958, p. 10) as a return to the lost paradise in the Old Testament sense. In general, Gauguin is a painter who (like Beckmann later) developed a quite extensive iconology of his own which so far has been investigated only in parts, not as a coherent whole. Hence the present difficulty in estimating how much of this prophetic role of Gauguin's is literary and how much true piety. Or how much sincerity there is in the picture the *Market* (now in Basle). It is supposed to be the market of young girls, who give themselves away according to a strict ritual – a folk equivalent to Toulouse-Lautrec's brothel, but one that can be interpreted either like Flotow's cheerful opera *Martha*, which also presents a maidens' market to the big-city public, or like the frown of Tacitus, who confronts the decadent ladies of Rome with the strictly regulated morality of the German women. When one also sees (and reads in Gauguin's own words) how Egyptian painting of the New Kingdom from the graves of hundred-gated Thebes influenced the arrangement of the women's bodies on the surface of the picture – in the profile position of the head, the knees, the feet – one realizes how this fugitive was pursued by his education even to the South Seas.

PLATE P. 174

Two generations later, when tourism has become the natural thing, it is difficult to estimate how much sentimentality and illusion were already contained in 1890 in the attempt to return to the 'primitive life' and how far Gauguin could have implemented the same decision – to break through the bonds of convention and decadence by means of personal artistic activity – even in Europe itself, like William Morris at Kelmscott or Henry van de Velde at Uccle.

However that may be, the Art Nouveau which in van Gogh is only perceptible in the twisting lines and the arrangement of the surface, in other words only in a field confined to painting, was with Gauguin a genuine, irresistible urge to regeneration through the practice of a craft. This is apparent even in his mode of producing a painting. Gauguin was concerned in the development of *cloisonnisme*, the application of colours to the canvas in patches firmly enclosed by edging lines, which are often blue. This style of painting was called *cloisonnisme* after the outlines of metal wire between which the molten enamel was poured in medieval enamelled plaques. People's vision had already been so radically transformed by Impressionism that it did not strike anyone that these blue borders might have something to do with the shadow cast by a body.

Gauguin also played a leading part in the development of the Art Nouveau colours, the violet, yellowish white, brown, pale blue, carmine which are kept discreet, so to speak, by the priming.

Above all, the urge to make things himself turned Gauguin into a genuine potter. And here one must hesitate before adding: into a genuine sculptor, for the tendency of Art Nouveau was not to replace conventional painting by conventional sculpture but to seek fields where the new artistic expansion could find expression

without encountering academic conventions. Hence the interest in ceramics, furniture and later wood-carving – all fields in which one certainly met respectable master craftsmen trained in a firm tradition, but not colleagues from the École Supérieure des Beaux-Arts. Menzel was still 'the boss', who instructed and trained his wood-carvers. Gauguin was the first to carve and cut the wood himself, and by doing so came to experience quite unparalleled sensations of enjoyment, of naturalness.
The swing to primitivism, the express renunciation of the refinement attainable by conventional craftsmanship and now also by the precision of the machine – there are so many romantic elements in Gauguin, yet on the whole he was the man who introduced a revolution that was inevitable.

SEURAT

Who shut out whom? Did the artists shut out the scientists, so that the latter have since ceased to have any artistic view of the world? Or did the scientists shut out the artists, so that artists have ceased to have any genuine place in a social structure still completely dominated by science and technology? So that they are bound to feel like outcasts, like showmen, clowns, parasites?
This is the situation depicted by Seurat, the purest 'artist' and, as a transmuter of forms, the most significant person in the whole century. His life was too short (he died of an infection at 31) for us to be able to form any notion of him as a man; perhaps he had no private life, although he is said to have given an impression of quiet resolve. It looks as if he was purely a painter; at any rate we know of no ventures into other branches of art and it seems unlikely that he made any. While other men – van Gogh, for instance – were partly something other than 'artists', Seurat seems to have concentrated all his energies on one goal alone – on transmuting and re-creating form; not on saying something fundamental, but on doing it. But he could have done this just as well in architecture; his chosen medium of painting could have been exchanged for another medium.
It is not that his paintings had no content. On the contrary, they were at first on Parisian subjects, rather like those of Manet: river-bank and sea-shore scenes – which change later, however, into coloured asphalt; urban people – who change into chess-board figures. Then, towards the sudden end of his career, come shows, parades, stage scenes, the circus. Nor did he avoid discussion. On the contrary, he conducted a studio conversation in the fullest sense of the phrase; he had a theory that was meant to give painting the precision of a scientific method; though it could only be applied by personal decision, personal discretion and rhythm, and was thus quite unscientific. These were studio conversations in which methods of painting may well have been discussed more often and more exclusively than in any previous Impressionist gatherings. His own method was called *pointillisme*. The last vestiges of the warm, clinging brushstroke were to be eradicated, the brushstroke which had fondled objects, like one of Manet's brush-strokes. What the painter saw and what he painted were to be inexorably divided by a mode of production based on quite firm rules. It was not real painting any more but a process of stippling, of filling the area to be painted (sometimes great walls, six or seven square yards of them!) with dots, and rectangular, round or rhomboid

dots at that; nothing was left to personal inclination, and certainly not to chance, from which artists today await salvation. At that time people were bound to connect and compare this so-called *pointillisme* with the Impressionism that had preceded it, or with the scientific theories about colour then current. Today it looks closer to the lines of which a television picture is composed, to Vasarely's or Riopelle's treatment of data or Günther Uecker's boards full of nails. Seurat's blobs of colour stand on the canvas in the same way as the heads of the nails slant across the board. Any kind of personal handwriting is renounced, the individual element is suppressed and the punched card is created, at any rate in principle. Seurat said in self-defence to his painter friend Angrand: 'You see something poetic in what I have done. But I only apply my method, that's all' (Zahn, p. 5.) Seurat's world of show-business seems to be the same as the world of opera and cabaret we meet in Degas and Lautrec. But no friendship links us (or Seurat) to the artists portrayed; there is no fellowship with them before and after their work; they are seen exclusively 'from in front'. Or again not 'seen' either symmetrically from the front or eccentrically from the back, but seen without perspective (this is the start of the perspectiveless age), simply recorded. On the other hand the figures are given a veritable ground-plan (the shadow of the vaulting clown in the *Circus*) and the stamp of a pictorial script with which one can report on the event itself, its accomplishment in space, and the meaning of this event.

PLATE P. 175

Just as the finest line and the tiniest dot that could be made with the silver-point were outbid by the grain of photographic emulsion – and subsequently the wave-length of the light ray by that of electronic apparatus – so precision manufacture, the accuracy of the machine, was bound to outbid the finest handwork, which after all remainded dependent on the human eye and on the tactile capacity of the five fingers. I remember how a historian of architecture said, on the occasion ot the report on the measurement of Greek temples, that a method of measuremenf involving a possible error of more than three millimetres was useless for Greek temples; heavens alive, if in the case of an electron accelerator (which is much bigger than a Greek temple) our precision engineers allow themselves an error of a thousandth of a millimetre, the electrons would be hurled all over the place! The moment at which the work of the human artist is so completely overtaken by technology in the field of precision is at the same time the moment at which the artist makes his decisive about-turn. He resolves to give up trailing along behind the accuracy and realism obtainable through technology and to proceed instead in the opposite direction, searching for the sort of patterns of life which cannot be grasped analytically, for the symbols by means of which one can point to the reality behind. He decides to look for a language in which one can make oneself understood once again, a language which quite definitely cannot be used for mere reality, mere research, mere recognition, mere progress.

How will the people thus shut out react? For in this genuine secession of the artists it is not only a matter of the artists isolating themselves but also of those from whom they part – scientists as a whole – being excluded from the artists' world. Previously scientists had been convinced that both sides – they themselves and the artists – wanted the same thing, to wit, the description of a world seen in optical perspective. On closer examination it becomes clear that this desire had seldom been uniform; only in the centuries since the Renaissance, and even then more as a result of misunderstanding than of agreement. But if the scientist Du Bois-Reymond already felt excluded by Böcklin, if it filled him with rage that art should look different from the materials for a scientific experiment, how very much more decisively excluded would he have been bound to feel from all subsequent art! Since then scientists have seen art working busily and effectively, but artists refuse to confirm, as they had done since the Renaissance, that scientists are also on the right track. They decline to confirm the artistic – one might almost say the religious – inspiration of science and to be the good conscience, so to speak, of analytical enquiry.

The excluded artists have sought to react by enunciating the principle of *l'art pour l'art;* art wishes to be corroborated only by art, to exist only for itself. In spite of the apparent rightness of this principle, in spite of all the snobs art has since (as ever) produced – what a misunderstanding! Art never wishes to be alone; it wants to create something recognizable, 'to speak with other tongues' which will enable people to understand who belongs to its realm – and art is convinced that everyone belongs to it and has always done so. There have been many centuries in which there was no analytical science, but there has never been a century without this artistic understanding.

The secession of art: the question is whether ordinary people can subsequently find their way along the path taken by the secessionists. Even the Impressionists had been a secessionist movement; but since they remained inside optics, since they still saw the world in perspective, it was possible, for the last time, for mankind as a whole suddenly to turn and adopt the viewpoint of the Impressionists. And – for one last time – the scientists could turn with them; but the standpoint of the Cubists was outside their range.

There had been a transitional period once before – after an age of boldly illusionistic painting – when the object was to convey an act of worship, its architectonic arrangement and its meaning: I refer to the period of early Christian painting. When a Tunisian mosaic (another variety of *pointillisme*!) was intended to depict an early Christian basilica, it was constructed in a style remarkably similar to that of Seurat's *Parade*. The left-hand half was arranged like a basilica; in other words, it had near and far sides, with a row of people below, seen from the back, and the opposite row of people higher up facing them, with burning flames above them. The right-hand half was arranged like an apse, that is, with the manager (the priest) on the podium (the choir), whence the 'act of worship' was projected into the 'space for worship' between the two banks of people opposite each other. This arrangement, which comes out much more clearly in the *Parade*, because a rectangular (basilical) ground-plan can be assumed, is also carried over to the *Circus*, although the circular arena would really require another figure and the right-hand section really ought to be a central path, for in a circus the way in from the stables to the ring lies on a central axis. Here it is turned into a right-hand section, an apsidial form, seen from the side. Starting from the top, we have the band (corresponding to the angel music in the mosaic of an apse vault), the reflection of the

FIG. 15
FIG. 14
FIG. 14
PLATE P. 175

circular ring in a mirror, the curtain (which played such a big part in early Christian ceremonial), the ring-master's colleagues (corresponding to the elders who would sit on the lower benches in an apse), and finally the ring-master himself, corresponding to the officiating priest. The action is projected to the left – the acrobatics, the mise-en-scène. Right in front comes the symbol for roundness; it is a curtain in the clown's hand; in an earlier sketch it seemed still to be a rope, over which he would make the speeding lady rider jump.

The arrangement of the left-hand side shows, instead of a curve, which would correspond to a circus, benches as rigidly straight as those along a race track. This part of the picture can be compared with late Roman reliefs of chariot races. It is amazing that in 1890, when illustrations of late Roman reliefs, such as those on the base of the Theodosius obelisk in Constantinople, were not yet in circulation, the artist Seurat should arrive at the same formal idiom, at a new creation based on a very ancient pattern. If late antiquity at that time was transforming secular rituals into the hierarchical ones to come, it was much the same with Seurat: he sacralized an event in which his contemporaries could see only secular entertainment.

How was it that Seurat arrived at the same graphic arrangement for his stage, his spectators and his actors as was to be found in early Christian painting? Was it a necessary solution, the only one possible if he wished to give more than a perspective view? He could have found other solutions in Japanese graphic art. Was it as necessary in late antiquity as in the late bourgeois period, in 1890, that art should be given a new content? What is the new content? In late antiquity it was the epiphany of the saint, the sharing in grace, hierarchy. What is it in Seurat? It is easier for the time being to reply with a negative: individual personality fades away, to be replaced by facelessness. Between Lautrec and Seurat lies the break between individualism and the mass. With Seurat it is the mass: a sum of patterns, of types, without any personal destinies. It is still the mass with Medardo Rosso: destinies blown together. In Lautrec there is no mass; even the girls from the brothel are individuals. Seurat himself is at any rate the clown who pulls the curtain up and down, a universal clown. Even this is outside anything Lautrec could have felt. Lautrec could never have painted himself as the man who pulled the curtain up and down. And it is also understandable that this self-appointed clown, this universal clown, should escape into the grimace of a Punch-and-Judy figure. No one could bear to see himself as the man who pulls the curtain up and down on the whole world, unless he no longer saw himself as an individual human being but simply as a representative.

So far as the equestrian acrobatics are concerned, there are photographs of Lipizzan stallions jumping with both fore and hind legs outstretched, obviously a pretty difficult feat of dressage, which looks unnatural but is suggestive for the depiction of great speed. Naturally Seurat was familiar, just as Degas was, with Muybridge's snapshots of galloping horses. But he rejected the recorded image, he stuck to the idea. The whip-crack is for its part almost an 'object'; it became the independent symbol of Art Nouveau. The skirt and hair, blown upward, signify joy according to Seurat; they have an upward-pointing lily shape. The same form

Vincent van Gogh, *Sunflowers*. 1888. Oil on canvas. *Height 36 in., width 28 in. Bayerische Staatsgemäldesammlung, Munich.* *Cf. p. 167.*

Paul Gauguin, TA MATETE *(The Market)*. 1892. Oil on canvas. *Height 29 in., width 36 1/2 in. Basle, Kunstmuseum.* *Cf. p. 168.*

Georges Seurat, *The Circus.* 1890/1. Oil on canvas. *Height 6 ft., width 4 ft. 11 in. Paris, Louvre. Cf.* *pp. 170, 171, 177.*

FIG. 14 – *Georges Seurat, The Parade. 1887–1888. Diagrammatic sketch. Cf. p. 171.*

pointing downward would signify grief. In short it is no longer a question of art in the sense of aesthetic beauty but of the communication of news, of information. In the *Circus* numerous very precise facts are conveyed. Seurat is already behaving more like an engineer, or an architect, who would rather give the exact ground-plan and elevation of the building than a picture of it in perspective. Thus these pictures of Seurat's contain the roots of the spatial graphics of the 'Stijlgruppe', the Bauhaus, in the period between 1917 and 1930.

PLATE P. 175

Why does Seurat wish to communicate so much data about the circus? Is the show as such so important to him? For he did not live in the atmosphere of the circus as Lautrec lived in the atmosphere of the dance-halls. Nor for that matter did he live in the atmosphere of the *haute bourgeoisie*, as Manet had. Where did Seurat live? Was he an outsider who had not yet found his place? Lautrec was warm-hearted, honourable, lovable; but he did not change anything; he simply spread warmth. Perhaps Seurat did not change anything either. But he gives very early warning that a change is in progress. He is a reliable seismograph. From the point of view of the history of art Seurat is more important today than Cézanne; there are many art lovers who accept and comprehend the landscapes of Cézanne without any difficulty, but reject Seurat as the first distorting, incomprehensible painter of 'modern art'. But after all Seurat was born much later than Cézanne.
The 'school' of Seurat, Paul Signac and others tried to convert the treatment of data into terms of painting, but they had no information to communicate. Naturally enough; how could anyone else have said clearly what not even Seurat could embrace 'in words'?

Edvard Munch, *Puberty*. 1894. Oil on canvas. *Height 5 ft., width 3 ft. 8 in. Oslo, National Gallery. Cf. pp. 141, 180.*

FIG. 15 – *Mosaic of an early Christian basilica from Tunisia (reversed). Cf. p. 171.*

MUNCH

Munch was twenty-nine when, in 1892, the Berlin Society of Artists broke up on his account. Max Liebermann, who took over the leadership of the secession movement, said: 'Others act as if they could do more than they really can. Munch is a clever man; he does it the other way about'. Munch was forty-five when (in 1908) he had to seek a cure in a Copenhagen sanatorium. Into this period (1892–1908) falls his great achievement as one of the founders of twentieth-century art. In Berlin he lived in a Bohemian circle whose members included the writer August Strindberg, the Polish writer Stanislaw Przybyszewski and the art critic Julius Meier-Graefe. Przybyszewski was married to a young Norwegian girl, 'very slim, with the figure of a Madonna, with a laugh that drove men mad'. Munch himself said: 'I do not understand how my nerves stood up to it. I sat there at the table and could not say a word. Strindberg talked. I thought the whole time: doesn't even her husband notice anything at all? First he will probably go green, and then he will be furious. I painted some pictures of these people, including one that I called *Jealousy*. It is the picture with the green face in the foreground and beside it a man looking at a naked woman. I had travelled to Paris to arrange an exhibition there. Then they arrived and I had to depart with my pictures, for it was the very two that I had painted, him green and her naked. Nothing came of the exhibition in Paris.'

FIG. 16

Munch underestimated the Pole. Przybyszewski was a steadfast Bohemian; he looked at the picture carefully, understood what it was meant to express and remarked: 'That is what it looks like inside the brain of a man who is robbed by another of the woman he has chosen for himself. The wild prehistoric fight for woman has become a cultured, sad, cowardly, stupid, resigned brooding.'

But Munch's colleagues, who in 1894 published the first book on him, saw much more. They saw, ten years before the publications of Sigmund Freud, that in Munch there was at work a force which was something other than the mere gift for line and colour. They saw that they were confronted with 'the creations of a somnambulant consciousness, commonly known as the subconscious'. They saw that 'the subconscious in Munch was far older than the young brain, that it was infinitely more receptive than the brain, that it was the force that made Munch's creations convincing, the reservoir of warm, pulsating life.'

They saw, and we see today too, that in Munch the recognizable heads, figures and landscapes no longer lived together on a sort of artistic stage on which they could talk to each other and meet each other. Rather is the head, green with envy, arranged frontally, like the reflection in a mirror, or like a poster that shouts at us. It is only a head, of an indefinable size. The scene beside it on the canvas does not occur on the same plane; it is an idea, a hallucination. Previously, with the means of the earlier relief-stage, brooding and inner compulsions could not be painted. Munch made it possible. He tore to pieces the previous fabric of art and replaced it with a language of symbols. And his language is not the interrelationship of symbols, but precisely the fissure, the gap between them, the gap permitting a glimpse of a world beyond, which provokes in us unrest, anxiety, sudden recognition.

Munch was an example of the doctrine, later given a scientific basis by Freud, that a sensitive person, a person who has been shocked, suffers from his early childhood experiences. Munch tried to free himself from these impressions by painting them, by drawing 'his situation'. The Munch family was an old, respected middle-class family with a good deal of talent, indeed almost prone to the danger of religious ecstasy. His mother died when he was a child, and again and again he tried to paint a 'dead mother' and the horror of the child left behind. The elder sister died after a long sickness which oppressed the whole family and which praying did little to lighten. Munch painted the *Sick Girl*, first in a middle-class scene in a middle-class room, then simplified to the two heads of the child and the mother: the mother's head bent and in shadow, that of the child erect and illumined, so that the imperceptible transition to transfiguration becomes visible. He painted the *Death Chamber*, with the people left behind standing in it. Previously they were focussed on a common centre, like a family; now, in the presence of death, they break apart, the space between them swells to the front and becomes unbridgeably wide. Anyone who wishes to stay alive must ensure that he finds a way out into the open air.

What Munch has to say about love is equally hallucinatory, subconscious and super-sensitive. A half-grown girl sits naked on the edge of her bed, a giant shadow like a sack beside her; slowly it fills with anxiety and sex (Hodin). A couple stand locked in an embrace, naked; their heads are barely recognizable – just a streaky white mass. They think they are alone and in reality the whole street is watching; or, rather, the street itself is not watching, but it is clear to us standing in front of the picture that this loving embrace, which the two persons regard as their most intimate possession, is in reality taking place with ghastly publicity.

Since these are frontal pictures one might be tempted to put them alongside Toulouse-Lautrec's posters. But when Lautrec paints a poster he is thinking of those strolling past and wants to invite them in. With Munch everything has

FIG. 16 – *Edvard Munch, Jealousy. 1896. Lithograph. Cf. p. 178.*

different origins, which must be enumerated: the street scenes in Oslo, which begin with a public concert and then turn into agoraphobia, with the walls of the houses tilting forward and displaying windows like eyes, while on the other hand the people advance towards us windowless, eyeless. Then the 'shriek', which leaves us wondering whether fear is being experienced or disseminated. One must remember this in order to understand the murderous means used by Munch, even in *Puberty* – the slimy paint, the pillow, body and shadow together forming a kind of propeller. But one should also know that it has been proved that the stimulus which made Munch paint this picture was a graphic drawing by Félicien Rops, *Le plus bel amour de Don Juan*, in which the shadow is still a giant figure of the seducer throwing his cloak around him. It is also not unimportant to point to the cavalier opposite Manet's barmaid. But Munch no longer looks for the guilt in a seducer, in a social class, in an absence of morality, in others. What he paints is a part of his own life. No wonder that this man arrives at the point where he is threatened with collapse himself, where the 'shriek' seeks to force its way out of him yet remains inaudible, where the structure of his lithographs breaks

PLATE P. 176

apart into horizontal, perpendicular and abruptly plunging lines. Once again this break-up, this absence of coherence in the drawing is the symbolic language intended to make us realize that we are surrounded not by a connected world that can be surveyed in perspective, but by uncomprehended and incomprehensible fragments, that it is these very gaps and shadows that give us our only intimation of something basically different and yet to come, something threatening. Munch's sister had collapsed under this burden into illness and insensibility. Munch's nature was strong enough not to give way in the sanatorium, strong enough to emerge from it into the world again. A crisis of another sort might have awaited the outwardly cured painter, namely the drying up of his artistic inspiration now that it was no longer nourished by childhood experiences and overpowering eroticism. However, his artistic genius now showed its strength. He was rich enough in colour and form to create a second and just as amazing body of work. This second half of his artistic career (up to 1944) is much more similar to the achievement of other contemporary masters, men like Matisse and Bonnard. Neither the world nor art as a whole is called in question any longer; on the contrary they are enriched by beautiful, cheering creations. The themes are no longer hallucinations but clear, objectively viewed subjects: man as worker, as a social being, snow-shoveller, mechanic, mason, returning from the factory. Or movement and its pictorial representation – the galloping horse, the running dog. Or the decoration of a festive room with murals: the hall of the university in Oslo, the dining hall of a factory. Landscape too now becomes a section of the earth seen on a large scale, comprehensible in its geological forms. The foothills of the mountains are no longer dusky in the winter night, the night of the soul; instead they lie in bright sunshine. As for the portrait, Munch had a talent for it both before and after his crisis.

As we have said, for powerful, unmistakable achievements Munch is the equal of any artist of our age. Yet his lasting importance will rest not on these works of artistry in the narrower sense but on the circumstances and visions of his first period. At that time it was he who turned to account the Nordic capacity for dreaming; the midnight sun and the eternal snow. In those days, before 1900, he lived on the subconscious; in those days he showed that the world does not come to a stop beyond the limits of consciousness but goes on infinitely further.

ENSOR

James Sidney Ensor's life began two years earlier and ended five years later than that of Munch, who lived to be eighty-one, but Ensor had only one period of genius, between 1880 and 1900. He was artistically burnt out like van Gogh, cut off in his prime like Seurat, but he outlived himself by half a century, ludicrous and very famous.

Ensor too put his own situation into his work, in a very personal way and much more directly than the early Picasso and Rouault, who came next, with their generalized lyrical references to themselves as vagrants. Since his father was an Englishman he was familiar with English romantic painting – Turner, John Martin, Whistler. His father is said to have been physically very strong, to have tried to build up an independent position for himself in America, to have failed

FIG. 17 – *James Ensor, Mirror with skeleton. Pencil drawing.*

and to have returned to Europe. From then on he lived in his wife's establishment in Ostend, in her knick-knack and souvenir shop, which dealt in everything sold to holiday-makers at a seaside resort, everything brought back by sailors from abroad, from buckets and spades and picture postcards to stuffed crocodiles and exotic masks. The father: sitting like a respectable citizen in his armchair. The father: a beggar in front of an iron stove. The father: at a shabby table with a bottle of spirits, wearing a mask; and before him the mother, also with a mask – and a rod. The father: with a fiddle by a stove that is no longer burning, on the floor the husk of a man, with death's head and palette (thus the son's own activity too – frantic painting – is art that wins no bread). The father: as a skeleton in an armchair, looking at a Chinese water-colour scroll. The skeleton (and now we pass right over to Ensor's own plight) pulling a pickled herring from its own teeth. It is usual to point to the implied pun, *l'hareng sour*, *l'art en sort*, *l'art Ensor*, but in so doing one misses the opportunity to reflect on this first self-portrait of Ensor – in the form of the sacrificed beast.

For the series of disguises in which Ensor depicts himself is easily penetrable. All these pictures of the encounter with self, the avoidance of self, arise from the unendurability of being obliged to see his own face, his own situation in the way prescribed by nineteenth-century 'realism' with its sound common sense; or

rather from the perception that the so-called 'real' situation is grotesque, unreal, not to be spoken of.
It is true that Ensor's first self-portraits, painted when he was a young man, are executed in the heavy colours of Belgian painting, a high artistic culture, developed and disseminated by gifted and intensive painters, who created something akin to what was produced by the Munich school and Leibl in Germany, or Fattori in Italy, in other words very good painting but not French Impressionism. The Belgian painters did not change over to painting everything in light and colour; they continued to recognize the existence of darkness and applied their colours with a broad knife on a hard foundation.
Now for Ensor himself: as a beetle, beside other insects; and this is 1888, in other words twenty-five years before Franz Kafka's *Verwandlung (Metamorphosis)*, a story that plays such an important role in the literature of the twentieth century. Then the self-portrait with the woman's hat, thirty years before Marcel Duchamp's *Rose Selavy*. The reflection in the shape of a death's head and the big pictures with death amid masks are no longer versions of the earlier *memento mori* motif of the Middle Ages, nor are they *Death as a Strangler* or *Death as a Friend*, to mention two woodcuts by Alfred Rethel which were famous at the time. Death is no longer the adversary and terminator of life, and in general no longer the naïve and crude notion which the Middle Ages had of death (or, to put it more cautiously, which the Middle Ages may have had according to the usual view). From the medieval Dance of Death and its verses it would be impossible to arrive at Rilke's prayer, 'O God, give every man his own death', just as it would be impossible to proceed from the medieval view of animals (as soulless, as man's possessions) to the horses and riders of Marino Marini. Death is much more intertwined with us, death is much more we ourselves, than earlier centuries, including the nineteenth-century 'establishment', could have imagined. When Ensor sees himself in the mirror in the likeness of a death's head, he is not learning that he will die, but very carefully testing himself to see what proportion of him belongs to the domain of death. When he paints the masks he is testing to find out how much of man is a role, a valid assertion, a persona – or whatever the psychological terms are – just now or always. He recognizes himself in another mask. The task imposed on the artists between historicism and functionalism is that of extending the realm of reality, far beyond the limits of the 'really visible'.

FIG. 17

The self-portrait as Rubens: how clearly this poses the problem of historicism. It lies parallel to the problem of death: how impossible it would be for man to avert his eyes deliberately from death as an aspect of the world. Similarly, how impossible it is for people to avert their eyes deliberately from the past as an aspect of the world. Historicism, in the clothing proper to it, is a nineteenth-century encounter with self, a self-recognition; it was ridiculous to regard it as a style that could be abandoned at will.
Ensor's self-portrait as Ecce Homo. Once again we have to quarrel with the view of 'sound common sense', this time in the guise of a highly intellectual art critic, who says that in the nineteenth century such references to religion, to Christianity, are not genuine. On the contrary: Ensor's demonstrative concern with Christ

and His miracles is much more genuine than the critic's view that the Middle Ages were pious while people like us in the nineteenth and twentieth centuries have lost their centre; as if a Middle Ages, or indeed a humanity in general, that had not 'lost its centre' were conceivable at all.

The herring, the beetle, the woman's hat, the death's head, the Rubens head, the Man of Sorrows are six encounters with self. The banal reaction would be: what eagerness, what inventiveness in the search to escape himself. Not very different from this attitude is the comment: what an amazing breadth of personal life, what a wide examination of self in unexpected contexts. A further slight shift of emphasis brings us to this consideration: the concept of disgust, which has been explored further and further in the twentieth century, in literature up to Sartre, disgust with oneself, the intolerable element in one's nature, occurs here and is endured by a completely isolated young man on his own.

For if we will not accept the truth of the religious factor and of Ensor's encounters with himself, then the *Entrance of Christ into Brussels* and the engraving the *Cathedral* are not true either; and what would then be left as truth? For the artistic touch, the geography of bright colours, the improvisation of this *Entrance of Christ*, which dates from 1888, points beyond anything contemporary into the twentieth century – beyond Impressionism, Post-Impressionism and even Expressionism. Work of this kind does not arise simply out of Flemish folklore and processions.

Ensor's creative force was spent after ten years and although he lived on for a long time after that it was not vouchsafed to him, as it was to Munch, to experience a renewal of his artistic power. He remained in Ostend, became famous, was awarded titles and decorations, and honoured beyond measure on every birthday; a statue was put up already in his lifetime. He became one of the indispensable sights of the town, lived in a room crammed with furniture over the knick-knack shop and played on the harmonium ballet music which he composed himself. Photographs were produced in which ladies in ballroom dresses crowded round him in the poses they knew to have been painted by Ensor thirty years earlier in his mask pictures.

CÉZANNE

Cézanne commands our awe; but that is not all. In an environment that was to turn to objects (Art Nouveau), he is the purest embodiment of a painter. But that is not all either. He contains a world, and therefore signifies and compels a pause. Anyone who has arrived at Cézanne has reached the goal, like someone who has arrived at Goethe.

That by 1900 he was so old, born so long ago, was part and parcel of the phenomenon of Cézanne; he could not be younger. Only now, after so many younger men, did he make an impact, and at once he was clothed with the authority of a classic. He was filled with his destiny, with loneliness, with hatred of his father, with memories of the Arcadia of youth. Kurt Badt has shown this in one of the most attractive books ever written on modern art. The myth only arose when Cézanne came to paint; so long as he only wrote letters it was a depressing, petty-bourgeois business. The themes indicated by Kurt Badt are convincing precisely

Paul Cézanne, *Mountains in Provence*. 1878–1880. Oil on canvas. *Height 21 1/2 in., width 29 in. Cardiff, National Museum of Wales, Gwendoline Davis Bequest.*

Pablo Picasso, *Les Demoiselles d'Avignon.* 1907. Oil on canvas. *Height 8 ft. 1½ in., width 7 ft. 9 in. New York, Museum of Modern Art. Cf.* *pp. 190, 191, 193.*

because they remained subconscious. Cézanne carried these depths about with him, but his attention was not concentrated on them at all. Just think with what joy later artists experiment with their psychological depths, enriching them with what they have read and making them predictable, with the result that these depths cease to be subconscious. Just think, too, with what concentrated intensity Cézanne worked at the problems of his painting, at the *réalisation*, and try to imagine what explosive force would have been released if Cézanne had made himself aware that here lay one of the great possibilities of the art of the future. Nothing of the sort is to be seen; indeed nothing of the sort was possible with this shy being, in whom the power of the subconscious rests on the very fact that it is kept repressed by his own conscious mind.

For he is a great traditionalist. What is art? Painting, pictures. To him the idea of an anti-art is inconceivable. Inconceivable, too, the idea of a Musée imaginaire in which the production of easel pictures is only one aspect of the Art of the World, and one confined to a few centuries. Where does one learn to paint? In the Louvre, of course, in Cézanne's view. The large number of copies which he made of old masters (in other words, recently dead modern masters, beginning with Leonardo and Giorgione) is not to be explained by the suggestion that Cézanne was shy of working from living models, that he used sculpture as nature.

What are the subjects of his pictures? The human figure, the portrait, still life, landscapes. The human face grows emptier and emptier because it is only occasionally that friends of some character sit for him; he is confined to people he encounters by chance – the gardener, Marie Fiques. At the same time the content becomes tremendous when he paints himself in a series of self-portraits, like Rembrandt. The still lifes are also thematically limited. They are not *natures mortes*, loaded with symbols, nor are they costly delicacies of the sort which the Dutch artists of the seventeenth century had painted. Nor again are there any complicated reflections on glasses, as there are in Manet's work. On the contrary, Cézanne paints chests of drawers, solidly made by craftsmen, table-cloths as thick as layers of cement, and a great many apples.

He gains identification with nature from landscape, as is perfectly possible for him. His subjects are quite limited in number. It is certainly not the helplessness of advancing age but the need to return that takes him back again and again to the same 'motif'. (Turner could not have achieved this kind of limitation. He puts his world together out of many different stimuli, which were not in fact 'motifs').

Then there is his intricate way of painting a picture, with everything done uniformly all at once. It could be compared with the way in which a tree grows green as the year advances: buds on all the branches at the same time, and then in regular succession, but always all at once, leaves, blossoms, fruit. This is quite different from the way in which Leibl painted; Leibl had such a precise plan of the picture in his head that he could begin with a hand or an eye and completely finish this detail before going on further. For Cézanne the canvas was first of all a transparent web, in which the growing work had to be stretched everywhere at the same time and kept in equilibrium. Hence his comparison with spheres,

cones and cylinders. One could say of a spider's web that it was like a large number of trapeziums; the spider's web too can only come into existence all at once as a whole. The remark about spheres, cones and cylinders was not made by a painter aiming at the reproduction of three dimensions; consequently they were not meant to remain three-dimensional bodies. What was meant was the way in which they sank into the surface of the picture. One needs to throw a handful of wooden spheres, cones and cylinders on to a sheet of water and see what curious outlines they form. What Cézanne meant and what he painted was what cuts the surface of the water. This surface tension could only be condensed into a 'picture' very slowly and patiently; even the spaces in between had to be kept fluid as long as possible before everything hardened into the surface which was the *réalisation*. Attention was directed simultaneously to this surface in front and to the Montagne Ste-Victoire in the background. However, one did not come to know the mountains through the picture, but through the mountains what a picture was.
Does the 'motif' occur in different lights? Or even in different impressions, as with Monet? Is it not the case, as with the earliest surviving photograph (by Niepce, 1826), that the exposure lasts so long that all kinds of light occur in it, shadows both of the morning and of the evening? A distribution of shadow confined to one part of the day would imply a sort of theatrical view, and with it a special kind of object; the web-like structure of the picture would be destroyed. If the 'motif' is supposed to have been seen from several sides, then it must have received light from several sides.
This process of solidification was first perfected in the 'seventies, in the *Maison du pendu* and the *Railway Cutting near Arles*. Only in retrospect, after the picture is built up and the paint laid on with the knife, does one realize that one has also learned something about the cutting, that one has learned to see it as a parting between two banks of the earth, that one has learned something about the railway, something quite different from the information conveyed by the confident Monet's clouds of smoke.
It would in fact have been incomprehensible if Cézanne had lingered any longer with the Impressionists than for a brief accidental period. And how lonely he must have felt when the Impressionists had their great triumph, which he could only regard as a fleeting success.

Women Bathing: this is an attempt, like Rodin's, to depict a whole world: the unhistorical, in other words contemporary, presence of all painting. But Cézanne here came into conflict with himself; what was missing was the 'identification' with the motif, the French connection with the female world. The father's world in Cézanne has been revealed by Kurt Badt; but has Cézanne any direct connection with the 'mothers'?

Women Bathing does not possess the foreground area, that is, the finished part – for much the same reason that the Festival Hall in London does not possess the foreground area. It is impossible to 'make' something complete before it has 'grown' complete. Can Cézanne be described as an experimentalist? No, because he does not experiment. He produces one picture after the other, tirelessly, never fully satisfied, but not probing at random. The words 'tireless' and 'laborious' are always recurring in his own testimony.

CUBISM

Other events in Paris form parts of a consecutive series – they represent the intensive life of a school of painting in which what happens next always develops out of what has gone before – but Cubism is a different sort of artistic event; it could not have been planned in advance, it was not foreseeable and even retrospectively it cannot be classified as a development that was obvious. Cubism did not have to come. It is an accomplishment of pure genius, unthinkable without Picasso and Braque, the two artists who created it.

It is not sufficient to measure Cubism against the events which preceded it, against Cézanne, for example, and his utterance about spheres, cones and cylinders. Or against the discoveries of modern physics, chronological thinking and conquest of the fourth dimension, which appear again in a hazy form in Cubism. This attitude is always connected with the wish that the artist should have 'seen it in advance', that he should turn out to be more progressive than progress itself.

Likewise, it is only partially correct to call Cubism an art which has done, in an overpowering way, what art always must do: bring men into the proximity of the sacred. This is quite an old idea, and at the same time a very modern one, for it is employed by the ethnology and search for symbols which have succeeded 'Functionalism'. The artist who discovers a new form does not do it for the sake of 'the unknown'. This expression comes from Willy Baumeister, and as with all such sayings one must be clear what one means by it. The unknown cannot just be what one did not know before; otherwise the artist would come too close to the research scientist, whose task it is to explain the unknown in nature. It cannot be simply a question of the artist moving from one room into the next. Rather must the search for the unknown be preceded by the artist's perception that what has gone before is not in fact already familiar. Repetition of the known is very much one of the artist's tasks, in the same sort of sense that it is one of the mother's tasks to give every new child the already familiar maternal love, or the priest's task to offer anew every day the familiar sacrifice of the Mass. If we were to reject the known simply because it is familiar, we should be acting like the inquisitive or bored person; it would be confusing art with change. The decisive factor is rather the artist's perception that the already known is at this particular moment no longer exerting any healing effect. It may well still be quite sound and will one day radiate its beneficent influence anew; but now, at this particular moment, it is ineffective. And what the artist seeks is not the unknown as such but whatever can heal, whatever moves people again and has a form which provides a meeting-point.

Meeting-point: another important word. The new form is not created for itself alone; it must lend itself to communication, people must be able to gather round it. As for healing, I do not think that this can be explained any further. It is certainly not a question of something that will 'work', as it is with an industrial problem. It is more a vista perceived; salvation seems to be something transcendent, as opposed to the finite perfection of what has gone before. A work of art is something that shatters perfection. Not salvation itself, but the path to it, is opened up again. If salvation were promised directly, it would be religion, revelation; and art is neither of these. The compactness of artistic form is never salvation itself. But art keeps the road open. The artist believes that healing exists and he acts accordingly, even though he might declare himself sharply anti-religious and refuse to allow his art to be yoked to the service of an already revealed religion.

It is not sufficient to examine only those ideas about Cubism which were discussed by the Paris school of painters. These ideas lead to Fauvism and to Matisse, but not to Picasso and Cubism.

Picasso's previous path was by no means a dead end; on the contrary. The pictures of his blue-and-pink period link up with the preceding period. His *Woman Ironing* presupposes the ironing women of Degas, but no longer buxom enough to yawn; emaciated, laden, with thin, angular limbs and joints, a foretaste of Bernard Buffet. His families of circus artists were a continuation of Lautrec, Seurat, even Watteau. The child is sad, the artist sad, and then again unexpectedly athletic, opposite the Lolita-like girl on the ball. The ape is the personification of sadness because it is on exhibition, has to be funny. The woman is either emaciated too or decking herself out for the ball, while the husband has to stay at home. On top of this there were the swift abbreviations, the economical shades, the delicate etchings. In fact Picasso had reached the point of being launched. Ambroise Vollard wanted to put him under contract. But to Picasso himself the period had suddenly come to seem empty; it no longer contained any connection with past and future; he could not have prolonged it.

Matisse was able to stick steadily to his work; early Fauvism too had already piled up mountains of colour and given colours an existence in their own right as things; he could develop all this further. But Picasso had to get away from himself, from elegies on the artist's life. He had also to 'objectify' himself; he had to express himself in a much harder, less sentimental way, less blue-and-pink. The pink period had been a withdrawal, so far as forms were concerned, into a soft classicism, with the faces tender and graceful and the arms raised, so that the armpit was disclosed. Beside the beautiful woman another was placed, clothed but not innocent, not reproachful, but simply to hold the mirror. Then came the shock, the sudden change in approach: once again two women were painted, but fat, sack-like, hard, in the style of Spanish Romanesque frescoes. Traces of these two women are still to be seen in the two middle figures of *Les Demoiselles d'Avignon*.

PLATE P. 186

Away from sweetness: a test of courage. For with his previous pictures Picasso had been on the road to success. The lonely, impoverished Spaniard did what is so difficult in the twentieth century: he changed a style which he had invented and people had recognized. Away from sentimentality – of course, this did not yet mean 'to ugliness'; there was no anti-art in the change, no Dada. It was the impulse towards reality. It is true that Picasso still painted himself looking sad in the self-portrait of this period, but it is no longer a sentimental sadness; it is a hard sadness, reflecting the firmness of a character now mature enough to meet the demands that were to be made upon it in the future.

Picasso wanted to paint a universal picture. Fauvism had attempted the same enterprise. Matisse's *Bonheur de vivre* was the transference of the eternal theme of Arcadia to the present day; the lines were like Art Nouveau, the colours were new, but not incomprehensible to eyes used to Impressionism and Post-Impressionism.

Carefully Picasso prepared a big canvas. He wanted to demonstrate that he could handle an 'eternally valid' subject. He took up again the subject of the brothel (the title *Les Demoiselles d'Avignon* came from a Barcelona street called Avignon Lane which contained a brothel), which Toulouse-Lautrec had already mastered, treating it more calmly and less sentimentally than he would have done in the 'blue period'. The theme of death: in the sketch the death's head played its part. The theme of good and evil, in the sense of the medieval moralities. The still life, inset in Manet's way: the longer Picasso worked, the more involved with the waning moon his symbolism became. Above all, the theme of the judgement of Paris. As we have said, Lautrec had already transposed it into the present far more objectively in his salon pictures; in comparison Picasso's attempt was almost a relapse into the nude figures of classicism. But naturally the brothel theme always hung together with the choice, the presentation, of the female body. The seaman as Paris disguised in front of the three goddesses – all this is well known. The curtain motif, a very old one, recently used again by Seurat. The large-bodied forms: the colours are still pink and blue, as if the picture were a continuation of Picasso's early period, but there was a hard layer over everything and the outlines were sharp and clear, so that the forms fitted in smoothly beside each other.

PLATE P. 186

A coat of a new kind of azure was to be laid over the whole picture. This had been done hundreds of times before, but instead of the solidification which Cézanne had attained by going over his work in this way the result was something like a new kind of plaster for a wall, with coarse brush-strokes beside each other, and scratches. Before this last layer could be applied to the whole picture the brush-strokes began to come to life. What had happened? Picasso had found his way to a quite different 'language', to a different script.

Up to now, all that has been asserted about this different language is that it shows a kinship with Negro sculpture. It is not suggested, of course, that the new forms came from Negro sculpture, but that Picasso, in the search for a possible language of his own, hit upon forms which had already been developed as a result of similar impulses, which confirmed his own feeling. His new forms were to be flat and yet modelled. To Europeans the remarkable thing about Negro sculpture, which they had never seen before, was the contrast and interplay between plastic form and the tattooing of the surface. The former was eminently plastic, the latter was spread all over this plastic surface. One thinks one has the tattooing on a Yoruba head flat before one, but in reality it bends round to the back of the head. But is the opposite possible too? Should one be able to accept tattooings that seem to bend round like a screw yet are on a flat plane? The result would be a flat plane that creaks from sundering while in reality it is held braced. For certain graphic patterns make the human eye whirl. (The same effect could be achieved with colour; this was later investigated by Hölzel and Itten and their school. Today Pop and Op art is flirting with it).

But the fateful encounter with Negro art was only one of the events of this year. It was a question of finding not only a new form (or even a new fashion) but a new writing, the test of which had to be whether it became comprehensible. The invention of writing, of vehicles of information, is very ancient, ever necessary and always blossoming out. In Picasso, the Spaniard in Paris, there rose to the surface not only the memory of an Avignon Lane in Barcelona, not only the memory of Iberian sculpture and Romanesque Catalan frescoes; there rose a new thrust of ornament in the sense of writing – the greatest new discovery of ornament that the twentieth century has so far experienced.

Ornament: in this very year the Viennese architect Adolf Loos equated 'ornament' with 'crime'. He said: 'Ornament is squandered labour and therefore squandered health. This was always so. But today it also means squandered material, and both together mean squandered capital.' In other words, he regarded ornament as decoration, as something external, instead of as the heart of all art. What short-sightedness, conditioned by the period in which he lived! In the same year, 1907, the American architect Louis Sullivan built the National Farmers' Bank in Owatonna – an intensive example of the ceaseless reflection on ornament that was part of his creative activity. This ornamentation of Sullivan's belongs alongside the examples of Cubism proper created by Picasso and Braque after the *Demoiselles d'Avignon*; one must simply be in a position not to overestimate the superficial details of a different dialect.

In other words, in the twentieth century, too, the necessity arose – and found the right artists and forms – to create a 'script' through which men could make themselves understood. A picture should say something, it should inform, not just be beautiful. To convey information one needs a script. We are accustomed to recognize certain black lines as letters, to combine them into words, and finally, looking at these words, to form the mental picture they are meant to evoke Thus:

<table>
<tr><td></td><td>Hair</td><td></td><td>Hair</td><td></td></tr>
<tr><td></td><td></td><td>Brow</td><td></td><td></td></tr>
<tr><td></td><td>Eyes</td><td></td><td>Eyes</td><td></td></tr>
<tr><td>Ear</td><td></td><td>Nose</td><td></td><td>Ear</td></tr>
<tr><td></td><td>Cheek</td><td></td><td>Cheek</td><td></td></tr>
<tr><td></td><td></td><td>Mouth</td><td></td><td></td></tr>
<tr><td></td><td></td><td>Chin</td><td></td><td></td></tr>
</table>

– this is an arrangement that means something to us because we understand that these signs are meant to convey a face, even when we can see no art or beauty in them. The optical picture of a face seen in perspective would put everything in a certain visual angle; it would certainly convey more of what is seen, but it would give less stimulus to our own inner vision. Now let us not forget that our

neighbours employ other symbols – *œil*, *Auge*, for example – for the same pieces of information. Or just say the individual word twenty times in succession slowly, aloud; note how it degenerates into a meaningless noise and no longer evokes the mental picture. This will make it clear that the necessity is ever arising to find a language, a script, a vehicle of information that is valid, hard and resistant.
The hardness of the previous surface of the *Demoiselles d'Avignon* was still not sufficient; a different kind of hardness had to be sought. Now came the surprise that Negro art employed something of the same sort to convey information, expressed itself in this way and had thereby discovered other artistic combinations. One simply had to get rid of the idea that artistic forms could only cohere through being in correct perspective. The connection between them can be quite different; not only through immediate juxtaposition on the canvas – a curve beside a straight line, a network beside a lenticulation – but also through the interweaving of ideas, so that the connection lies in the symbolism.
Picasso set about going over the whole picture, indeed painting it afresh. The separate hieroglyphs for nose, eyes and mouth on the right now become movable components if they are no longer kept in one particular place by optical accuracy – and this allegedly 'right' place had in fact turned out to be arbitrary. The upper head looks like an assumed mask – and why not? Negro art too consisted partly of masks. The lower head is even more radically altered. A possessive female attitude becomes a dubious male attitude. The head twists out, glides into a hand like a shovel, becomes its own image of doubt, a self-portrait. And the process which Picasso later had to repeat on innumerable occasions – the fact that, alongside the beauty of the models, alongside the goddesses, one is incapable of remaining a 'self', that one feels changed into an old man, a bull, an ape – here occurs for the first time. The eyes can no longer remain beside each other, the mouth cannot keep its position.
At this point the picture came to a halt. The artist lost heart at the idea of having to go over everything again. The picture's original state, which had been almost a unity, almost beautiful, has not been preserved, nor is its new state a unity. The artist was overcome by restlessness; Kahnweiler and other friends were brought to see the picture; finally it was put away, and that was how it was found later, the lava of an eruption, the document that illustrated the origin of Cubism. Of course, Braque was involved too. He had developed independently, with no blue-and-pink period; his early painting had been influenced rather by Fauvism. But now he worked for years, in close collaboration with Picasso, to develop and master Cubism. It is difficult to conceive what temporary isolation this enterprise was bound to lead to, this enterprise of acquiring something which to anyone else was bound to look incomprehensible, although the purpose behind it was to find a new means of communication. Since neither of the two was a wanton or deliberate rebel – scarcely ever has such a profound transformation been accomplished by such thoughtful, reserved men – the work was concentrated on a small number of fronts. Not on colour; this was reduced to a quite small spectrum of shades from grey to yellow. Not on subjects; the ambitious universal theme of the *Demoiselles d'Avignon* was not tackled again; the selection of themes employed

PLATE P. 186

was quite small – the nude, the still life, the portrait, the musician, hardly ever landscape. There were no boldly unbalanced designs; on the contrary they were quite simple, centralized ones, classical formulas – nothing eccentric of the sort introduced by Degas and Gauguin. Quite tranquil scenes; no temporal elements. Musical instruments, but no acoustic sounds or notes. Only one thing was attempted and really achieved: the interweaving of the visual symbols connected with the subjects – mandoline, head, jug, table, chair – with the symbols of the surrounding space; stuffing the shadows under the surfaces like ballast under railway lines.

Surrounding space: this was first of all simpler, more objective than the metaphysicians of modern painting depict it, as if a third or fourth dimension were included. The frame was part of the 'thing'. So long as a painting was comparable with a theatrical stage, a proscenium or frame could be arranged round it. The frame round *Plato's Symposium* by Feuerbach is a good example. But if the picture ceased to be a peep-show, yet nevertheless was to become more of a thing, the change had to affect the erstwhile frame as well. Picture symbol and frame symbol had to be similar to each other. If the Futurists said, 'The noise of the street invades the house', one could say by extension, 'The frame invades the picture.' Of this too there were important earlier examples. In Mannerism and its love of ornament there are all kinds of convolutions. Not only the picture itself in the middle; not only the charter with bent-up or tattered edges; not only the metalwork or the stone boss; but on the intellectual side, writing that could be read, and on the physical side figures holding coats of arms, cherubs, musicians, standard-bearers. Completely different worlds, yet combined to form a unified work. It had already been like this in Roman painting, which we know best from Pompeii. It had had its day in Spain as well, and so had Mannerism. If one can see Iberian sculpture and Romanesque painting come to life again in Picasso, the language of Mannerist ornament does not lie much further back and can likewise experience a spontaneous, intuitive resurrection.

PLATE P. 136

In comparison with examples of Mannerism, Cubist pictures suddenly lose the provocative look they might have so long as they were put alongside only the so-called 'real' picture of the nineteenth century. They become simpler, more comprehensible, more inward, indeed we dare say: more beautiful than the restless creations of the sixteenth century.

The way in which the real creators of this art, Picasso and Braque, remained in the background, while the noisy exploiters, from Metzinger to Gris, pushed themselves into the foreground, with printed recipes for the production of Cubism, is one of the most interesting chapters in the story of twentieth-century art. But these people were much rather successors of Cézanne; primitive pieces of sickly sweetness made their appearance. No one else could really master Cubism or really express himself in it.

After the interweaving had been on the whole successfully achieved the individual surface could be coloured again. A return to colour became possible, and also a return to greater differentiation of detail; when isolated it can become more objective. It can acquire patterns, indeed it can even contain patterns before

George Braque, *Girl Playing the Mandoline*. Oil on canvas. *Height 29 in., width 24 in. London, Mr. Roland Penrose's Collection.*

ASTRA
CONSTRUCTION
AGIC

Gino Severini, *Dynamic Hieroglyph of the Bal Tabarin.* 1912. Oil on canvas. *Height 5 ft. 4 in., width 5 ft. 6 in. New York, Museum of Modern Art.*

Pag. 196. Robert Delaunay, The *Eiffel Tower,* 1909. Oil on canvas. *Height 18 1/2 in., width 15 in. Paris, Sonia Delaunay Collection.*

Pag. 197. Umberto Boccioni, *Movement in Space.* 1913. Bronze. *Height 44 1/2 in., Milan, Galleria d'Arte Moderna.*

they are laid on. About the same time architectural draughtsmen developed the spray process, while graphic artists developed filter printing and other methods of distributing colour. Wall-papers are employed which already bear definite colours and patterns printed on them. Even earlier, letters, bits of words and pieces of newspaper had been stuck on. The so-called *collage* came into existence. If it did not attain the multiplicity of layers of Mannerism, it did immediately become a method. The impermissible turned into the fascinating, the seductive. The method had to be thought out and investigated; it was the beginning of the experimental phase of modern art.

The *collage* also embraces the mutation, the metamorphosis, to which Picasso has devoted considerable periods of his later life. However, it will be impossible to devote individual chapters to all the techniques which now become possible, just as it is also impossible to find a place in this book for every artist active in the twentieth century. Many techniques became legitimate once the whole conception of art has been opened up in this direction, once the basic assumption of classicism (and of the Academy) had been abandoned, the assumption that artistic reality is something different from the reality of nature; once Leonardo's thesis had been abandoned, the thesis that it was the task of art to produce a recognizable rendering of nature in all its visible continuity, and that the highest rank was held by that art which had to achieve the biggest and most sophisticated transposition, namely, painting.

But the great variety of these techniques and the features common to all of them can best be discussed in the context of Futurism, which threw up a large number of important, pressing, unavoidable questions, with less constraint and greater logic than the French, even if it also achieved fewer valid solutions.

FUTURISM

Around 1910 the whole of Europe was in a ferment. The 'marriage' between science and art had been dissolved. For four hundred years both partners had been convinced that what lay before their eyes was also reality; science investigated it and art depicted it. They were also convinced that there was a clear dividing line between reality and art. Nothing really 'real' could be incorporated in a work of art; all reality had to be transposed into art's ideal model of representation. For four hundred years both partners, science and art, had relied on the presence of the other and on its holding the same beliefs. Now all the presuppositions were changed. The scientist ceased to investigate by attentive observation with his two eyes. As soon as he began to use microscopes and telescopes the artist's naked eye could no longer follow him. Quite different aspects of nature were discovered – chemical, mathematical, indescribable, almost inconceivable interrelationships. How could painters have 'represented' a chemical formula of whose importance they had learned? On the other side artists had discovered the 'thing'; they had broken through the taboo dividing art from reality. Whereas according to the classicists ornament and handicraft had only followed the ideal world of high art at a carefully prescribed distance, they now moved into the centre of the stage. Art was no longer what hung on the walls of museums but the house, clothing, chair, handle with which one lived. The thing itself was art, not its representation, not its arrangement in an artistic space. Conversely, art itself was to become like a thing that one could use in daily life, not just on Sunday mornings.

The work of art was no longer isolated, either in an ideal space or within a single branch of art. No more painting without a traversable space, to which it referred; no more space without time in which to tarry; no more tarrying without noise which arose at the same time. The total work of art, which the nineteenth century had visualized as an orchestration of individual genres complete in themselves, became something simultaneous that was already all-in-one in conception, in imagination. *The Noise of the Street Penetrates into the House*, the title of a famous futuristic picture by Umberto Boccioni, would surely have been inconceivable as the theme of a picture to Hegel or Wagner.

Both partners of the modern period, now ending, emerged from their fixed positions, from the perspective mode of thought which had presupposed an intensive but motionless 'I'. The twentieth-century scientist no longer stood still while he carried out his investigations; he realized that he himself changed. It was the same with the artist. But, as in a marriage, only the partner was reproached when the change became obvious. And so we find, not once but repeatedly, that scientists and technologists demand of artists that they should have clung locally to the old abode, to the old conception of reality, the old perspective mode of depiction, which they themselves, the scientists, had long ago abandoned. They do not see that the old house could now contain only a puppet, not a partner.

How cool and collected the two Cubists Picasso and Braque were during the decisive years, how little they allowed themselves to be diverted from their chosen path by the loud challenges issued, becomes clear when one reads the Futurist manifesto with which, in 1909, the Italian diplomat and writer Tommaso Marinetti summoned lyric poets, and later, in 1911, painters, to fresh deeds: 'We want to sing of the love of danger, of courage and boldness and rebellion; we hold the view that no work that is not aggressive can be called important; we are already at the very head of the century and we shall be the vanguard; space and time are already dead, we are already in a different condition; we want to glorify war and militarism, the only hygiene for the whole world, patriotism, the gesture of the liberator, the beautiful idea for which one dies, and contempt for women. We want to destroy the museums, the libraries, the academies; we want to fight against moralism and feminism, against opportunism and utilitarianism. . .' And then follows the famous sentence: 'There is a completely new kind of beauty, the beauty of speed, and a racing car is more beautiful than the *Victory of Samothrace*.'

It was the first time that lyric poets rather than dramatists or novelists felt that they were the real revolutionaries. In 1910 Marinetti was joined by a group of painters: Umberto Boccioni, Giacomo Balla, Luigi Russolo, Carlo Carrà, Gino Severini, with just as rabid a manifesto, which at the very moment when it was read out was already toppling over into the opposite of what was intended. This was part of the Futurists' programme; they were experts in the art of creating a productive hullabaloo, as their caricatures show. They hired the biggest theatres

in the biggest cities and by means of well-directed publicity succeeded in attracting thousands to their performances, during which poetry was read, pictures were painted and music was tested out, and at which after a short time indescribable uproar reigned.
Perhaps the forms taken by Futurism were somewhat noisy, perhaps their solutions to the problems they raised tended to short-circuit them, perhaps the engineers who had built the racing cars were somewhat in advance of the artists who found them beautiful, perhaps nationalism led to the First World War, perhaps the dream that Futurism would be the art of the new Fascist Italy was only of short duration and was shattered by the return to the imported forms of communication and the grandiose classicism of all dictatorships; nevertheless the impulses behind it were legitimate. For example, the Futurists said 'speed' and devoted themselves to motoring; they studied the serial photographs of men walking, horses jumping, girls dancing, which had been produced since the 'eighties and transposed this kind of picture into a *pointillisme* painted with hard spots of paint. But the unintentional result was a graphic web that can only be understood as a picture of movement by derivation; it looks more like an abstract picture (Balla). Or they depicted the study of eddies, formed of currents of air, the lines of rapid movement and called the result *dinamismo*; this too was stimulated by photographs of the eddies of air caused by flying bullets.
Even with the Futurists, movement was at first noted in other things, while the painter himself stood still. But later they painted the motion in which one is oneself involved; the fixed point is the outside world past which one is carried. For example, they paint the inside of a cab, or of an underground railway carriage; the stations flash past outside, indicated by scraps of the inscriptions on them, and the rattling motion inside is also depicted. Thus the world is experienced from the interior of a vehicle, a car, a tank; it is the basic experience of modern transport. It signifies the relativization of one's own standpoint – a presupposition of all present-day thinking.
In his picture of dancers Severini followed Cézanne much more closely than the Cubists did. He split up the surface of a picture into individual areas with pure colours. He produced a mosaic, a piece of inlaid work, so to speak. This approach was still based on the presupposition that the whole area of the picture was something seen; that what was not seen was not present. The Cubists would not accept this; they wanted to reach realities that lay behind the surfaces seen by the eye. The Mannerists had produced these secondary layers by means of intellectual sequences with the most various levels of content. The Cubists wanted to attain this interweaving through means of depiction alone; they did not wish to employ either different subjects or other times or speeds. Through this concentration they reached purer solutions.
But it must be recognized that the attempts of the Futurists to paint simultaneous pictures throw more light than Cubism does on an important point of departure of the twentieth century, namely the realization that we ourselves change, that we ourselves shift, are shifted, are driven. Looking at a Cubist picture, one might think that the painter regarded himself as a fixed point; in front of a Futurist

picture one would not think that. In Braque's picture a mandoline can be recognized, but it makes no sound. 'The noise of the street' does not penetrate into the Cubist studio.

The word 'Futurism', however fleeting any future may be, is a temporal concept and as such nearer to the aims of the Futurists than the word 'Cubism' is to those of the Cubists. Really the task was to make time depictable – a burning task which artists had to face. The expression 'simultaneous' – the most important word after 'futuristic' and 'dynamic' – meant above all 'happening at the same time'. Later, the logical conclusion was to be drawn that chance, the momentary occurrence, the 'happening', was the real moment of art. What the visual impression had been in the context of the optical approach, chance is in the context of time.

It was the impulse from outside that led to Italian Futurism, not the constantly fluid attitude to form of a stable school. That is also why it was a poet who wrote its programme. In a sense the phrase 'Futurist manifesto' – both words in it – is the perfect example of the Utopias and calls to action which have proliferated since 1910. In contrast to the solid progress of the nineteenth century, which seemed to produce concrete results, we now have shouts that become shriller and shriller – and at the same time a growing scepticism whether every further step, every won or lost war, every new 'ism' really does bring the future, social equality, the new art any nearer. Everything always remains somewhere ahead.

People are beginning to realize that art and happiness simply do not lie ahead at all, to be attained after a period of time, but in us, over us, outside time and future. To that extent the Futurist manifesto, which refers even in its name to some kind of future, is the most obvious, most daring piece of Utopianism that there could possibly be.

Alongside Futurism, and in a sense in opposition to it, there arose suddenly Giorgio de Chirico's *pittura metafisica*. It grew in the same environment, among the Italians in Paris, but from a totally different nineteenth-century root. The comfortless instruction at the technical high school where Chirico was trying to learn his profession (he too was originally an architect, like Ernst Ludwig Kirchner) gave rise to the ideal reconstruction of Roman forums and acropolises. These views which the pupils were required to produce were almost identical with the empty spaces which Chirico made out of them, apart of course from the addition of loneliness and melancholia. Historicism paired with Roman greatness produces fear. The peopling of these spacious squares with symbolic figures, with a lofty tower (the 'Mole Antonelliana' in Turin, 550 feet high), with a child playing with a hoop or with a monument that cast a shadow, was the next development, after Chirico had seen what had come into existence under his hands. Then came the dolls with bandaged heads, the empty sheaths and rulers, the factories in picture frames. After that came the sophisticated elongation of the perspective, the soundlessness, the abolition of time, which is indicated on the clock towers but does not move on. All this was a counter-blow to the noise and speed of Futurism, but so closely related to it that Carrà and Severini found no difficulty in henceforth expressing themselves through *pittura metafisica* instead of Futurism.

EXPRES-
SIONISM

PLATE P. 207

After Art Nouveau's thorough exploitation of joy in the object came horror at the macabre aspect of the object, at the aquarium-like nature of the whole world. Kokoschka's *Still Life with Dead Sheep* is an arbitrary construct; it has no such thing as a 'motif' – certainly not the white mouse, a laboratory mouse. So the whole thing is a laboratory table, a dissecting-table, on which Lautréamont was so keen. It is anti-Cézanne: against the round-cheeked apples. And it is anti-Cubist: against the neutralization of the objects depicted, which are only allowed to be there as layers of the picture and are not themselves a mandoline, say, or a harlequin. Anti-Marc: against the assertion that in the animal kingdom all is harmonious. Consider the tortoise and the mouse: they are like members of the *Wandervögel* movement or the animals in the tale *Die Bremer Stadtmusikanten.* Then there is the newt, for which a glass tank has to be specially added; it is amazing how simply one can apply blue and then say 'that signifies glass'. The tomato – anything but an apple of love. The worn-out earthen pitcher, the exotic hyacinth, the snake, the snail. All backed by the flayed lamb. Perhaps this lamb and the impression it makes, its accusing look, its complaint, its (formerly Christian) humility were the starting-point of the whole picture. It is as if the tortoise had eaten into the lamb, like a rat; it is not just in front of the lamb. The remaining areas of the picture are simply painted over; they have no content and nothing further to say. Or are there outlines of mountains on the left and plants on the right, nearer the foreground? Is the scattered, discarded collection of objects to be regarded as a kind of landscape painting, as is sometimes the case with Delacroix's still lifes?

The whole thing is done expressly in colours, and as the colours are scratched off here and there, lines incised, and the cracks round the lamb possibly allowed for in advance, the whole picture can be described as 'flayed'. A certain nakedness is laid bare; perhaps for many people it reaches the pitch of pain and joy. Surrealism did not yet exist.

Young Kokoschka grew up in Vienna. He was twelve years younger than Hugo von Hofmannsthal; however, he was not 'precocious and tender and sad' but possessed by a searing fury to express himself. *Murder, Hope of Women* had already been written, drawn and performed, though it is true that Paul Hindemith's music was needed to give the shrieks a duration that made this one-act play really performable.

It is difficult to understand retrospectively what fascination can be exerted by young men whose talents are only just developing. 'Speaking with tongues', the 'yeah, yeah' of the Beatles does in fact lend strength. The twentieth century is full of such groups. The most natural of them was that of the 'birds of passage', the *Wandervögel,* but it hardly had anything to do with art. Artistic people had to stir themselves, as in the 'Brücke' movement in Dresden. This group's programme was quite inarticulate: 'We count as belonging to us everyone who reproduces directly and without falsification whatever it is that urges him to create.' Their pictures had something of the holiday afternoon about them. How different were the groupings in Paris, which were all connected with the studios, with the milieu of the 'Parisian school'. So strong was Paris that the very term 'Expressionism' is a variation on 'Impressionism', which did in fact come from France, which must have seemed to the young to have only just appeared, and which had to be resisted like the Academy, authority and historicism. On the other hand, the growth of the Munich Blaue Reiter, which is usually counted as part of German Expressionism, was quite different. The very name Blaue Reiter (Blue Rider) is not expressive, and the group was led not by youthful enthusiasm but by the superior intelligence of Kandinsky, who was no longer a young man; nor was Jawlensky. In addition there were the comparatively tranquil, if youthful, temperaments of Marc and Macke.

The 'content' of Expressionism came from the individualists, from Nolde, Barlach, Beckmann, Kokoschka; they developed the ideas of van Gogh, Munch and Ensor. The other typical work of Kokoschka's reproduced here, *Die Windsbraut* (the *Tempest*), was first exhibited in 1914. It was immediately described by Wilhelm Hausenstein as the most important picture in the exhibition (that of the Munich Secession); at that time it was still called *Das grosse Boot* (the *Big Boat*). The title *Windsbraut* (lit. *Bride of the Wind*) can be given to the picture because of the bridal element, not because of the wind. Anyone who has noticed the jetty in the top right-hand corner knows that the picture is one of a long series of statements about dreams and water. Klinger's *Glove*, Hodler's *Boat*, Max Ernst's element of water in the *Semaine de bonté* are among its nearest relatives, as also are the reclining couple at the foot of Bartholomé's sepulchral monument in the Père Lachaise cemetery in Paris, or the youthful reclining couple of Rodin – naturally Rodin, who made it possible to represent hovering and drifting. But it is also a self-portrait; it is an existential picture, comparable with Dürer's *Melancholy* and Rubens's *Late Self-Portrait with Hélène Fourment*. It is a work of absolute genius; full of genius in the painting, in the loneliness, in the experience of love which it reflects – and what a woman it was that Kokoschka was able to paint.

PLATE P. 208

Alma Mahler, daughter of the Viennese landscape-painter Schindler, lived and loved her way through four branches of art. She was first married to Gustav Mahler, the only one of her husbands who was older than she was, almost twenty years older, and the only one for whose art she had any creative capacity of her own; with the others she must have concentrated her indescribable intensity on just being there. She must have lived the content of twentieth-century art, namely the direct collision, or rather the identity of spirit and sexuality. Oskar Kokoschka lived with her for four years; the *Windsbraut* signified the dénouement. It is impossible to estimate what flashed from one human being to another during these four years. Then she married Walter Gropius and helped to found the Bauhaus, for example by bringing Johannes Itten to Gropius. Finally, after music, painting and architecture, she married the writer Franz Werfel, her man-child, as she herself described him. How easy it is to shrug one's shoulders over her book, *My Life*; but what a woman!

PLATE P. 208

The boat or the shell or the wave in which the lovers drift is still closed at head and foot, as though it kept out the raging waters. But amidships the water is already swirling in and they are already sinking: an age-old symbol, or rather

FIG. 18 – *Wassili Kandinsky, Preliminary sketch for an etching, 1916.*

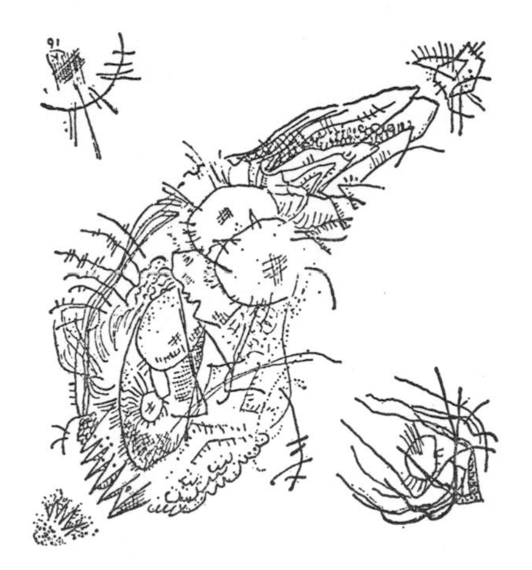

the daily experience of people who feel themselves drifting. The woman's sleep is deep and trusting, yet what tension, what watchfulness, what concentration is apparent in the compressed features. The man lies unsleeping with torn breast, hands worn out by work, like those of Dürer. How deeply significant it is that he has these introspective hands, almost in the middle of the whole picture, where the woman has shimmering arms. But he is no longer touching her. The inescapable loneliness, the knowledge of the demonic element; it is a very definite self-portrait, in a definite situation, more accurate than most self-portraits painted with the help of mirrors. The Romans said *fert unda nec regitur*; but they were referring to a straightforward destiny which one really ought to control, not this watery mass.

There is yet another element in the picture: landscape. After objects and people, landscape is Kokoschka's third domain. And undulating landscape at that; this is to be found even in the *Windsbraut*, though the troughs have been brought close and made to look huge. Kokoschka must really have studied the landscapes of Rubens, for his results are similar: the collaboration, the coincidence of clearly given topography, enhanced to signify the surface of the earth, the experience of history. An event in the landscape, indicated not so much through human figures, as with Rubens, but through atmosphere, changes of light – and sometimes also through boats, bridges, houses which man has characteristically inserted in the landscape. They are modern panoramic landscapes; one can order a landscape of a definite district from him (people do this) and not be disappointed. But these landscapes only developed later. In the *Windsbraut* the landscape is still a spiritual state.

KANDINSKY

Just as we assert on the one hand that 'objective' art can have a spiritual as well as an illustrative content – thereby disagreeing with those twentieth-century artists who wish that one always had to paint abstractly – so we also disagree with those who wish to permit only objective painting. In both styles one must above all have something to say: 'One human being speaks to another through something

FIG. 19 – *Oskar Kokoschka, Portrait of Herwarth Walden. Pen and ink drawing. Cf. p. 212.*

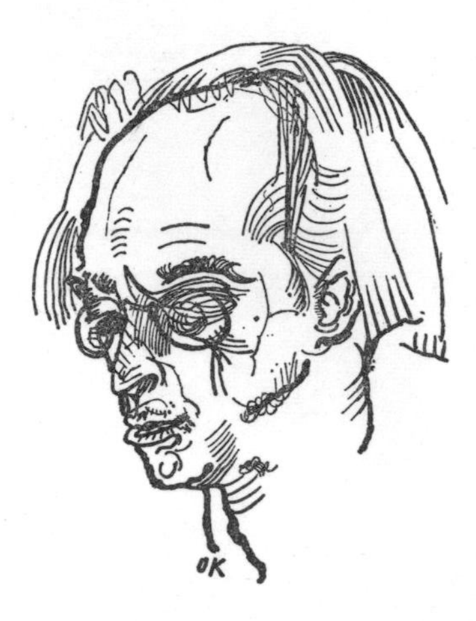

superhuman – the language of art' (Kandinsky, writing in the programme of the New Artists' Association, Munich, 1910). Mere objects do not produce any art, nor do mere colours and lines, however beautiful and evocative they may be. One must have something to say, something 'spiritual', and that is the other vocable that Kandinsky employed.

The conception of non-objective painting goes back a long way, at least as far back as the Romantic period, and at the beginning of this century many artists – Strindberg, van de Velde, Schmitthals, Ciurlionis, Hölzel, Kupka – were on the brink of it; nevertheless it was one individual, Kandinsky, who really achieved the transition. Looking back, one is tempted to say that it could have been no one else.

Kandinsky came from a well-to-do middle-class Russian family; he was a lawyer, a scholar, an ethnologist and at the beginning of a university career. At the age of thirty he decided to decline an appointment at the university of Dorpat and went instead as a painter to Munich. He lived in Germany from 1896 to 1933; even if we do not count the years from 1914 to 1921, when he was back in Russia, his stay in Germany lasted for thirty years. Of all the artists associated with the Bauhaus, he stuck it out the longest, from Weimar via Dessau to Berlin, from Gropius via Hannes Meyer to Mies van der Rohe. But in 1933 he was forced to retire to France.

Everywhere where he was recognized he was also the leader. First because he was older and more mature and had seen more of the world, second because he was more intelligent and thoughtful, and third because he was chivalrous. When a 'Phalanx' was founded in Munich in 1901, Kandinsky was the president; when a 'Neue Künstlervereinigung' ('New Artists' Association') was started in Munich in 1909, he was again the president. If there was a *Blauer Reiter (Blue Rider)*, Kandinsky could perfectly well have said, 'I am the Blue Rider' for both words were full of his imagination and his chivalry. There could have been neither a 'Grüner Reiter' nor a 'Blauer Wanderer'. It is a combination of words that is

Oskar Kokoschka, *Still Life with Dead Sheep*. 1908. Oil on canvas. *Height 35 in., width 45 1/2 in. Vienna Dr. Reichel's Collection.* *Cf. p. 203.*

Oskar Kokoschka, *Die Windsbraut (The Tempest)*. 1914. Oil on canvas. *Height 6 ft., width 7 ft. 4 in. Basle, Kunstmuseum. Cf. pp. 150, 204.*

Pag. 209. Wassily Kandinsky, *Unnamed Improvisation*. 1914. Oil on canvas. *Height 50 in., width 29 in. Munich, Städtische Galerie, Gabriele Münter Stiftung. Cf. p. 211.*

Piet Mondrian, *Composition*, 1921. Oil on canvas. *Height 1 ft. 8 in., width 1 ft. 6 1/2 in. Basle, Kunstmuseum. Cf. p. 213.*

striking and untranslatable, like Dada and Bauhaus, Fauvism and Tachisme. And in any case there was no so-called artists' association. There was the editorial board of an almanac, which was called the 'Blaue Reiter'. The editors were Kandinsky and Franz Marc, and they decided who should be accepted as a contributor.

From Russia he always retained piety (recollections of cathedrals and icons), nobility (lofty castles; even cannons do not signify war but boldness) and an intelligent knowledge of folklore (costumes, bridal crowns, good fairy and witch, bird of paradise, butterfly, flowering meadow). It is said that he came to know fairy-tales in the German language from his grandfather's time. His early paintings are composed in deep colours like pages from a picture book, and the signs of what was to come are already quite clear. The subjects, for example storm-clouds, are carried out in graphic forms which look like prints. For every subject – clouds, hair, flowers, clothes – there is a different graphic form, a special stamp. Colour and graphic stamp are developed separately. He does not draw with colour nor does he squeeze the paint from the tube or apply it with a knife.

The subjects: lighting emerging from the clouds, rays emerging from the sun, dryads emerging from trees, fairies from meadows, tired women sitting by hedges – and these forms, which up to 1916 are drawn in full over and over again, subsequently remain hidden in Kandinsky's so-called non-representational symbols as certainly as male-and-female are concealed in Mondrian's horizontal-vertical patterns. The fact is that this generation of artists was born in a world of objects – Kandinsky was 44 when he painted his first 'non-objective' picture – and they could no more stop understanding the significance of objects than Mondrian could stop understanding Dutch or Kandinsky Russian, even if they later used other languages. It was only the next generation of artists that no longer had any objects and no longer understood what could be expressed with them. It didn't understand Russian either.

The connection between Russian onion domes and Bavarian onion domes is evident; so is the link between the foothills of the Alps and masses of colour and cloud. Since that is so, one cannot imagine that the transition would have been possible in any other landscape. The colours, the forms, the stamps, the transcendental, 'spiritual' element in art become so strong that previous subjects become invisible. But this is the point: they become invisible; it is not a question of their no longer being there. The transition was quite slow and logical; it was spread out over four years and more. It is only retrospection that makes it look like a 'sudden' illumination or decision. Any of Kandinsky's 'improvisations' can be translated back almost stroke by stroke intro representational terms; an apocalypse, for example, with the four winds in the corners, the cartographical border round the world as in medieval maps, the mountains of the world and monsters on the diagonals. Alongside it a drawing with signs that can still be named: jagged teeth which could be rays, dots like flowers, lines like rain, circles like suns, bars like prohibitions. Opposite this I have placed a drawing of Kokoschka's, to show how in the same year the same dots, lines, curls, bars recur, clearly distinguishable in a drawing which as a whole fulfils the function of a

PLATE P. 209

FIG. 19 'portrait' (that of Herwarth Walden). Kokoschka never felt the urge to work non-objectively.

Kandinsky always retained these added representational indications. But in the fifty-year-old painter's early phase everything is still possible, everything is contained; in every work birth occurs afresh, the whole cosmos. In many-sidedness these works are ahead of those of all his successors; in them one could trace the programmes of all that was later split up into the characteristic styles of each individual painter.

Naturally when in 1921 Kandinsky returned from Russia and from the Russian revolution (which ceased to employ revolutionary art and went over to having revolutionary politics preached in the most traditional – and hence comprehensible – forms possible), when he went to the Bauhaus, he created stricter forms, ones more akin to the basic mathematical shapes, not indeed spheres, cones and cylinders but the circle, the triangle, the square, the dot and the line, in other words strictly two-dimensional forms, not solids. But these figures were so imaginatively varied, merged with such bright colours into the space around them, that the result was a completely new phase.

And there is yet another change in the last decade, in Paris, when the symbols become more arid, the additional elements clearer, the interpretative element more objective; when the positive half of the picture is balanced by a negative half, or when (in pictures with titles like *Everyone for himself*) the spiritual entities, each in its own chessboard field, look like the figurines of Schlemmer, the *mâles* of Marcel Duchamp.

One can imagine that to Kandinsky himself each form hung together with the other, not only formally but in a spiritual language as real and as incomprehensible to strangers as the language of dolphins. It is almost certainly impossible for a new language to become completely comprehensible within the space of a few years, for the process requires not only that a creative spirit should discover an ingenious system of conveying information but also that an adequate number of people should become accustomed to this new language. This was hindered on the one hand again and again by political upheavals; the effect of the opposition of Bolshevism, Fascism and National Socialism to modern art should not be underestimated. It was also hindered on the other hand by the vast number of abstract painters who now appeared upon the scene, each of them imbued with the desire to speak an idiom of his own and to express his own individuality. The result was that people became used to the linguistic chaos of abstract art, not to one single learnable language. It was a generation of artists in whose work abstract forms moved away even from the abstract, in the literal sense of the word; hence the attempts to discover new words, concrete or formless or – what? No universally accepted word has yet been found. It was a phase in which the promise of the early days, namely that the new manner would be universally comprehensible and universally employed, was not fulfilled as quickly as expected. Will there be a third generation? I will not assert that the promised kingdom of the abstract will never come to pass, but it will not come so quickly, and not now in this century. But at any rate since Kandinsky, since those years 1910–1914, abstract painting exists. And it had to be Kandinsky and no one else who invented it, not a group of wild innovators, of angry young men. On the contrary, the man who acted thus was also a thoughtful man, who did not recognize chance and had no time for trances or unconscious painting. This fifty-year-old painter was the furthest advanced; the transition was slow and irrevocable. 'The spiritual in art': many of the arguments in his book have turned out to be untenable, but not this central assertion that it is 'the spiritual' that brings art into being.

MONDRIAN

If Mondrian had not existed it would have been necessary to invent him. In other words, somewhere or other the extreme in abstraction, in the mathematical approach, had to be tried; it was needed like a lighthouse on the last cliff, to show people in which direction they were sailing – assuming, that is, that one wants to have fine art within the limits of the visible and not beyond all frontiers in the no-longer-present, in the 'liberated nothing' of a man like Malevitch. Mondrian is this extreme point.

Only the flat surface is allowed. The inadequacy of traditional languages, which can no longer contain our thinking, brings the consequence that Mondrian's expression *Nieuwe beelding* is not very clear. He translated it himself into French as *Néo-plasticisme*, because in many languages *plastique* or plastics is a general term for any artificial material. However, one has to be a bit careful about using the word 'plastic' in connection with Mondrian, for it has sculptural connotations and Mondrian expressed himself with extreme consistence only as a painter, on a flat surface. Even this he did only because he believed that in this way he was expressing the 'constant equilibrium', after the restoration of which everything in the world, not only art, would attain a new harmony.

PLATE P. 210

Only the horizontal and vertical are now admitted. Naturally they are much more than mere mathematics. The fundamental divisions of life are contained in them – male as against female, land as against sea, rest as against growth, and other ideas as well. These ideas have not been read into the painting retrospectively; it was from them that Mondrian's forms and demands arose; he thought them through. He was born in 1872, and it was not for nothing that he belonged to the Symbolist generation and studied anthroposophy.

Only the three primary colours, red, yellow and blue, are admitted, plus black and white as non-colours. This extreme in simplicity, as we have said, must be definable; it must be distinguishable from all the other possibilities of art, from representational art, the massing of space, *tachisme* and so on. It must be possible to formulate it as an axiom (a doctrine). But here instead of a doctrine we have Mondrian, a human being with a character of his own. He has 'made himself available'. It is a fundamental, almost deliberate error on the part of opponents of modern art to assume that 'making oneself available' means complete devotion, inability to do anything else. According to this view, a Gothic person must have always moved in a pointed way because the Gothic script and Gothic shoes are pointed. Similarly, Mondrian, it is assumed, could only draw straight lines with a ruler. But Mondrian's handwriting is known: it is a soft hand, rounded in the Dutch style. His physical appearance is known: he was a slender, sensitive, silent man. Thus different styles in the same man, then? How could just one of them, his artistic style, be described as 'his style'?

It would be much more appropriate to equate it with self-sacrifice, with the sensitivity of a seismograph, with a spiritual flair for the unknown. It is certainly an artistic act of will, with all the consequences, all the dangerous moments, which an excessive exertion of the will is wont to produce in the human personality. There was the break with his closest friends ('because in Mondrian's view Theo van Doesburg had forsaken the principles of Neo-Plasticism by using the sloping line in his works, Mondrian would no longer work with him' – Seuphor, p. 149), the frequently displayed aversion for trees ('I remember how once, dining in Albert Gleizes' house, he asked if he might change his seat so that he did not have to see the trees of the Bois de Boulogne. Later, after 1934, this scene seems to have been repeated with Kandinsky at Neuilly and with Arp at Meudon' – Seuphor, p. 74) – but how wrongly this anecdote would be interpreted were it not known that Mondrian devoted years decisive for his development to the study of trees.

Mondrian is the product of an extreme purification. He is an example of the profoundly comprehensible, necessary urge of the artist living now to assume responsibility himself for what he does, not to embark on expressing himself with ideas, images, feelings whose scope he cannot check, and therefore to concentrate on those utterances and forms which he can determine himself and thus answer for himself. This means more and more complete exclusion of the environment, greater and greater concentration on form. *L'art pour l'art* did not mean, however, as was imputed, that artists did not wish to hear any more criticism, but that they themselves were their sternest, strictest critics, and consequently denied themselves easy access to, and facile employment of, non-artistic (non-formal) elements. This purism is one of the strongest currents running through the period from historicism to functionalism.

If one tries to look at it the other way round, as if it were will-power alone that had made 'Mondriaan' (the earlier, Dutch way of writing the name) into the real Mondrian, one gets nowhere at all. It is quite obvious that Mondrian did not become one of the fixed stars of modern painting just because he was an inflexible character. It was just as certainly not because he was a mathematician. It was because he was a great artist, and more sensitive than his contemporaries even in his 'pre-Mondrian' period.

And now, how can this man's doctrine exert any influence? The Utopia of *stijl* and neo-plasticism is over and done with: it was no more than a personal inspiration. Can we not see very clearly in the case of Mondrian that he was only able to become the Mondrian of neo-plasticism because he had previously been the Mondrian of the Belgian Academy, of the Fauves, of the school of van Gogh? That he was only able to abstract because he had something to abstract from, namely his exceptional training in the forms of representational painting?

And alongside Mondrian must be placed, for the same reasons, Kurt Schwitters – likewise a friend of Theo van Doesburg, likewise a member of the 'Abstraction-Création' group, which had previously been called 'Cercle et Carré'. But Schwitters drew the opposite conclusion from contemporary existence: he was not a purist, but an eclectic.

MARCEL DUCHAMP

The sculptor Raymond Duchamp-Villon, one of the three Duchamp brothers, has remained famous for his *Horse*. An earlier version could still be interpreted as very late Impressionism: horse and rider jumping over a fence. In the final version the ankle joint has been replaced by a crankshaft and a bumper, and speed (which in Umberto Boccioni's work was frozen as a passive swirl of air) is represented by an active blast from rocket-jets. This work is unique; it is the moment at which art moves over from the recognizable figure of a horse (by means of which artists had depicted power and speed for three thousand years) to the symbols 'h.p.', the basis on which the power of modern machinery is calculated. This changeover could not be pursued by the sculptor, for his life and work were cut short by the First World War. However, the idea was taken up by the younger brother, Marcel Duchamp, who out of this moment of universal significance forged a substantial and coherent achievement.
Chess was always being played in the Duchamp family. The pictures painted by the young men, who had at first portrayed these games as family scenes in conventional perspective, changed into pictures in which the chess-board once again became the canopy of heaven, a 'world scene', with staggered levels, with the struggle between the white and black principles. The pieces were no longer moved to and fro with the hands but with the head, by thinking. King and Queen found themselves encircled by 'swift acts' – and these were no longer acts of presence of mind but at the same time floating 'acts' in the double meaning of this word, floating nudes. The great artist returned later to the ever-present mental and symbolic world of chess.
There now came into play two factors to which only a Frenchman could be receptive. First, spiral staircase pictures, which came from a long western tradition and more recently straight from Degas; and, second, the vast and still largely unexplored domain of sexuality.
The figure of a *Melancholy Young Man Shaken about in a Railway Train* could still be understood as a continuation of Futurism, or as a self-portrait; at that time Marcel Duchamp was travelling to and fro between the capitals of Europe. But the melancholy young man turned into the *Nude Descending a Staircase*, the picture that formed the centre-piece of the 'Armory Show' in New York in 1913 and from which (or at any rate from this exhibition) modern American art sprang. As a result, Duchamp migrated to America, where he became an American in the same sense that Picasso has become a Frenchman.

PLATE P. 219

Superficially the picture has something in common with Cubism: it is painted in a few very delicate colours, almost entirely shades of yellow.
The staircase signifies art as movement, as link between above and below, as an irradiating force; Degas had already produced, in his spiral staircase, what was possible in this direction in the still firm context of perspective vision, of sober ballet training. In many respects Duchamp's design is more classical, because it is less broken up than the slender thighs, the light frilly skirts that glide past the

window in Degas's picture. With Duchamp the staircase is not something winding and descending, but a stationary pattern.

Another comparison will help to make clear what happened between Degas and Duchamp. What began to exert an influence was Leonardo's magnificent anatomical drawings, without which many features of the twentieth century would be inexplicable. An unsurpassable draughtsman and researcher had made visible the interrelationships of the various parts of the human body: its physical structure, the bone structure, the musculature, the details of comparative anatomy and the circulation of the blood (but not the nerve mechanism or the chemistry of the body). His drawings had accurately explained the complicated three-dimensional body, proceeding from point to line, from line to surface, from cross-section to three-dimensional representation (once again, just up to this boundary, not up to the new train of thought of the twentieth century, according to which a three-dimensional body must be preserved in just the same way in a fourth dimension, but cannot explain it, in the same way as the two-dimensional surface can be understood as a cross-section of a three-dimensional body without entirely explaining it). Instead of visible shapes Leonardo had drawn thin abstractions of layers of muscles; these abstractions indicated, like wires, the starting-points and directions of movement – the pull of a muscle, the streaming of the blood to the heart. A similar conversion of what is seen into what is happening – and in particular the transition from girl to woman – now became for a number of years one of Duchamp's principles of thought and representation: he invents all kinds of ingenious pumping, distilling, contact, injection, sloping, spreading and flooding processes, and tries to make them clear to himself and others. Not, it is true, like Leonardo in firm alliance with science (or, as it would have to be in the twentieth century, with bio-chemistry and an intellectualized technology), but along a path of his own in a way that makes one feel dizzy, underpinning and bracing himself from one idea to the next. He does all this with an artistic virtuosity no less amazing that that of Leonardo; in fact actually with beauty, if also with the hopeless isolation of present-day man. It is not the artist who has renounced the alliance with science and technology. Duchamp would not have been afraid of any hard work to make himself familiar with science if there had been any sense in the enterprise, if there had been any prospect of agreement. But science no longer expresses itself in pictures, indeed not even in words, but only in numbers, isolated letters, signs and hermetic symbols.

PLATE P. 219

Already in the *Nude Descending a Staircase* the forms are not just visual images but also cross-sections, directions of movement, contact-plugs. This is completely the case in the following works, which Duchamp finally gathered together in a total work of art, the *Large Glass*, in which with the aid of grinding-mill, lubricating machine, capillary separation and spray-work the group of 'Bachelors' (chess figures as similar to each other as clothes-pegs) attains the just as complicated and prepared stratification of the 'Bride'. Now everything is in the literal sense a giant micro-section, a pointer to the fourth dimension, an attenuation between two sheets of glass, a protest against the assertion that painting must start from a flat surface – as if the flat surface existed in itself, as if it was anything but convention. Dust settles over the scratches on the surface: a 'dust-dial' instead of a sun-dial. That the panes of glass were cracked in the course of transport could be seen as a 'happening'.

But already innumerable combinations have come into existence. Switches are made with lightning rapidity between language and painting, between painting and the construction of machines, between the machine and physiology. The craftsman, the producer is being replaced by the thinker who controls an automatic process. At a definite spot the 'ready-made' work of art comes into existence – and the phrase itself is a primer of this sort. What is found contains the process of finding.

When a bird-cage holds not the bird, but sugar, as if it were a sugar box – not sugar, but imprisoned cubes of marble, no, imitation ice cubes; when a thermometer is already included, to measure the temperature – but already the shock could make us shiver, we could sneeze: this is the key-word of this chain of combinations, *Why Not Sneeze?*, the title of this particular 'ready-made'. Or, more simply, a clothes-hook is taken from the wall and screwed to the floor; really this is only a move from one wall of the room to another, but previously it was a clothes-hook, now it is a 'man-trap'. Or the upper part of a clothes-stand is hung on the ceiling. Previously the object was supposed to carry hats; now it is one of the first mobiles. Selection, the fixing of an unexpected time, the altered context turn the object of daily use into the ready-made work of art.

Criticism of one's own attitude, of one's own activity, is taken so far that the shift over into 'anti-art' is unavoidable. Anti-art (the word was taken up at once by the Dada movement) always has reference to art; it is not outside the humanity that has to express itself in forms and symbols. But it is outside the framework of previous values, outside the works of art previously put together individually by artistically trained hands. In precision the machine has overhauled the individual craftsman; and the number of objects it can produce is far beyond what the individual can manufacture. If art is to go on existing it must be sought in other realms, in the realm of creativity – the term was discovered at that time and was just as compelling, in other words just as inevitable, as anti-art. Paint by hand? 'He sees the whole of Paris as a picture-factory debasing painters into hired labourers' (Paul Wember). The ceaseless activity of a man like Picasso would seem to Marcel Duchamp like ceaseless repetition.

It is logical, at any rate in the context of his own way of thinking, that Duchamp should replace painting by playing chess, that is, replace the solution of artistic problems by solutions or endless variations of prescribed rules. Just as Picasso is the prisoner of his painting, so Duchamp is the prisoner of his attempts to find solutions. Having to abide by the rules makes it possible for him to go on living.

DADA

Twentieth-century art has created two new words superior to all the wretched -isms, words that a child can lisp, words than can be enunciated in all languages: one is Dada, the other is Bauhaus.

In Zurich in 1917 the Dadaists produced the only genuine anti-art of the twentieth century. They were the only ones who could do it with a good conscience, with an

FIG. 20 – *Kurt Schwitters, Merz drawing from Merz* NO. *1, January 1923.*

unassailable conviction of their own rightness. Their position as émigrés was unequivocal; they had all fallen out, each in his own way, from the marching columns of their countries, the revolutions, the First World War. They lived on an island and realized that previous formulas of salvation had brought only destruction.

They were not nearly so well informed about themselves as artists and that was precisely why their consciences were so clear. They thought that art consisted only of what they called bourgeois academicism. Their self-confidence would have been somewhat less overweening if they could have realized how many revolutionaries had already preceded them in the field of art during the course of the nineteenth century; and still less overweening if they had realized that they

Marcel Duchamp, *Nude Descending a Staircase*, No. 2, 1912. Oil on canvas. *Height 4 ft. 11 in., width 3 ft. Philadelphia, Museum of Art. Cf. pp. 215, 216.*

Max Ernst, *Le Juif au pôle nord*. About 1934. Oil on canvas. *Height 21 in., width 26 in. Zurich, Kunsthaus.*

themselves, so far as art was concerned, were not paupers, but more like the snobbish sons of parents of proved wealth, which the sons regarded in the moment of rebellion as quite inexhaustible, as something simply to be taken for granted. It was not a revolt of the poor and hungry, but of the overfed.
They may have thought that they could do away with the archaeologists, burn the museums and put history out of action, but all the same they possessed a noticeable desire for life. A real 'anti' attitude would be bound to deny life itself; whereas in reality they had an exceptionally strong will to live. Their cynicism was an aggressive, positive attitude, not only to life but also much more directly to the spiritual factor which Kandinsky had described as the essence of art.
The unconditional urge to 'do something', the cabaret-like élan, the made-in-a-moment attitude, the theatrical exhibitionism – only once in this century did all this occur with such idealistic enthusiasm. The Futurism that had preceded it was no so influential, and all the later repetitions of it were second-hand, more laboured, shriller.
There was an eminently literary element in the Dada movement and it is difficult to know whether to introduce its members rather as poets than as artists: Hans Arp with the cloud-pump, Kurt Schwitters with the 'Ursonate' and Anna Blume, and Hugo Ball with the 'Lautgedicht', not to mention Tristan Tzara and Richard Hülsenbeck.
The application of literature and fine art to printed graphics was a splendid achievement of the Dadaists: the break-up of the traditional line, the change in type, in thickness, in direction; the new arrangement of previous fragments; the possibilities for advertising – again something essentially akin to cabaret.
There is a quite legitimate connection between Dada and photography, an almost surprisingly slight one, though it is much greater than in the case of the other groups of artists – Brücke, Blauer Reiter, Orphism, Fauvism, Futurism, Cubism – which did not accept any connection at all with photography. Did the 'Sturm' produce any photographic exhibitions? The Dada movement's members included Man Ray, Hans Richter (with the further step into films), Hannah Höch – and this means almost straightaway again Rayogramm, montage, in other words exaggerated, artificially enriched photography, not the simple tatters of reality out of which Schwitters built up his 'Merzbilder'.

FIG. 20

It is true that the *collage* was not invented by the Dadaists, but it was only with them that it acquired its true significance. Previously, in Cubism, it had been a piece of artistic preciosity, a useful patch of colour, part of an ensemble intended as a whole to be art. But now it came into the hands of Kurt Schwitters, the collector, who takes it on himself to decide what is important and what is not. Gold is not to be regarded as valuable just because other people pay a lot for it; art is not valuable just because elsewhere great collections of it are made. To collect the things oneself is what counts – to collect something that has been thrown away, something that one has found, something with a memory attached to it, to incorporate it in a work, guess its possible significance in the new context, and even instinctively feel this when the object is still a tram ticket or a match-box. On top of this basic attitude, which is possible in any age, there was the special factor of the first inflation. For the first time in this century daily needs could not be met; string, corks, paper, all the ugly detritus of reality acquired a value – the refuse of inflation was much more valuable in those days than the glossiest goods of today's mail-order houses.

A bit of wire, a bit of print. In other words, the problem of life: what hangs together and lives, what threatens to fall apart and to be dead? The tendency towards a centre of life – a principle as enigmatic as the building activities of termites, as the flight of a flock of birds. Why does the branch not break so long as it is 'alive'? And why does it break when it is no longer alive? The Dada artist is like the rainmaker in N.R. Nash's play: he brings things to life. It is true that he can make himself objectionable by not keeping the rule that things must be thrown away.

The aim in any case is to produce a shock effect, the flash of lightning that has always made recognition possible in a dream. This recognition occurs at the edges, in the torn parts, indeed in the very operation of tearing. Hence the doctrine of the later *Life* photographers, with their technique of illuminating life. And hence the logic of the tearing, an (allegedly) as unfailing means of producing the shock. Chance as an element in art. The chance occurrence. The mutation, the metamorphosis. The express determination to avoid looking for anything, so that chance can play its part. Keeping oneself open – this determination now becomes a sort of experiment. (What corresponds to Dada in the nineteenth century? Does chance exist already in any concealed form? 'I walked in the wood wherever I fancied, and my intention was not to look for anything' – Goethe.)

Alienation. How long has this expression been in existence? There has always been alienation – in Dürer, in Mannerism, in charades – but it was not so demonstrative, not so definitive as it can be today. Nor did it involve the same somersault into the positive: alienation as compost heap for the new plants, *les fleurs du mal.* Out of the scrap metal something new is welded together. The torn newspaper with the world 'Commerzbank' on it produces 'Merz-bau'. 'Now we'll "merz" ', Schwitters used to say when he was sitting in a café with someone. This makes Schwitters, the complete opposite of Mondrian, just the same sort of lighthouse on the edge of the last cliff. 'Merzbau' can really exist only in imagination. It is always growing. It is untranslatable (though the last 'Merzbau', in England, has just been moved out of the barn into a museum). Assuming that 'Merzbau' were accepted, how would it be displayed? 'At the end of the passage on the second floor of the house that Schwitters had inherited, a door led into a not very big room. In the centre of it stood a piece of sculpture in plaster. At this time, about 1925, it filled about a quarter of the space and reached almost to the ceiling. But it was not just a piece of sculpture; it was a living document, changing every day, of Schwitters and his friends; a collection of cavities, an assemblage of concave and convex forms causing the sculpture to bulge in and out. Each of these special forms had a 'meaning'. There was a Mondrian-cavity, and cavities or hollows for Arp, Gabo, Doesburg, Lissitzky, Malevitch, Mies van der Rohe and Richter. There were also hollows for his son and his wife. Each hollow contained very personal belongings of all these people. He cut some of my hair off and put it

in my hole. A thick pencil, purloined from Mies van der Rohe's drawing-board, lay in his space. Many of us had several holes, according to how Schwitter's spirit moved him – and the column grew. When I went back three years later the column had changed. None of the little hollows and bulges which we had 'inhabited' earlier was visible any longer. 'They are all deep inside now', Schwitters explained. They were in fact covered up by the monstrous growth of the column, hidden by other bulges, new people, new forms, colours and details. A sort of vegetation that never ceased to grow. Earlier the column had looked more or less like a construct; now it was more curved. But, above all, the column's enormous growth had caused it to burst the seams of the room, so to speak. As Schwitters could not add anything more to it sideways if he still wanted to be able to walk round it, he had to go upward. As owner of the house he gave notice to the tenants above, broke through the ceiling and carried on with the column on the next floor. I never saw it completed.' (Hans Richter, *Dada.*)
The 'Merzbau' was a pure dream work of art, a sort of 'world interior', like an Egyptian *mastaba* transported to Hildesheim or Vienna or Manchester. We enter full of wonder and see their creators' world all round us. But what about the incantations? Or the similarity with the state bedroom at Herrenchiemsee? Or with a space capsule, which is also full of indicators and knobs and heated clothes and carefully counted calories? Or even the so-called driver's cabin of some fairly big piece of machinery – an automated assembly-line or even a locomotive? In the space capsule too one can do nothing. Really one just sits inside it and flies. And what does flying mean to a space-traveller outside the pull of gravity? These are not far-fetched comparisons, but simply the realms in which an artist's imagination ranges in so far as he too is a contemporary and a newspaper-reader, in so far as he too is moulded by the news, adapted, pre-formed, industrialized in his opinions. He can only save himself from all this technological perfection by means of a Dada act – only to fall undeniably into the comic, the curious, the non-adapted.
We have put Mondrian and Schwitters together in the same section of this book because they are at opposite poles. Contemporaries without any question, and concerned in the same way with the so-called reality of this century, which must be shaped and made apprehensible to man. While Mondrian thinks that he can heal by means of the strictest asceticism, Schwitters is the man who loves little details, the man who has no programme except the programme not to have one. 'My ultimate aim is the union of art and non-art in the Merz world-picture. Quotations in poetry, sentimental pictures as parts of paintings, the incorporation of consciously sentimental and consciously bad sections in the work of art, etc.'

SURREALISM

The term 'surrealism' was originally coined by the poet Guillaume Apollinaire in 1917 and was developed into a manifesto by the poet André Breton in 1924: 'Surrealism: pure, psychic automatism, through which one seeks to express the real course of one's thinking orally, on paper or in any other way. Instinctive thinking without any control by reason and outside all aesthetic or ethical considerations.' Thus Surrealism arose in the field of literature. However, it was neither through this emphasis on automatism nor through poets in general that Surrealism became one of the important forms of expression of this century, but through painters. There are only a few Surrealist writers, but in Marcel Jean's book on Surrealism in the fine arts some seven hundred names are mentioned; in other words, more or less all the artists of our age.

Surrealism was preceded by *pittura metafisica*, which was developed in all essentials by Giorgio de Chirico. He was preceded by Dada, and many artists belonged first to the one and then to the other movement. Surrealism verges on '*objets trouvés*', on 'Neue Sachlichkeit' and 'magical realism'. It is continued in Pop art and Op art. Surrealism is in danger on one side of becoming a political action group. The danger on the other side is empty modishness.

Sigmund Freud's teachings are not mentioned by Breton, but they have more in common with Surrealism than automatism has, for dream and depth psychology work with concrete images, not just with instinctive ideas.

Salvador Dali remodelled François Millet's *Angelus* and gave every figure and every object in the picture a 'paranoiac' interpretation. He remodelled the *Island of the Dead* and Böcklin was discovered to be one of the fathers of Surrealism, after the France of the Impressionist period had taken no notice of him. Max Ernst assembled his novels-in-pictures out of the details of the woodcuts in early nineteenth-century journals. And why should we stop at the nineteenth century? We can ask if there has ever been any century in which the attitude known in the twentieth century as Surrealism cannot be traced. It is very frequent, indeed almost the main current, in the European sixteenth century; but there we call it Mannerism. It is present in the first century; there it is known by the general title of Pompeian painting.

Take one of the puzzle-pictures of the Mannerist period, an allegory of nature (an engraving by Maerten van Heemskerk): *Natura naturans* and *Natura mechanica* are made to confront each other, for it was clear to the men of the Mannerist period that Nature has two apparently irreconcilable sides: lush, organic growth on one side, and on the other a strict legality which can be grasped in mathematical formulas and measurements. Perhaps present-day physics teaches that the opposition between the organic and mathematical aspects of nature seems to disappear in the field of concepts of energy. So today one would have to depict the irreconcilable elements in another way, possibly like Max Ernst, by showing a forest of fish-bones on one side and Euclid and Pythagoras on the other.

I certainly do not wish to go into the question of the difference between religion, magic, superstition, cabbala, gnosticism, shamanism, myth, allegory and symbolism, or that of their connection with Surrealism. But we can no longer say that Surrealism is a discovery that distinguishes the twentieth century from all preceding centuries. The contrast is not between Surrealism and the other millennia of human history, but between Surrealism and the nineteenth-century Realism that immediately preceded it. The problem does not lie in the twentieth century but in the nineteenth. It springs from the exaggerated importance – greater than ever before – which realism acquired in the nineteenth century. Only so long as there was as much faith in realism as there had been in the last few generations

FIG. 21 – *Max Ernst, Collage from 'The Lion of Belfort', 1934. Cf. p. 117.*

could something called Sur-realism detach itself in the way it did, could such an impulse develop, could indeed be produced at all as we have seen it produced. For it is based on the fact that the individual components of the 'real' can be separated from each other and distinguished with a clarity that only we have developed. It is the product of a generation that can separate chemical compounds, isolate genes, cultivate different viruses. In the same way we can also isolate artistic styles from each other and consequently combine them artificially. We can isolate – and this is the basic pattern of the Surrealistic process – the component parts of realism and put them together again in a new way.

Surrealism simply makes something clear, carries it into the realm of the absolute, a process which has always been an aspect of art. The danger of the twentieth century is that it is so good at isolating; it separates all the facets of art and consequently exaggerates them, makes each of them direct, exclusive, absurd, or rather impossible. For in fact it is not absurd at all, but simply logical. The only trouble is that it is one-sidedly logical and as a result comes near to being ill adapted for life. One might compare the many special developments which have sometimes caused earlier species of animals to die out.

PLATE P. 229

Dali's war picture is unthinkable without the monumental sculpture of the nineteenth century, and also without the age-old postures of alleged victory: the high-swung sword, the exhibition of the slaughtered adversary's head (in the language of the nineteenth century, the hereditary foe; in that of the twentieth century, the subhuman being), the proud foot placed on the corpse. Now the head rises even higher than the sword, the hilt of the sword swells into a woman's breast, and the monstrous phantom towers over the bare, distant landscape, between the dried-up red on the right and the vivid blue of the mountain behind. There is no vegetation in the picture. For the Spaniard Dali, lushness always means flesh; for the northerner Max Ernst, it means plants. Already, too, the next device of surrealistic composition has been introduced – the collision between the over-life-size and the inhumanly small and distant, the use of perspective in an age that no longer believes in perspective. Between the two hands (and they are two right hands; victor and vanquished have thus grown together) stands the tiny figure of the bureaucrat, who studies, laboriously immersed in his own thoughts, the switches on this inflated monstrosity and presses the buttons, the punctilious armchair murderer.

The rage of the Pharisees, the distaste of the devotees of *peinture pure* cannot alter the fact that this is a magnificently painted picture and that it must have existed, in front of these clouds like the entrails of heaven, first as a vision and as a whole in the artist's imagination before it could be assembled out of the individual components of realism.

Dali's probably most famous picture bears the title the *Persistence of Memory*. It was painted in 1931, and some twenty-five years later Dali painted the same ideas in a picture of which the content is the same, but what had previously hung together is now falling apart into orderly ruins. The watches have gone limp and hang over the bare branch of a tree or over the cube of stereometry. Or they are as red as tomatoes and are being eaten by ants. Or they lie like a saddle on a

tired horse. Time for us is so closely connected with the watch that we might think it had become a part of our body. Now this domesticated time grows soft, melts like wax and lets its head droop.
We move over in this picture out of one concept of time into another concept of time. Take the representation of power: there was a period when increased achievement meant more slaves. Afterwards it was a question of horse-power. We still speak of horse-power, but we mean internal combustion engines. And already we no longer reckon by h.p. but by units of atmospheric pressure and things like that. It is the same with time. There was time that ran through the hour-glass, then the time measured by the wheels of the watch. Now comes a kind of time that is no longer indicated mechanically but chemically; one will have to read off the softening-point, the melting-point of watch-time. Already atomic fall-out has become a measure of time, and half-life has become a current concept. Surrealism can take literally concepts, words that had once been images. If the chance notion is a happy one, the words become images again.

PAUL KLEE

As I have already said, what was exceptional about the Bauhaus was not the architecture or the work on individual problems of industrial design but the collaboration of exceptional men. Furthermore, the exceptional works of theory written in this period were produced by painters: by Itten, Schlemmer, Albers, Kandinsky and, above all, PaulKlee.
Klee's theoretical utterances are collected in the publication *Das Bildnerische Denken*. The relevant drawings are reproduced in this book, so as to make the text comprehensible. The book also contains reproductions of those of Klee's pictures in which the method of drawing under discussion is applied. As a result, comprehension, comparison and investigation in depth are possible, and all from a didactic not a historical point of view.
The main part of the book consists of lectures given at the Bauhaus in the years 1921 to 1930. The legendary Bauhaus instruction, which in the meantime has been passed on, via pupils and posterity, to preliminary classes in painting and crafts all over the world, is here (and in Itten's books) preserved in print. Klee's teaching is the most precise, inexorable and comprehensive analysis extant of painting as it was practised at that time.
Anyone who could find the energy to work through and absorb this teaching page by page, drawing by drawing, definition by definition, would subject himself to an amazing training. What would he really gain? Unawares, against his will, the reader arrives at a completely different position. It is not just a case of learning with wonder about the life of a great artist. The reader is transported, almost coerced, into a whole fresh language and mode of instruction. He has to be instructed in a language which the teacher once invented for himself. I repeat, it is the teaching, the analysis on which Klee based his own creative work during the Bauhaus period. During each stage of his life a creative artist not only alters the present but also creates a new past and future to go with it. The analysis which the forty-year-old Klee wished to have as his starting-point, and which he consequently tried to pass on to his pupils as instruction, was intellectually con

ditioned to suit the needs of a forty-year-old man, but it was not the sort of analysis that could be worked out by a man of twenty or sixty. Early and late in life a man is much more intuitive, much more relaxed in attitude, and not so worried about working on rationally worked-out principles. One has only to pick up any drawing of Klee's from the period round 1911 and another from the period round 1939 to see that the nervous line of the early period and the lapidary line of the late period come from quite different layers of his personality. In other words, Klee himself did not become Klee or remain Klee according to the teaching contained in his lectures.

For Klee's early period, from 1898 to 1918, there are the diaries, just as self-contained as the *Bildnerische Denken* but – and this is the point – quite different. The entries are not arranged by dates but by numbers. No. 934 runs: 'Misery. Country without bonds, new country, without a trace of memory, with the smoke from an alien hearth. Unbridled! Where no mother's womb carried me.' No. 935 runs: 'The big animals mourn at the table and are not satisfied. But the cunning little flies climb over mountains of bread and live in a city of butter.' In between are the words: 'Between 934 and 935 the war broke out.' Any other diarist would have written: 'Between 31 July and 2 August 1914 the World War broke out.'

Klee made the phenomenon of the 'inner emigration' a reality long ago, twenty or thirty years before it became, in the Second World War, a generally practised, indeed essential, habit of the intellectual. Emigration whence and whither? For, after all, the Klee of those days did not emigrate from Germany; he allowed himself to be called up and became a member of the *Landsturm*. It is not an emigration from a hated environment but emigration out of historical time. Entry No. 952 reads: 'I have long had this war in me. Therefore spiritually it does not concern me.' This means that Klee's art (the art of the twentieth century) scarcely contains historical time in it any longer. It is impossible to date a work by Klee or one by Pollock by historical periods (categories of historical, political time). They differ radically, in the same way as Klee and Jackson Pollock themselves do, but they no longer differ as being 'from the period round 1920' and 'from the period round 1950'. They have nothing to do with chronological styles.

In Klee's diaries we do not find a narrative of consecutive events but the power of the synchronous, which shatters all earlier associations with a quiet irresistibility. The gradual growth of a static kernel with a ring for every year. It is a question of changing over into a different period of time. In an ordinary person the breakaway from the historical, and also from the contemporary, becomes mere thoughtlessness, the attitude which says 'it doesn't concern me.' With a genius, time no longer elapses but begins to come to a halt, to fulfil itself. What is true is that the signs of a post-historical age are beginning to be apparent in both ordinary people and geniuses.

Inward or spiritual emigration is also concerned with other ties, for example with marriage and the erotic side of life. What is recorded about the case of Klee's baby son Felix would be completely uninteresting if it showed merely the conscientious father. But it shows the integration, one might almost say the incapsulation, of the erotic element in this artistic organism.

Salvador Dali, *Premonition of the Civil War*. 1936. Oil on canvas. *Height 3 ft. 8 in., width 2 ft. 9½ in. Philadelphia, Museum of Art.* *Cf. p. 226.*

Paul Klee, *Ad marginem.* 1930, worked over again 1935/6. Water-colour and ink on paste-board. *Height 18 in., width 13 in. Basle, Kunstmuseum.*

It is not as if the Bauhaus (and Klee with it) had expounded a language of art, or even simply of art training, that now had to be employed for all eternity. It is true that in those days the world of misunderstandings, of historical periods, of non-forms was cleared away and the world lying at the root of individual creation discovered. But in the course of this more attention than ever before was devoted to the technical processes connected with drawing. This can only be understood by reference to the whole twentieth century's interest in engineering, to the joy in experiment which is a part of the scientist's and technologist's make-up. That one should seek to couple a given beginning – a point, a line, a surface, a colour – with all imaginable variations of a similar and different kind, cross it, boil it, make it evaporate – this is the chemist's mode of working, but in earlier centuries it was not that of the artist. Dürer and Rembrandt, like Klee, drew lines and instructed young apprentice painters, but they would not have stopped to think that they were setting a point in motion in a particular direction, and that they therefore had to reflect on the nature of point, direction and motion. They would simply have spoken forthwith about whatever they wanted to produce, Madonna or landscape, or whatever it might be. That one must look beyond technique into an infinite distance, that one must have the arrow in the butt before despatching it – this 'art of archery' would be in opposition to the analytical methods of the Bauhaus. It is extremely remarkable that Zen Buddhism, 'Gestalt' philosophy and the integral approach to learning languages should have all become known and taught in the West at the same time as Klee's analytical method.
But we are talking as if this analytical method were Klee's final aim. That is precisely what it is not. It is 'a dance round a central point', an unparalleled intensity of concentration on his own activity, but it does not hold, as in Rilke's famous poem, 'a great will bemused'. Just the opposite: it is a central point from which a ceaselessly tensed receiving and transmitting intelligence revolves in all directions, like a radar beam.
For Klee certainly controls his creative thinking very precisely, but the result is never self-isolation; he always remains in contact with the 'other', with the world; and a tested, tried, examined world at that, from music *via* literature to the growth of nature, from the theatre and opera *via* fear and hope to everything human. All these subjects appear in the titles of his pictures, and they were not provided by literary friends but created by Klee simultaneously with the pictures. They represent a maximum of what can be achieved by simultaneous self-examination and observation of the outside world, of what can be understood and depicted, or rather encoded, in this fashion. A whole world seen and organized from the drawing-board.
For again Klee is typical in the format of his works, in the work he gets through at his table. He is not limited to the 'optical surface' of the world, like the Impressionists who were his predecessors in control over artistic means. The liberation of painting from the peep-show, from the idea of a framed picture on the wall of a room, drives the painter (or the creative artist) at one extreme to walls in general, to the vast expanses of skyscrapers, since architecture produces at the same time not only grids of innumerable windows but also windowless strengthening slabs

of unheard-of size – and the so-called painter's imagination has to grapple all at once with thousands of square yards and seek to 'organize' them.
The other extreme is that exploited by Klee: the material of creation lies on the table, is contained in a show-case, is seen from above; it no longer has anything to do with the uprightness or straightness of the wall of a room, but much rather with the crowded appearance and omnipresence of the page of a book, which can also contain everything.
What a wide span, then, is covered by the 'art of our world', which saw the simultaneous production of Monet's *Nymphéas*, good examples of the above-mentioned 'wall-size' painting, of encirclement by the vertical, the surface of the water reflected in the sharpest optical sense. On the other side there is Klee's *Underwater Garden*, the size of a sheet of paper, in which the growing and interweaving under the surface become visible, with letters and cartographical symbols, as if there were traffic signs under water too.
Just as wide as the difference between Klee and Monet is that between Klee and Edvard Munch, who at roughly the same time painted the sun as the giant centre of a mural in a university nall, shining over the fjord, uniting human and plant life, science and history.
In contrast to that, the star in the tiny Klee picture, the sinister destructive sun, the fireball, the pill.

EPILOGUE

The fireball, the pill – Cheops would understand that. He would think of the pill which the Egyptian scarab pushes along in front of itself, the constantly recurring sacred symbol of the religion of Amon. The beetle has placed its world-egg in the ball of dung: Cheops would think of the origin of the All from the despised Nothing. He would also think of the underwater journey of the sun, which in the evening embarks in the nocturnal barque in the west and travels back deep beneath us to its rising in the east. In the creative, burning circuit of the sun he would honour the incomprehensibility of God.

Every earlier king built cities; so do we. Each of them tried to produce good architecture; so do we. Each overestimated his own achievements; so do we.

When we are left to ourselves, when we have to overcome our emotions, it becomes clear that our own age does not stand outside time. There is more reason to stress the elements that persist, that are always present, than those which seem strange, which seem new and incomprehensible.

There is no good reason for mistrusting the art of the period which is dealt with in this book. We can see the transformation that has taken place. Its great pace is only apparent; any art historian can adduce earlier centuries in which the changes were just as constant. We see an unceasing succession of exceptional artists and achievements. We can see the deep sincerity in them. This is much more important than the occasionally evident streaks of capriciousness and arrogance.

APPENDIX

CAPTIONS TO THE APPENDIX OF PLATES

1 – Richard Wagner, first performance of the *Meistersinger*, Nuremberg, 21 June 1868.
2 – Marc Chagall, unveiling of the ceiling in the Paris Opéra, 23 September, 1964.
3 – Production of the *Rheingold*, Act I. The Rhine Maidens. First performance, Munich, 22 September 1869.
4a – Paris Opéra, auditorium. Ceiling by Marc Chagall. Photo Agence Rapho, Paris.
4b – Ceiling by Eugène Lenepveu. Photo Marburg.
5 – Vilshofen, bridge over the Danube. Augsburg-Nuremberg Engine Works, 1872. Photo H. G. Evers (1936).
6 – Augustus Welby Pugin, *True Principles (The Present Revival of Christian Architecture)*, 1843.
7 – Pennell, *Street Scene in New York*, 1913/14.
8 – Spain, Valle de los Caídos (Guadarrama), detail: St. Mark and lion. Photo by H. G. Evers.
9 – Exhibition at Darmstadt (Mathildenhöhe), 1901: A Document of German Art. Olbrich house, Habich house. Architect: Joseph Maria Olbrich.
10 – House of Two-dimensional Art. Architect: Joseph Maria Olbrich.
11, 12, 13 – Caricatures from *Ein Überdokument*, Darmstadt, 1901. Drawn by Paul Bürck.
14 – Auguste Rodin, *Balzac*. Photo Edvard Steichen.
15 – Gottfried Schadow, etching: Memorial to General von Dieten, 1794.
16 – Auguste Rodin, *Squatting Woman*, 1882, head. Munich. Photo H. G. Evers.
17 – Auguste Rodin, *Je suis belle*, 1882. Paris, Rodin Museum. Photo Marburg.
18 – Auguste Rodin, *Je suis belle*, 1882. Paris, Rodin Museum. Photo Marburg.
19 – L. H. Sullivan, Iowa, Merchants' Bank, 1914.
20 – The Bauhaus team, Weimar, 1923.

„Habt Dank der Güte
aus tiefstem Gemüthe!
Und darf ich denn hoffen
steht heut mir noch offen
zu werben um den Preis
dass ich Meistersänger h iss?"
„Oho! Fein sacht! etc. etc.
2
3

5
6

9
10

ÜBERDOKUMENT"
OLBRICH·HAUS
HAUS HABICH
EIN ÜBERDOKUMENT
EIN ÜBERDOKUMENT.
HAUS DER FLACHHEIT

11

12

13

15

16

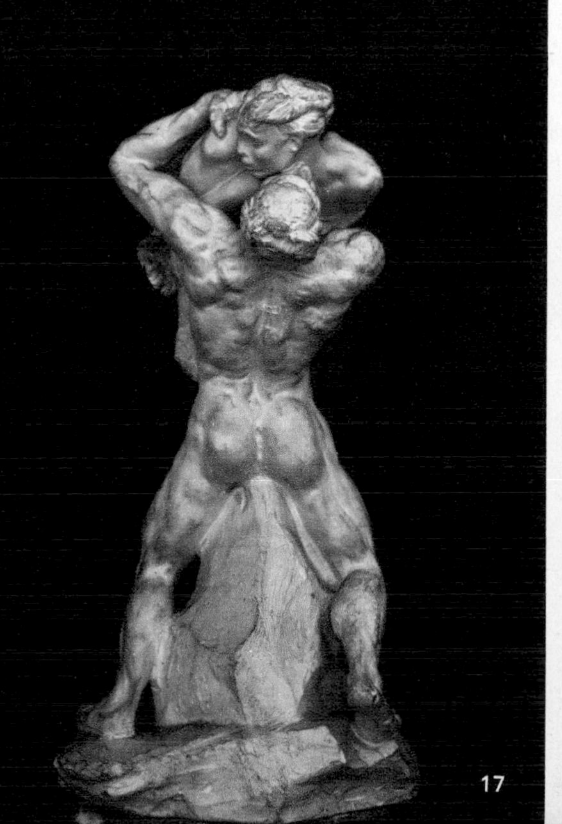

17

18

CHRONOLOGICAL TABLE

	POLITICAL HISTORY	ART	LITERATURE, MUSIC ETC.	SCIENCE AND TECHNOLOGY
1860	Italian War of Liberation (Garibaldi)	Ensor*	Burckhardt: *Die Kultur der Renaiss. in Italien* G. Mahler*	Bullock: Rotary printing press
1861	Wilhelm I. King of Prussia (1871–1888: German Emperor) Prince Consort Albert†	Rietschel† Garnier: Grande Opéra in Paris Monti: *Sleep of Sorrow* and *Dream of Joy* Manet's début at the Salon Maillol*	Firm of Morris & Co. founded Rudolf Steiner*	Reis: Telephone
1862	Bismarck: Prussian prime minister	Scott & others: Albert Memorial (to 1871) Feuerbach: *Iphigenie* Monet, Renoir, Sisley at the Atelier Gleyre Degas: first pictures of horse-races Klimt*	Debussy* Schnitzler* G. Hauptmann*	
1863	Lincoln: Proclamation emancipating slaves American Civil War Lassalle: Universal German Trade Union	Delacroix† Manet: *Dejeuner sur l'herbe*, *Olympia* Signac* van de Velde* Munch*	Salon des Refusés in Paris: Manet, Whistler, Cézanne, Pissarro et al. d'Annunzio* Bahr* Holz*	Huxley: Theory that man is descended from apes
1864	Geneva Convention Marx: First International Ludwig II: King of Bavaria (to 1886)	Klenze† Toulouse-Lautrec* Jawlensky*	Ricarda Huch* R. Strauss*	
1865	Lincoln†	Kiss† Mengoni: Galleria Vittorio Emmanuele II in Milan Busch: *Max und Moritz*	Vollard* First performance: Wagner's *Tristan and Isolde*	Kekule: Discovery of the circular form of the benzene molecule Mendel: Heredity laws
1866	North German Confederation	Gibson† Poelaert: Palace of Justice in Brussels Courbet: *Deer in the Forest* Monet: *Women in the Garden* Kandinsky*		Transatlantic telegraph cable
1867		Cornelius†. Ingres† Marocchetti† de Chavannes: Murals in Museum at Lyon Cézanne: *Railway Cutting*	Marx: *Das Kapital*, I Verdi: *Don Carlos*	Nobel: Dynamite Siemens: Principle of electric dynamo

	POLITICAL HISTORY	ART	LITERATURE, MUSIC ETC.	SCIENCE AND TECHNOLOGY
1867		Bonnard* Kollwitz* Nolde*		
1868		Corot: *The Woman with the Pearl* Makart: *The Plague in Florence* Renoir: *Sisley Couple* Slevogt* Vuillard* P. Behrens*	Stifter† Brahms: German Requiem St. George*	
1869		Overbeck†. Carus† Carpeaux: *The Dance* (from 1866) Matisse* Poelzig* F. L. Wright*	Berlioz†	Mendeleyev and Meyer: Periodic system of chemical elements Brehm: *Life of Animals*
1870	Franco-Prussian War (1870–1871)	Repin: *Volga Boatmen* Courbet: *The Wave* Denis* Barlach*	Schliemann: Excavation of Troy Verdi: *Aida*	Monier: Reinforced concrete
1871	Bismarck: German Empire	Scott & others: Albert Memorial in London (from 1862) Whistler: *Arrangement in Grey and Black (The Artist's Mother)* Rouault* Kupka* Balla* Feininger*		Darwin: *Origin of Species* Maddox: Photographic dry plate Maxwell: Light = electro-magnetic wave
1872		Schnorr v. Carolsfeld† Schmid: City Hall in Vienna Trübner: *Brawling Boys* Whistler: *Old Battersea Bridge* Beardsley* Mondrian*	Grillparzer† Diaghilev*	
1873		Piloty: *Thusnelda in the Triumphal Procession of Germanicus* Marées: Neapolitan frescoes Feuerbach: *Plato's Symposium*		
1874		Abadie: Start of Sacré Coeur in Paris First Impressionist exhibition in Paris	German Archaeological Institute in Athens founded K. E. Osthaus* v. Hoffmansthal* Schoenberg*	Billroth: Discovery of streptococci and staphylococci

	POLITICAL HISTORY	ART	LITERATURE, MUSIC ETC.	SCIENCE AND TECHNOLOGY
1875		Carpeaux†. Corot† Bandel: Hermannsdenkmal (from 1836) Menzel: *Iron Rolling Mill* Böcklin: *Triton and Nereid* Barye* Villon*	H.-Chr. Andersen† Th. Mann* Rilke* Ravel*	
1876		Bandel† de Chavannes: Ste. Geneviève frescoes in the Panthéon, Paris Degas: *Absinth Drinker* Renoir: *Dance at the Moulin de la Galette* Rodin: *The Age of Bronze* Brancusi* Duchamp-Villon* Gonzales*	G. Sand† Schiemann: Excavation of Mycenae Marinetti*	Koch: Discovery of the anthrax bacillus Otto: Four-stroke cycle engine
1877		Courbet† Monet: *Gare Saint Lazare* Kubin* Dufy*. Kolbe*	Gobineau: *The Renaissance*	Edison: Cylinder phonograph
1878		G. G. Scott† Fernkorn† Cézanne begins his constructive period Malevitch* Hofer* Freundlich*	v. Stephan: International Postal Union founded in Paris G. Kaiser*	
1879		Semper† Viollet-le-Duc† Daumier† Redon: *Dans le rêve* Klee* Picabia*	«La Vie Moderne» founded Dostoyevsky: *The Brothers Karamazov* Keller: *Der grüne Heinrich*	New York: Electric light Siemens: Electric locomotive Edison: Carbon filament lamp
1880		Feuerbach† Lenbach: *Bismarck* Böcklin: *Island of the Dead* van Gogh begins to paint Dérain* Kirchner* de Chirico* Purrmann*	Apollinaire* Jacobsen: *Niels Lyhne*	
1881		Drake†. Monti† Klinger: *The Glove* Manet: *A Bar in the Folies-Bergère*	Dostoyevsky† St. Zweig* Bartok*	Meisenbach: Facsimile

	POLITICAL HISTORY	ART	LITERATURE, MUSIC ETC.	SCIENCE AND TECHNOLOGY
1881		Renoir: *Canoers' Luncheon* Picasso* Léger* Gleizes* Lehmbruck* Carrà* Pechstein*		
1882		Fowler-Baker: Forth Bridge Gaudí: Start of Church of Holy Family in Barcelona Braque* Boccioni*	D. G. Rossetti† Joyce* Stravinsky*	Darwin† Koch: Discovery of the tuberculosis bacillus
1883		Manet† Seurat: *Une baignade* Heckel* van Doesberg* Severini* Bartning*	Wagner† Marx† Nietzsche: *Also sprach Zarathustra* Kafka* v. Webern*	
1884		Makart† Sacconi: Vittorio Emmanuele Monument in Rome Wallot: Reichstag, Berlin Uhde: *Suffer the little children to come unto me* Seurat: *La Grande Jatte* Modigliani* Schmidt-Rottluff* Beckmann* Société des Indépendants (to 1911)	D.-H. Kahnweiler* Th. Heuss*	
1885		Spitzweg† Tuaillon: *Amazone* Renoir: *Grandes baigneuses* van Gogh: *Potato Eaters* Delaunay*. Laurens*	J. P. Jacobsen† V. Hugo† A. Berg*	
1886		Bartholdy: Statue of Liberty, New York (1871–1884) unveiled van Gogh in Paris v. d. Rohe* Kokoschka*	Liszt† Benn*	
1887		v. Marées† Klinger: *Judgement of Paris* Archipenko* Chagall*	Trakl* Mendelssohn* Pevsner*	Hertz: Electric waves produced in space and observed Daimler: Car with petrol motor

	POLITICAL HISTORY	ART	LITERATURE, MUSIC ETC.	SCIENCE AND TECHNOLOGY
1887		Duchamp* Gris* Macke* Schwitters* Le Corbusier*		
1888	Emperor Wilhelm II (to 1918)	Zumbusch: *Maria Theresa* Ensor: *Entry of Christ into Brussels in 1888* van Gogh in Arles Cézanne: *Boy with Red Waistcoat* Rodin: *The Burghers of Calais* (from 1885) Symbolistic group «Nabis» Albers*. Arp* R. Bissière*. Chirico* Itten*. Schlemmer*	Strindberg: *Miss Julie*	
1889		Eiffel Tower in Paris (from 1887) Dutert and Cottancin: Palais des machines, World Exhibition, Paris Jenney: Ladder Building Gauguin: *Le Christ Jaune* Baumeister*. Marcks* Sophie Taeuber*		Hollerith: Punched card calculating machine
1890	Bismarck dismissed	van Gogh† Cézanne: *The Card Players* Munch in Paris Gabo*. El Lissitzky* Morandi* Tobey*. Zadkine*	Heinrich Schliemann† G. Keller† Hamsun: *Hunger* Morris: Kelmscott Press	Koch: Tuberculin
1891		Seurat† Lautrec: *Moulin-Rouge* poster Gauguin goes to Tahiti M. Ernst*. Dix*	*Revue Blanche* (Natanson Brothers) Wedekind: *Frühlings Erwachen* Prokofiev* Carl-Zeiss Foundation	
1892		Wolff† Berlin: Künstlergruppe XI and Freie Künstler-vereinigung Munich Secession Neutra* Hülsenbeck*	Walt Whitman† Hauptmann: *Die Weber* Debussy: *Prélude à l'après-midi d'un faune* Honegger*	Siemens†

	POLITICAL HISTORY	ART	LITERATURE, MUSIC ETC.	SCIENCE AND TECHNOLOGY
1893		Munch: *The Shriek* Matisse and Rouault in Moreau's studio Grosz* Miro* Scharoun*	Vollard: Gallery opened *The Studio*, Engl. art magazine O. Wilde: *Salome* Tchaikovsky†	Diesel: Diesel engine Schmidt: Superheated steam locomotive Behring: Diphtheria serum Nansen: North Pole expedition with the *Fram*
1894	Dreyfus Affair	Klinger: *Brahms-phantasie* Munch: *Puberty* Beardsley: *Salome* Gilles*. Nicholson* Soutine*	Lou Andreas-Salome: *Friedrich Nietzsche in seinen Werken*	Hedin: Tibet expedition (to 1897)
1895		Hodler: *Eurythmie* Gauguin goes for the second time to Tahiti Cézanne: *Bathers* (various versions up to 1905) Kollwitz: *Weavers' Revolt* (to 1898)	Gustav Freytag† Fontane: *Effi Briest* Periodical *Pan* Hindemith*	Röntgen: X-rays v. Linde: Condensa-tion of air Pasteur†
1896	Fr. Naumann: Nationalsozialer Verein	Messel: Wertheim store in Berlin M. Rosso: *Lady with Veil* Kandinsky and Jawlensky in Munich	Bruckner† Clara Schumann† Brahms: Four Serious Songs Munich magazines *Simplizissimus*, *Jugend* Paris: *L'art nouveau* gallery founded Coubertin: Olympic Games in Athens Tristan Tzara*	Nobel†
1897		Eckmann: Swan tapestry Endell: Atelier Elvira in Munich Viennese Secession (Klimt)	Brahms† Gauguin: *Noa Noa* Loie Fuller dances at the Folies-Bergère	Marconi: Wireless telegraphy Krische and Spitteler: Artificial material galalith
1898	O. v. Bismarck: *Gedanken und Erinnerungen*†	Moreau† Puvis de Chavannes† Beardsley† Leipzig Memorial (to 1913) Rodin: *The Kiss*, *Balzac* Minne: Fountain (execution: 1906) Moore* Calder*	Fontane†. C. F. Meyer† *Ver Sacrum*, perio-dical of the Viennese Secession Koldewey: Excavation of Babylon (to 1917) Zola: 'J'accuse'	Marie Curie: Discovery of radium and polonium Bölsche: *Love Life in Nature* (to 1903)
1899	The Hague: Inter-national Court	Segantini† Sisley† Nolde a pupil of	Karl Kraus: Periodical *Die Fackel* Artists' colony at	Elster and Geitel: Start of atomic physics

	POLITICAL HISTORY	ART	LITERATURE, MUSIC ETC.	SCIENCE AND TECHNOLOGY
1899		Hölzel Vordemberge-Gildewart*. Aalto*	Darmstadt Johann Strauss† Schönberg: string sextet *Verklärte Nacht* R. Huch: *Die Romantik* (to 1902) Rilke: *Weise von Liebe und Tod* Schnitzler: *Der Reigen (La Ronde)* F. G. Lorca*	
1900		Leibl† Phalanx group founded Capogrossi*	Paris: Centenary Exhibition Nietzsche† O. Wilde† Freud: *Interpretation of Dreams* Evans: Excavations in Crete begun	Planck: Quantum theory
1901	Queen Victoria†	Böcklin† Balzico† Toulouse-Lautrec† Olbrich and Behrens: Mathildenhöhe in Darmstadt Picasso: Blue Period (to 1904) Marino Marini*	Verdi† Shaw: *Caesar and Cleopatra* Strindberg: *Dance of Death* Th. Mann: *Buddenbrooks* First art education day in Dresden	Marconi: Wireless telegraph across the Atlantic
1902		Klinger: Beethoven Monument (from 1886) Slevogt: *d'Andrade as Don Juan* Maillol: *La Méditerranée* Nay*	Zola† Osthaus: Folkwang Museum at the Hague founded Warburg: Warburg Library founded (to 1933 in Hamburg, then London) C. Neumann: *Rembrandt* Avenarius: Dürerbund	Virchow†
1903		Gauguin† Pissarro† Whistler† Klimt: Painting in the hall of Vienna Univ. Klee: grotesque etchings Barbara Hepworth*	Salon d'Automne in Paris founded Th. Mann: *Tristan* Hauptmann: *Rose Bernd*	Wright brothers: First powered flight de Vries: Mutation theory Ford: Motor Car Company
1904		Bartholdy† v. Lenbach† Bazaine*. Fr. Bott* Dali*. Estève* Germaine Richier	Deutscher Künstlerbund founded Dvořák†	Boveri: Chromosomes recognized as bearers of hereditary features Elster and Geitel: Photo-electric cell Rubel: Offset printing

	POLITICAL HISTORY	ART	LITERATURE, MUSIC ETC.	SCIENCE AND TECHNOLOGY
1905		Lederer: Bismarck Memorial in Hamburg Wagner: Post Office Savings Bank in Vienna Hoffmann: Palais Stoclet in Brussels Picasso: Pink Period (1905/1906) Matisse: *Luxe, calme et volupté* Paris: Les Fauves Dresden: Brücke founded	R. Strauss: *Salome* H. Mann: *Professor Unrat* Rilke: *Stundenbuch* Gorky: *Mother* Dehio: *Handbuch der deutschen Kunstdenkmäler* (to 1912) Sartre*	Einstein: Relativity theory
1906		Cézanne† Ernst Josephson† Matisse: *Joie de vivre* Birolli* Poliakoff* Ben Shahn	Ibsen† Shostakovich*	
1907		P. Modersohn-Becker† Olbrich: Wedding tower in Darmstadt Picasso: *Demoiselles d'Avignon*, beginning of Cubism	Deutscher Werkbund founded E. Grieg†	Hahn: Discovery of radioactive elements radiothor, radio-actinium, medothor I and II
1908		Wilhelm Busch† Hodler: *Exodus of the Jena Students, 1813* Picasso and Braque: early Cubist pictures Picasso gives a banquet for H. Rousseau in the Bâteau Lavoir Brancusi: *The Kiss* Kokoschka: portraits, *Kraus und Ebenstein, Trance Player* Bill* Vieira da Silva* Vasarely*	Worringer: *Abstraktion und Einfühlung* G. Mahler: *Das Lied von der Erde* Messiaen*	
1909		Olbrich† Behrens: AEG-turbine house in Berlin Picabia: *Caoutchouc* Nolde: *Last Supper, Pentecost* Munich: Neue Künstlervereinigung founded Corpora* Singier* H. A. P. Grieshaber*	Diaghilev Ballet in Paris Marinetti: 1st. Futurist Manifesto Kokoschka: *Murder Hope of Women* Bahr: *Das Konzert* Rockefeller Foundation for scientific research	Baekeland: Bakelite Blériot: Channel flight Ford: Model 'T'

	POLITICAL HISTORY	ART	LITERATURE, MUSIC ETC.	SCIENCE AND TECHNOLOGY
1910		H. Rousseau† Marc and Macke meet Matisse: *The Dance* Delaunay: *The Eiffel Tower* Kokoschka: *Forel* portrait Kandinsky: *Composition II*, first abstract water-colour Mirko Basaldella* Berlin: New Secession Boccioni, Balla, Carrà, Russolo, Severini: Futurist Manifesto	Walden: magazine *Sturm* Kandinsky: *Concerning the Spiritual in Art* (published in 1912) First Sonderbund Exhibition in Düsseldorf Rilke: *Notebooks of Malte Laurids Brigge* Anouilh*	
1911		Begas† Boccioni: *The Street Invades the House* Gropius: Fagus works in Alfeld (to 1914) Lehmbruck: *Kneeling Woman* Munich: the Blaue Reiter founded Kupka: *La Fugue en rouge et bleue* Manessier* Lardera*	H. v. Tschudi† G. Mahler† Hofmannsthal: *Jedermann* Bartók: *Duke Bluebeard's Castle*	Amundsen at the South Pole Funk and Terucchi: Start of vitamin research Einstein: *On the Influence of Gravity on the Expansion of Light*
1912		Kolbe: *Dancer* Heckel: *Canal in Berlin* Delaunay: *Simultaneous Windows* Severini: *Métro* Boccioni: *Development of a Bottle in Space* Duchamp: *Nude Descending a Staircase* Schwitters: *Lustgalgen* Marc and Macke meet Delaunay Nolde meets Ensor Mondrian: Tree series Afro Basaldella* Pollock*	Sonderbund Exhibition in Cologne Apollinaire describes paintings of Kupka, Picabia, Delaunay as 'Orphic' Kandinsky: *Concerning the Spiritual in Art* (written in 1910) August Strindberg† Nefertiti discovered C. G. Jung: *Transformations and Symbolisms of the Libido* R. Steiner: Anthroposophical Society founded R. Rolland: *Jean-Christophe* (from 1904) G. B. Shaw: *Pygmalion*	Krupp: Stainless steel
1913		Bonatz: Main railway station in Stuttgart Matisse goes to Morocco Nolde goes to South Seas	Kandinsky: *Retrospect* Delaunay: *Concerning Light* (trans. by Paul Klee) New York: Armory Show	Niels Bohr: Planetary system model of atom, spectral frequencies of hydrogen atom Geiger: Counter for radioactivity

	POLITICAL HISTORY	ART	LITERATURE, MUSIC ETC.	SCIENCE AND TECHNOLOGY
1913		Marc: *Tower of Blue Horses* Malevitch: *Black Rectangle on White Ground*, Suprematism Tatlin: Constructivism Dissolution of the Brücke Wols*. Reg Butler*	J. Pierpont Morgan†, Foundation of his art collection for New York E. Lasker-Schüler: *Hebräische Balladen* Th. Mann: *Tod in Venedig* Stravinsky: *The Rite of Spring* Klages: *Ausdruckslehre* A. Camus* Britten*	Bredow: Music conveyed by loudspeakers Ford: Conveyor belt for car factory Diesel†
1914	First World War (to 1918)	Duchamp-Villon: *The Horse* Duchamp: *Readymades* Kokoschka: *Die-Windsbraut* (Tempest) Chirico: Pittura metafisica Marc: Tower of the Blue Horses Klee, Macke, Moillet go to Kairouan Macke* De Staël* Chadwick*	Trakl† Christian Morgenstern† Werkbund Exhibition in Cologne London: magazine *Blast*	
1915		Zumbusch† Weissgerber† Carrà goes over to Pittura metafisica Malevitch: Suprematist Manifesto		Einstein starts to develop general theory of relativity
1916		Redon† Boccioni† Marc† Arp, Tzara & others: Dada Gabo: material constructions Armitage*	H. Bahr: *Expressionism* Rosa Luxemburg: *The Crisis in German Social Democracy* Anette Kolb: *Letters of a Franco-German Woman* Reger† Dada magazine: *Cabaret Voltaire*	v. Post: Pollen analysis
1917	Bolshevik Revolution	Trübner† Degas† Rodin† Rouault: *Miserere et Guerre* (to 1927) Stijl group: Mondrian, van Doesberg	Diaghilev, Cocteau, Satie, Picasso: Russian ballet *Parade* Dada magazines: *Dada, Rongwrong, 391* Magazine *De Stijl* C. G. Jung: *The Unconscious in Normal and Diseased Mental Life* Klages: *Handwriting and Character*	DIN standards committee founded

	POLITICAL HISTORY	ART	LITERATURE, MUSIC ETC.	SCIENCE AND TECHNOLOGY
1918		Hodler† Klimt† Otto Wagner† Schmidt-Rottluff: wood carvings of Christ Ozenfant and Le Corbusier: *Après le cubisme* (Manifesto of Purism) Novembergruppe in Berlin: Klee, Kandinsky, Barlach, v. d. Rohe Belling; later: Gabo	Apollinaire† Debussy† Wedekind†	Ostwald: Theory of colours, colour atlas Hahn†. Lise Meitner: Discovery of the radio-active element protactinium
1919	League of Nations, Comintern and Nazi party founded Ebert first president of Germany	Renoir† Lehmbruck† Monet: *Nymphéas* Schwitters: *Merz* pictures Poelzig: Schauspielhaus in Berlin Malevitch: *White Rectangle on White Ground* Dada groups in Cologne and Berlin Soulages* Vedova*	Gropius: Bauhaus founded in Weimar Film *The Cabinet of Dr. Caligari* Rosa Luxemburg: *Letters from Prison*† Bartning: *Vom neuen Kirchenbau* Fr. Naumann† Karl Kraus: *The Last Days of Humanity* Huizinga: *Autumn of the Middle Ages*	Rutherford: First artificial transformation of elements
1920		Klinger† Modigliani† Mendelsohn: Einstein Tower in Potsdam-Babelsberg Matisse: *Odalisques* Picasso: classicist period Baumeister: murals Gabo and Pevsner: Realist Manifesto Mondrian: *Néoplasticisme*	Ozenfant and Le Corbusier: magazine *L'Esprit Nouveau* (to 1924) Dada exhibitions in Paris, Cologne, Berlin Arp: *The Cloud Pump* Schönberg: Five Pieces for Piano (1920/1923) Film *Golem* (buildings by Poelzig)	
1921		Hildebrand† Gaul† Picasso: *Three Musicians* Kandinsky returns from Russia Mathieu*	Duchamp†. Man Ray: Magazine *New York Dada* K. E. Osthaus† Schlemmer: Triadic ballet Alban Berg: *Wozzeck* Honegger: *King David* Kretschmer: *Physical Development and Character* Film *The Kids*, Chaplin	Banting and Best: Insulin

	POLITICAL HISTORY	ART	LITERATURE, MUSIC ETC.	SCIENCE AND TECHNOLOGY
1922	Mussolini: Fascist *coup d'état* in Italy Rathenau†	Höger: Chile house in Hamburg Dix: *Trenches* Klee: *Zwitschermaschine*	Last big Dada exhibition in Paris Ehrenburg and El Lissitzky: *Objet*, Constructivist magazine Joyce: *Ulysses* Spengler: *Decline of the West* Howard Carter finds the tomb of Tut-Ankh-Amun Film *Nanuk the Eskimo* by Robert Flaherty	
1923		Steinlen† Sullivan† Perret: church in Le Raincy Duchamp leaves *La Mariée mise à nue* etc. uncompleted, gives up painting	Le Corbusier: *Vers une architecture* Schwitters: magazine *MERZ* (to 1932) G. F. Hartlaub coins the concept of 'Neue Sachlichkeit' Rilke: *Duineser Elegien*, *Sonette an Orpheus*	Röntgen† Bredow: Radio for entertainment in Germany
1924	Lenin†	Hans Thoma† Léger: *Ballet mécanique* (Film) Breton: Surrealist Manifesto	Schwitters: *Ursonate* Kafka†. Chief works appear in the next few years, edited by M. Brod. Valéry: *Eupalinos* Marinetti: *Futurism and Fascism* Puccini†	
1925		Corinth† Mendelsohn: Schocken store in Stuttgart Gropius: Bauhaus in Dessau (1925/1926) Kirchner: Group portrait of the painters of the Brücke Klee: *Fish Magic* Ernst: 'Frottages'	Arp and El Lissitzky: *Les ismes de l'art* van Doesberg: *Elementarismus* First Surrealist exhibition in Paris 'Neue Sachlichkeit' Film *Battleship Potemkin* by Eisenstein Rudolf Steiner† Klee: *Pedagogic Sketchbook*	Heisenberg, Born, Jordan Dirac: Quantum mechanics (*c.* 1925) World Wireless Union Barnack: Leica
1926		Monet† The Blue Four: Kandinsky, Klee, Feininger, Jawlensky Gaudí: main tower of the Church of Holy Family in Barcelona Hoetger: Böttcher-strasse in Bremen	Kandinsky: *Punkt und Linie zu Fläche* Zervos: *Cahiers d'art* Rilke† Berg: Lyric Suite Film *Metropolis* by Fritz Lang H. W. Henze*	

	POLITICAL HISTORY	ART	LITERATURE, MUSIC ETC.	SCIENCE AND TECHNOLOGY
1927		Juan Gris† Chagall: Illustrations to La Fontaine's *Fables* Gonzales: *Masques découpés* Stuttgart: Weissenhof estate	Malevitch: *The Non-objective World* Diaghilev: Ballet *La Chatte* Heidegger: *Sein und Zeit* Utitz: *Overcoming of Expressionism* Woolley finds royal graves at Ur	Lindberg: West-East Atlantic flight
1928		F. v. Stuck† Medardo Rosso† Poelzig: IG-Farben in Frankfurt-on-Main Aubette in Strasbourg decorated by Arp, Taeuber-Arp and v. Doesberg Hundertwasser†	Gleizes: *Kubismus* Dr. Gachet†, doctor, friend and supporter of Cézanne, Renoir, van Gogh Sudermann† Ravel: *Boléro* Brecht-Weill: *Three-penny Opera* Disney: first Mickey Mouse films	Fleming: Penicillin Heisenberg: Indeterminacy principle Köhl, Hühnefeld and Fitzmaurice: East-West Atlantic flight
1929	World economic crisis Stresemann†	Ernst: *La femme à 100 têtes* v. d. Rohe: German pavilion at World Exhibition, Barcelona Aalto: Sanatorium in Paimio Breton: 2nd Surrealist Manifesto Heinrich Zille†	Museum of Modern Art in New York founded Diaghilev† Claudel: *Le Soulier de satin* Remarque: *All Quiet on the Western Front*	Einstein: General field theory Butenandt: Research into sex hormones First television transmission in Berlin
1930		Ilya Repin† Le Corbusier: Swiss pavilion in the Cité Universitaire in Paris (1930–1932) v. d. Rohe Director of the Bauhaus in Dessau (to 1933)	van Doesberg: magazine *Art Concret* Exhibition 'Cercle et Carré' in Paris Musil: *Der Mann ohne Eigenschaften* y Gasset: *Revolt of the Masses* Films *The Blue Angel* (Sternberg), *Sang d'un poète* (Cocteau), *Sous les toits de Paris* (Clair)	First demonstration of television without wires
1931		van Doesberg† Calder: first mobiles Chagall begins illustrations for the Bible Empire State Building in New York	Burning of the Munich glass palace Schnitzler†	Edison†
1932	Briand†	Slevogt† Schlemmer: Bauhaus staircase Bauhaus in Dessau closed	Schönberg: *Moses and Aaron*	Cockcroft and Walton change nucleus of atom by bombarding with artificially accelerated particles

	POLITICAL HISTORY	ART	LITERATURE, MUSIC ETC.	SCIENCE AND TECHNOLOGY
1932		Abstraction-Création group in Paris Wols in Paris		Heisenberg: Positively charged protons, neutral neutrons Piccard: Balloon ascent into the stratosphere
1933	Hitler seizes power	Loos† Schmidt-Rottluff and Hofer excluded from the Academy Schwitters goes to Oslo, Klee to Switzerland, Kandinsky to Paris Bauhaus in Berlin closed	Public burning of books Laws in Germany to prevent 'hereditarily diseased progeny' St. George† F. G. Lorca: *Blood Wedding*	
1934		Gropius goes to London Hölzel† Ernst: *Une semaine de bonté*	H. Bahr† Th. Däubler† Prof. Karl Barth dismissed from post (University of Bonn)	Joliot-Curie discover artificial radioactivity
1935		Liebermann† Signac† Malevitch	Alban Berg† Carl von Ossietzky wins Nobel Peace Prize	Regular television in Berlin
1936		Poelzig† F. L. Wright: House over the waterfall Feininger goes to USA German Künstlerbund banned 'Degenerate Art' action Troost: Haus der Kunst in Munich	Gorky† F. G. Lorca: *The House of Bernarda Alba* Thomas Mann deprived of civic rights, goes to USA	Synthetic rubber 'Buna'
1937	Bombing of Guernica	Picasso: *Guernica* Beckmann goes to Amsterdam Moholy-Nagy: 'New Bauhaus' in Chicago Klee: *Revolution of the Viaduct* Brancusi: *Endless Column*	Arp: magazine *Plastique* Ravel† Film *La grande illusion* by J. Renoir Heuss: *Friedrich Naumann*	Marconi† Shirshov and Fedorov drift from North Pole to east coast of Greenland (to 1938)
1938	Kristallnacht	Kirchner† Rohlfs† Taut† Barlach† v. d. Rohe goes to USA Kokoschka goes to London Speer: Reich Chancellery	d'Annunzio† Film *Dance on the Volcano* by Gründgens	Hahn: Discovery of splitting of uranium and thorium nucleus by neutrons

	POLITICAL HISTORY	ART	LITERATURE, MUSIC ETC.	SCIENCE AND TECHNOLOGY
1939	Second World War (to 1945)	Maillol: *La Rivière* (to 1943)	Vollard† Auction of requisitioned pictures in Lucerne First exhibition of 'Réalités Nouvelles' in Paris Freud† Seghers: *The Seventh Cross* Steinbeck: *Grapes of Wrath* Saint-Exupéry: *Terre des hommes (Wind, Sand and Stars)*	Müller: DDT
1940	Bombing of Coventry	Klee† Behrens† Vuillard† Mondrian and Léger to USA Mondrian: *Boogie-Woogie* series	Cave paintings at Lascaux discovered Hemingway: *For Whom the Bell Tolls*	v. Ardenne: Electron microscope
1941		Minne† Jawlensky† Delaunay† El Lissitzky† Chagall and Ernst go to USA Beckmann: *Perseus Triptych* Moore: *People Sleeping in London Tube Stations during the Air Raids*	Joyce† Henri Bergson† Brecht: *Mother Courage* Werfel: *The Song of Bernadette*	
1942	Auschwitz: start of mass annihilation of the Jews	Gonzales† Schlemmer: Series of *Fensterbilder*	Musil† St. Zweig†	Fermi: Production of atomic energy by chain reaction of uranium fission
1943	Scholl sisters: The White Rose†	Denis† Schlemmer† Soutine† Taeuber-Arp† Freundlich†	Sartre: *L'Être et le Néant*	
1944	Stauffenberg & others: Attempt on Hitler†	Kandinsky† Mondrian† Munch† Maillol† Picasso: *Man with a Lamb* Laurens: *Sirene*	Marinetti† R. Rolland† Film *Ivan the Terrible* by Eisenstein	V-rockets Waksmann and Schatz: Streptomycin
1945	Bombing of Dresden Hitler† Mussolini† Atom bombs on Hiroshima and Nagasaki	Kollwitz†	Lasker-Schüler† von Webern† Haushofer: *Moabiter Sonette*† Bonhoeffer†	Atom bombs

	POLITICAL HISTORY	ART	LITERATURE, MUSIC ETC.	SCIENCE AND TECHNOLOGY
	United Nations founded Expulsions, deportations, refugees, etc.		G. Kaiser† Valéry† Werfel† Endurance film *Kolberg* by Harlan Film *Les Enfants du Paradis* by Carné	
1946		Moholy-Nagy† P. Nash† Le Corbusier: 'Unité d'habitation' in Marseilles Church at Assy	G. Hauptmann† Rembrandt's *Night Watch* restored	
1947	Cominform founded Marshall Plan	Bonnard† Kolbe† Neutra: Tremaine House Beckmann goes to USA Gilles: *Orpheus* series	Baumeister: *The Unknown in Art* Ricarda Huch† M. Dessoir† Th. Mann: *Doktor Faustus* Camus: *La Peste* Borchert: *Draussen vor der Tür (The Man Outside)*	Planck† Jet plane attains speed of sound
1948	Gandhi† Israel founded, Bernadotte†	Schwitters† Rome, Stazione Termini	Sartre: *Les mains sales* Works by Shostakovich Prokofiev, Kachaturian condemned as 'formalistic' and 'alien to the people'. Film *Bicycle Thieves* by de Sica	Kinsey Report 5-metre reflecting telescope on Mount Palomar, USA
1949	German Federal Republic founded German Democratic Republic founded	Ensor† Picasso: *Dove of Peace* Matisse: Dominican chapel at Vence (to 1951)	R. Strauss† H. Pfitzner† Camus: *L'état de siège (State of Siege)* Films: *Orphée* (Cocteau), *The Third Man* (Reed, after Graham Greene)	
1950	Berlin city palace demolished: in its place 'Marx-Engels Platz'	Beckmann: *The Argonauts*† Tessenow† Le Corbusier: Pilgrimage church at Ronchamp (to 1955)	Seuphor coins the concept 'Tachism' G. B. Shaw† H. Mann†	
1951		Wols† Heiliger: Hofer portrait Church at Audincourt Bill: High School for Design in Ulm	Schönberg†	
1952		Moore: *Ruling Couple* Manzù: *The Great Cardinal*		

	POLITICAL HISTORY	ART	LITERATURE, MUSIC ETC.	SCIENCE AND TECHNOLOGY
1952		Zadkine: *City without a heart*, memorial in Rotterdam de Staël: *Les Grands Footballeurs*		
1953	Workers and middle classes of GDR: Rising of 17 June	Picabia†. Gleizes† Dufy† Mendelssohn† Picasso: *La Guerre, La Paix* Baumeister: *Montaru I* F. L. Wright: Guggenheim Museum in New York Butler: *The Unknown Political Prisoner* (1st. prize)	Prokofiev†	
1954		Matisse† Dérain† Laurens† Perret† Heldt†		
1955		Léger† Hofer† Baumeister† Pechstein† de Staël† Utrillo† Scharff† Milles† Picasso: *The Women of Algiers* (Variations after Delacroix)	Kassel: documenta I Th. Mann†	
1956		Nolde† Feininger† Pollock†	Sedlmayr: *Revolution of modern art* (as an 'unmasking')	
1959			Kassel: documenta II	

(Compilation: Michler)

INDEX

(*Note.* – The numerals in italics refer to the plates and figures.)